The Ultimate Guide
to Unusual Leisure

Also by Stephen Jarvis (co-authored with Elaine Edwards)
and published by Robson Books

The Kissing Companion

The Ultimate Guide to Unusual Leisure

Stephen Jarvis

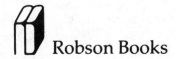

Robson Books

First published in Great Britain in 1998 by Robson Books Ltd,
Bolsover House, 5–6 Clipstone Street, London W1P 8LE

British Library Cataloguing in Publication Data
A catalogue record for this title is available from the British Library

ISBN 1 86105 164 6

Illustrations by David Candler

Typeset by Derek Doyle & Associates, Mold, Flintshire, North
Wales.
Printed in Finland by W.S.O.Y.

To my Great (in both senses) Aunt, Ivy Story; and to my old (in one sense) friend, Greg Holmes

Preface

'This book has its origin in my boredom.'

That was how I opened the forerunner to this book, *The Bizarre Leisure Book*, which was published in 1993. I told of how, fed up with the nine-to-five at a major industrial company, I was determined to make my leisure time as interesting and as varied as possible – so I learnt unusual skills (the bed of nails, the Japanese tea ceremony), tried out peculiar sports (toe-wrestling, peashooting) and joined extraordinary clubs and societies (like the Dozenal Society, who want the human race to count in multiples of twelve, not ten). After a while, colleagues at work would ask on Monday mornings, 'Well, what did you get up to *this* weekend?' It suddenly struck me: if people were interested, maybe I could *write* about unusual leisure activities – not only to recount the experiences and anecdotes, but also to act as a guide, to give people the contacts so that they could try out the activities for themselves. Thus, *The Bizarre Leisure Book* was born, recording my personal involvement with 150 unusual pursuits.

But it soon became clear that *The Bizarre Leisure Book* was not the final statement on the subject. Ever since that book was published, I have continued to find one or two new unusual leisure activities *every week*. If anything, there was too much material for a straightforward new edition of the original volume – and so, in writing this, *The Ultimate Guide to Unusual Leisure*, I have moved away from recording my personal experiences of each and every activity. This book is a mixture of in-depth coverage of certain activities, based upon personal experience, and a shorter treatment of others, based upon telephone interviews and/or a reading of the newsletters and other specialist publications produced by the various clubs, societies and enthusiasts. There are other differences, too, between this volume and its predecessor.

For one thing, this book covers unusual leisure on a worldwide scale, whereas in the previous book I concentrated upon the pursuits of the British. It should be emphasised that the headquarters of a given activity is largely irrelevant: most unusual clubs and societies have international memberships, off-beat newsletters have international readerships, and even in the case of unusual sports championships which are held in one particular country year after year, overseas participation is welcome.

The emergence of the Internet represents another difference between this book and the first. Websites and e-mail are commonplace now, whereas they hardly existed when the first book was published. In some cases, too, websites are replacing newsletters as a lower-cost means of establishing contact with fellow enthusiasts.

As before, there is the problem of how one defines an 'unusual leisure activity'. The vast majority of activities in these pages would be classified, without hesitation, as both unusual and leisure, but there are borderline cases. For instance, should one include a bizarre pressure-group, such as the Voluntary Human Extinction Movement? What about activities which have their underpinnings in religion, like the Institute of Pyramidology? Are there activities which are too politically incorrect to include, like golliwog collecting? Is it acceptable to feature activities which have humans as spectators, rather than participants, such as snail racing? There are no definitive answers to these questions but the activities I have covered seem to me to be of a piece. They all represent out-of-the-ordinary uses of one's spare time.

Stephen Jarvis

A note on the order of entries

In the listing of activities, I have often omitted words like 'The Society for' or 'The International Association of' – with the exception of groups whose full names are part of their charm. (Such as the International Association of People Who Dine Over the Kitchen Sink.)

Note also that there is a small section of activities which have a geographical or cultural bias towards the UK – these are listed together in the 'British Cultural Section'. (All other British-based activities are listed in the main body of the text.)

A

Alternate Worlds Enthusiasts

The past happened and cannot be changed: Adolf Hitler was a famous Austrian painter, Marilyn Monroe was the President of the United States, the Beatles' drummer throughout their career was Pete Best. Yet in the magazine *Alternate Worlds*, a journal devoted to speculative what-if history, you will find these facts disputed and other possibilities discussed . . .

In an alternate world, in a parallel universe, this book might have opened in that way. The possibility that history *could* have been different – that our present is just one of many options that might have resulted – is an issue that fascinates Michael Morton, a science administrator from Swindon, England.

In our universe, Michael actually does edit a magazine called *Alternate Worlds*, devoted to re-running and reinventing the past. When the first issue was published, the cover displayed a map showing Operation Sealion in progress – Germany's invasion of Britain in 1940 – with arrowheads showing the movements of the Panzer Divisions, as they broke out of Folkestone. Inside, there was a full analysis of how the invasion might have proceeded. ('On S-day +5, the Germans move up to 10 miles inland from their positions . . .')

'I liked history at school,' Michael told me, 'but I was always thinking, "What if things had gone differently?" Like, what if the Jacobites had come south in 1745 and taken London? Or, what if the Tudors hadn't been in control? Then I came across the *Encyclopaedia of Science Fiction* and it identified alternative history as a sub-genre within sci-fi. So I started to read books like *The Man in the High Castle* by Philip K. Dick, in which the Germans and Japanese win the Second World War. And there are also works by serious historians . . .'

He reached for the book *For Want of a Nail*, an alternative history of the American War of Independence by Robert Sobell. Opposite its title page was a map of North America: as well as an independent Quebec, there was an expanded USA, which swallowed up Mexico and the western coast of Canada. Smiling, Michael turned to the book's bibliography, which listed spurious source material – academic works which do not exist.

'This sort of thing just appeals to me,' he said, and he reeled off more possibilities. What if the atomic bomb had been developed in the nineteenth century? What if Elvis had been rushed to a hospital in 1977? What if Bill Clinton had become a saxophonist?

Of course, to many people such speculations will seem pointless. In response, Michael cites the work of quantum-theorists, who have posited the existence of not just one universe, but many, a *multiverse*. There may *really* be an infinite number of alternative realities, existing simultaneously and exhausting every conceivable path for history. (In another world, at this moment, you are murdering your spouse; in yet another world, your spouse is murdering you. Indeed, name any conceivable person, and there is a world in which you are married to, and murdered by, that person. Plus, of course, a world in which you are writing this sentence, not I.)

'Do you ever speculate,' I asked, 'on the what-ifs of your own life?'

'No,' he said. 'I agree with traditional Judaism that it is a sin to wish for something that is not possible. You can do yourself a lot of harm if you start wanting your own life to have been different.' Michael added that he was a practising Christian; and although Jesus Christ is one of the most popular figures for exercises in alternative history – what if Jesus had taken a more militant line than he did? – Michael's religious convictions do not waver.

'It may be a historical accident that I'm a Christian and Jesus Christ may not have been the Son of God, but I don't think about it that way,' he said. 'I believe Christianity to be true . . . though I am willing to listen to speculation that it might not be.'

Contact: *Alternate Worlds*, Michael Morton, 19 Bruce Street, Rodbourne, Swindon, Wiltshire, SN2 2EL, UK.

The Ancient Astronaut Society

I am looking at a photograph of an antiquity, a carved slab from Guatemala – but what does the carving represent? Is it a bear, or a warrior, or . . . wait, is it . . . is it a *spaceman*?

According to the Ancient Astronaut Society, you can see the helmet, the back-pack and the breathing apparatus. The Guatemalan stone is just another piece of evidence that, thousands of years ago, visitors from beyond the skies came to Earth to kick-start civilization; evidence that God was an astronaut.

Carrying on the work of Erich von Daniken (author of *Chariots of the Gods*), the society's members go on expeditions to such archaeological peculiarities as the two tracks cut into a mountain at El Fuerte, Bolivia: each track is 100 feet long, one foot wide, and four inches deep. As it says in their newsletter: 'The site could have been used as a catapult-type launch for spacecraft.'

But even if you're sceptical about the ancient astronaut thesis, the society does a fine job in adding what might be called a 'dot dot dot' factor to archaeology. For instance, they report that in a sand-quarry in Aiud, Romania, three objects were found buried to a depth of 33ft. The first two turned out to be mastodon bones, but the third was altogether different. It was a piece of metal plate, featuring two bored holes. The amount of oxidation indicated that the plate had been around for hundreds of thousands of years. Apparently, it resembles the landing plate of the lunar module . . .

Contact: The Ancient Astronaut Society, 1921 St Johns Avenue, Highland Park, Illinois, 60035-3105, USA.
(*For another archaeological 'dot dot dot' see the entry on Archaeo-cryptography.*)

Anglo-Saxon (Conversational)

In a corner of a City of London wine bar, three men sat talking about the weather.

'*Hu is thæt weder todæg?*'
'*Thæt weder is sciene.*'
'*Nis nan regn.*'
'*Ond seo sunne scinth.*'

Being the least fluent of the three, I needed to have the words translated as we went along. ('How is the weather today?' 'The weather is fine.' 'There's no rain.' 'And the sun is shining.') I repeated everything, and that was enough for me to feel included in the conversation. And when I said: '*We sittath on inne, ond we drincath ond we hliehhath*' ('We're sitting in the inn, drinking and laughing'), I was praised for my accent. For the hell of it, I asked, 'How do you say, "The cat sat on the mat"?'

'That's easy,' said Stephen Pollington. ' "*Se catta sat on tham matte*". It's not a different language, is it?'

3

In a way, that's true. It would be stretching things to say we were speaking our *mother* tongue, but it would not be unfair to call it our *grandmother* tongue. Old English, or Anglo-Saxon, was the form of the English language spoken up to about the year 1100, a language whose grammar and vocabulary unravelled when the Bayeux Tapestry was woven. Stephen, and the third man at the table, Alan Haymes, are members of Tha Engliscan Gesithas, or The English Companions, a group of enthusiasts for all aspects of Anglo-Saxon culture: language, art, architecture. Some members even re-enact the warfare – I wondered whether they gave their battle orders in Old English.

'No,' said Alan. 'I'm afraid that the ones who are good at the fighting tend not to be so good at the linguistic side.'

It was the linguistics which particularly appealed to me. Much of Old English is incomprehensible, and then you encounter phrases like '*ic eom*', which evolved into our 'I am', and 'he sæde', our 'he said'. The combination of the unknown shot through with the familiar leads to some of the keenest pleasures of learning a language. As you achieve fluency – by purchasing a language course, complete with tapes, from the Companions – hidden treasures are to be found in modern words: 'were-wolf', you discover, contains the old word '*wer*', meaning 'man', while 'nightingale' contains '*galen*', meaning to sing.

'Old English is different enough to be challenging and yet homely enough to be reassuring,' said Stephen. And he admitted that his private diary was written in nothing else.

Contact: The Membership Secretary, Tha Engliscan Gesithas (The English Companions), BM Box 4336, London, WC1N 3XX, UK.
Or: Mary K. Savelli, 514 Brown Street, Dayton, Ohio, 45402-2810, USA.

(The International Society of) Animal Licence Collectors

Perhaps only a numismatist truly loves money; and perhaps only the members of the International Society of Animal Licence Collectors truly appreciate dog ownership. Two such members are Marty and Trudy Doll – an American married couple with a collection of over 15,000 dog tags and assorted animal licences.

'People ask why,' said Marty. 'Well, you get some tags with interesting shapes.' He sorted through a handful: a bone from Michigan, a corn cob from Iowa, a kennel from New Jersey.

'And this one here is of such a sad dog,' said Trudy, pointing to a tiny mutt of metal. 'At least, I always think he looks sad – with his head hanging down.'

Together, the Dolls are two of the most active and committed members of the International Society of Animal Licence Collectors. They have hosted licence swap-meets in their house and Trudy is a former editor of *Paw Prints*, the society's newsletter. This publication is devoted to *all* aspects of animal licensing, not only dogs, but also cats, horses, cows, even *tortoises*. (In the deserts of Southern California, tortoises are considered an endangered species and anyone owning a tortoise has to glue an aluminium licence to the shell.)

'Not all of the members are animal lovers,' said Trudy. 'Some of them have probably never even owned a dog.' However, there are members who like their tags to *reek* of dog. 'Many of the guys refuse to clean their tags,' she said. 'So there's this cruddy green gook on the back from being worn around the dog's neck. Marty and I prefer to clean ours up.'

Contact: International Society of Animal Licence Collectors, c/o Bill Bone, 928 State Route 2206, Clinton KY 42031, USA.
Tel: 502 653 6060 E-mail: tagman@ibm.net

Apple Parer Enthusiasts

Mr G. W. Laverty describing his first encounter with an apple-paring machine in a New York antiques store:
'How it accomplished the peeling operation amazed me.'

Contact: The International Society of Apple Parer Enthusiasts, Mr G.W. Laverty, 735 Cedarwood Terrace, Apt. 735 B, Rochester, NY 14609, USA.

Archaeocryptography

I shall bore you and then awe you:

In its original complete form, Stonehenge consisted of 30 rocks in its outer circle, which held 30 lintels aloft, or 60 rocks in all. These rocks are arranged in a 360 degree circle, and if you multiply 60 by 360 it comes to 21,600. Take that 21,600, divide it by 51, and then divide again by 10. The result is 42.35294118.

Here comes the awe. The exact latitude of Stonehenge north of the equator is *51* degrees, *10* minutes and *42.3529* seconds. I'd better say that again: EXACTLY.

It's just a coincidence, isn't it? Stonehenge is an undeniable wonder, but it is *impossible* that its builders could have known about modern latitudes. Well, prepare yourself for the newsletter, *The Code*, edited by Carl Munck, an American who describes himself as an 'archaeocryptographer', from archaeo meaning prehistoric, and cryptography meaning code. Munck claims to have decoded over 200 ancient monuments in this way, from the pyramids of Egypt, to the Nazca Lines of Peru; and they all seem to 'know' their northern latitude ...

Contact: Carl Munck, Editor, *The Code*, PO Box 147, Greenfield Center, NY 12833, USA.

The Artillerymen

For emphasis and a sense of history – two things I need to discuss this subject – let me use a plural that takes no 's': these people fire cannon. I do not mean scale models – or, if I do, that scale is one to one. What I am saying is that the members of the Artillery Association own and fire full-size field-pieces, either reproductions or genuine items, but always a weapon that makes the appropriate noise.

'In a lot of ways,' said Ron Hill, one of the Association's founders, 'I don't like myself for liking guns.' He and I were in a pub, chatting over a pint, as he considered the distastefulness of instruments of misery. Set against the objections, though, he knew that he'd given a lot of pleasure with public displays and that his guns had raised money for charity. And since no shells or cannonballs were actually fired, the guns were harmless. 'The occasional burnt finger is about the worst that can happen,' he said.

As he spoke of how he wouldn't have minded living at the height of Britain's imperial power, of how he would have relished being a sergeant in a Victorian artillery battery, I wanted to know when his passion had started. Now in his fifties, Ron told me that his parents had taken him to Windsor Castle when he was seven. There was a large cannon on the outer terraces. 'That was it,' he said.

We drank up and then Ron drove me to the nearby Fort Coalhouse, in Tilbury, Essex. Resembling an amphitheatre, this is a historic fort which is open to the public. Once inside, I was introduced to members of the Artillery Association. They were in full Second World War battle-dress. Oh, and they had brought a gun: a genuine 25-pounder. I remembered that as a boy I had a model of one of these that fired matchsticks; a direct hit from this weapon on a fully-grown tree would leave you with *nothing but* matchsticks.

After we'd shaken hands, the members of the Association gave me the opportunity of sitting in the gunner's seat and turning the wheel that made the barrel traverse. Then Ron and I stood aside as a blank cartridge was loaded. The commander gave the order to . . .

Onomatopoeia: a word that sounds like the thing it describes. 'Bang' is a miserable attempt. Ron told me to open my mouth – an old artilleryman's trade secret for dissipating the effects of shock. Meanwhile, a member of the public, a mother with a child howling in her arms, was complaining to the artillery commander that insufficient warning had been given, that her little girl was seriously frightened.

I thought back to Ron's own childhood and the effect a single experience had had on his future life. I then looked at the little girl. I wondered whether we had started the career of an anti-war campaigner.

Contact: Ron Hill, The Artillery Association, 3 St David's Drive, Leigh-on-Sea, Essex, SS9 3RQ, UK.
Tel: 01702 558743
Or: *The Artilleryman* [a magazine 'dedicated to the advancement of safety and skill in the exhibition and competition shooting of muzzle-loading cannon and mortar'], RR1 Box 36, Tunbridge, VT 05077, USA.
Tel: 802 889 3500 Fax: 802 889 5627 E-mail: firetec@firetec.com

The Association for the Study and Research of .22 Calibre Rimfire Cartridges

'To me, it's part of a way of life,' said Richard Rains. 'After a long hard day at the office, I come down to my cartridge room to do some cataloguing . . .'

Richard is an ammunition collector – though not *all* ammunition, just one particular type: the .22 rimfire cartridge.

'My father was a gun collector, so I've lived with ammunition since I was a boy,' he said. 'And ammunition collecting isn't as expensive as gun collecting.' He explained that the .22 offered plenty of variation to collectors, because it was produced by many different manufacturers, and fired in every war since the American Civil War. There were also special versions of the .22 to collect: for killing cattle, for killing birds and rats, blanks for the movie industry, blanks for starter pistols, disintegrating bullets for shooting galleries, tracer bullets, and so on.

'Is it safe to have so much ammunition in the house?' I asked.
'As long as you don't go beating it with a hammer,' he replied.

Contact: The Association for the Study and Research of .22 Calibre Rimfire Cartridges, c/o Richard Rains, S. 4321 Bluff Rd, Spokane, WA 99204, USA.
Tel: 509 624 8772

Asterism

It is said that science fiction was abbreviated to 'sci-fi' by analogy to high fidelity, or 'hi-fi'. But the relationship is more profound than mere etymology.

'It has always been amazing to me that given the right melody one can be transported to far-off planets, faraway lands or a far-flung future,' I was told by Jeff Berkwits, the editor of *Asterism, The Journal of Science Fiction, Fantasy and Space Music*. 'And a lot of what goes on in science fiction is *about* music and sound. Think of *2001* and how different it would have been without music.'

The magazine, which has 'an estimated circulation of 2001 readers', contains reviews of CDs with titles like *Asteroid*, *Into Topological Space*, *Sonorities by Starlight* and *The Magnificent Void*. There are also articles about leading science fiction composers, such as Alexander Courage, creator of the theme music for the original *Star Trek* series. One learns that Courage is responsible for creating the sound of the ship's flyby. 'I went into the studio with a microphone,' he says, 'and when the Enterprise flew by on-screen, I blew from left to right into the mike, making a "whoosh" sound.'

But I haven't explained the magazine's title. 'Asterism' has a triple meaning: it is a term for a cluster of stars; it is a printing term for a symbol of three stars meant to draw attention to something on the page; and it is a mineralogy term for a starlike ray produced in certain crystals when a light is shone upon them. 'It's a six-pointed star that comes out of a rock,' said Jeff, 'so it's a rock star.'

Contact: Asterism, PO Box 6210, Evanston, IL 60204, USA.
E-mail: ASTERISMSF@aol.com

Astral Projection Techniques

'You go to sleep,' he said, 'and suddenly you find yourself in another world.'

I was at a public lecture in Hemel Hempstead, England. The subject: astral projection. You've probably heard of this. Otherwise known as the out-of-body experience, in this state the consciousness is supposed to unshackle itself from the flesh and wander forth as a living ghost. The lecturer claimed to have had thousands of these trips outside himself – it seems he's hardly ever in! He described the astral world as very like our own, with people, places and traffic. And the two worlds interpenetrate, so in your astral body it is possible to visit a sister in Canada, travelling 4,000 miles in ten to fifteen seconds. 'As you fly along, you may see icebergs, or the astral equivalent of Quebec,' he said. I put up my hand and suggested that all this might be a dream, but he disagreed most firmly. 'You have no control over a dream,' he said.

Astral projectors claim that *anyone* can master the techniques for inducing and then directing the experience. There are many methods of doing so. For instance, choose some object in your home – it could be a bottle, a statuette or anything else – and then memorize its every detail. Emblazon it on your mind so that you can call up a detailed image whenever you desire; and when you go to bed, recall the object – it should be the last thing on your mind before you fall asleep. With any luck, in the middle of the night, you will leave your body to seek the object.

I must confess that I have tried the latter technique with a key as my chosen object – though I have always remained inside myself, firmly locked up. Perhaps I should have persisted. As one enthusiastic astral projector told me in a letter:

'Once "out" you can do whatever you imagine or intend – walk through walls, ceilings and doors, fly through the air at will in any direction, travel to planets in other star-systems, shape-shift, gender change, and interact with a variety of spirit-beings, human and non-human. What more could you really want?! For free at that!'

Contact: A.K.V. Van Dam, 53 Hallett Way, Bude, Cornwall, EX23 8PG, UK. (Produces quarterly reports on astral projection and related themes.)

The Atlatl Association

One man and his atlatl could smash the Olympic javelin record. The atlatl – pronounced aht-laht-l – or spear-thrower, is a 19,000-year-old invention, shaped somewhat like a crochet hook, which increases the speed of a spear by, in effect, lengthening the thrower's arm. Nowadays it's the sort of thing you find only on an archaeological dig . . . or at a meeting organized by the World Atlatl Association, who have revived spear-throwing as a sport. (Their motto: 'Too long have I hunted mammoth alone.')

Contact: World Atlatl Association Secretary, Leni Clubb, PO Box 56, Ocotillo, CA 92259, USA.
Website: http://users.aol.com/tbprim1/WAA.html

Axe Racing

'Comparing this axe to an ordinary axe is like comparing a rally car to an ordinary saloon car,' Dafydd Cadwaldar told me, chopper in hand, when I met him at his home among the woodlands of Gwynedd, Wales. 'It's razor-sharp, and if you want to buy one you have to specially import it from either Australia or New Zealand.'

Dafydd is one of the leading exponents of *axe racing*, or competitive woodchopping, a sport in which men (and some women) sprint against each other, attempting to cut logs in half in the shortest possible time, using an axe or a cross-cut saw. So, he walked towards a pine log – which was held upright and steady in a metal stand – and he simply began to hack at high speed. How fast? A top axeman like Dafydd can cut through a 12in diameter log in about 20 seconds. I just stood watching, while the woodchips flew in my face like sea-spray.

Then, approaching a similar log, I attempted to follow his advice on axemanship. The idea is that, for maximum effectiveness, the axe-head should strike the log at an angle of 45 degrees. Suffice it to say that my blows did not appear to have been strictly measured by protractor.

There was more hope for me with the two-man saw. The technique is to *smoothly* draw the saw towards you, alternating with your partner. Here, the speed that can be attained is quite unbelievable: a top-flight two-man team can saw through an 18in log in seven or eight seconds.

'You could have a fairly powerful chain-saw, sharpened as much as you want, and you would beat the chain-saw with a two-man cross-cut saw,' said Dafydd. 'Manpower can beat horsepower anytime.' Though I slowed him down, I'll admit that it *was* satisfying when a disk of wood, that I had helped to cut, fell off the end of the log and settled in the sawdust.

'And, of course,' he commented, 'this is the only sport that will keep you supplied with firewood for the winter.'

Contact: Welsh Axemen's Association, Dafydd Cadwaladr, 'Bryn Meurig', Bethesda, Gwynedd, LL57 4YW, UK.

Tel: 01248 601592 E-mail: dafyddyfwyell@easynet.co.uk

Or: North American Axemen's News, Box 272, Webster Springs, W. Virginia 26288, USA.

Or: American Lumberjack Association, Shannon McBride, 18640 Midhill Circle, West Linn, Oregon 97068, USA.

Or: New Zealand Axemen's Association, J. Grimshaw, c/o PO Box 13, Te Kopuru, New Zealand.

Or: Australian Axemen's Association., D. Munday, 134 Noga Avenue, Keilor East 3033, Victoria, Australia.

B

The Bagpipe Society

So then it was my turn. Puffing hard on the mouthpiece, I inflated the bag till it was like a hot-water bottle fit to burst. I squeezed it against my ribs. Blowing again, and squeezing some more, out came a sweet sound, a remarkably sweet sound. 'You've done this before,' David VanDoorn's wife said. David himself confirmed that for a first attempt, I had played unbelievably well. 'Most people make the noise of a dying cat,' he said.

David runs the Bagpipe Society; and although that will immediately make you think of Scotland, the members are interested in the bagpipes of *any* culture. David's collection ranges from a reproduction English medieval pipe, to an enormous construction with multiple cowhorns, called the Grosser Bock, German for 'the bigger goat'. 'The term goat is used throughout the world to describe bagpipes,' he said, 'but traditionally, only billy goats are used for the bags. The air comes out of the female's nipples.'

Contact: David VanDoorn, 49 Osborne Rd, Hornchurch, Essex, RM11 1EX, UK.

The Bald Headed Men of America

My letter to John T. Capps III, the Founder of the Bald Headed Men of America, suggested that his organization could benefit from the pub-licity of an appearance in this book. 'Thanks,' he said, in his reply, 'we need a plug. (No pun intended).'

Yes, no pun intended – because one of the mottoes of the Bald Headed Men is 'No plugs, drugs or rugs.' Another is: 'God made many heads. The ones He was ashamed of He covered up.' Or, still on a religious theme: 'The Lord is just, the Lord is fair; He gave some brains, the others, hair.'

Every September, the Bald Headed Men gather for a convention at Morehead City (that's right) to celebrate baldness as a perfectly natural way to be. There are competitions for the shiniest bald head, the roundest bald head, the most kissable bald head and the smallest bald spot; not forgetting the bald look-alike event, and the bald-as-a-golf-ball putting contest. Heads are buffed and polished by a resident 'patecurist'.

And me? Okay, I'll admit that I don't have to bulk-buy shampoo. You got a problem with that? As Mr Capps says: 'It's what's *inside* the head that counts.' Where's that membership form . . .

Contact: Bald Headed Men of America, 102 Bald Drive, Morehead City, NC 28557, USA.
Tel: 919 726 1855 Fax: 919 726 6061
Website: http://pubweb.acns.nwu.edu/~pfa/bald.html
E-mail: JCapps4102@aol.com

Banana Label Times

'Don't even *think* about it!' she said.

My partner, Elaine, had caught me looking at a discarded banana peel that was lying on the street. As she had correctly surmised, I *had* thought about picking it up: regardless of the dogs that might have sniffed it, regardless of the dirty boots that might have trodden upon it. Yes, I wanted to turn the peel over, and see what it had to offer. This is what happens when one becomes a serious collector of banana labels.

It all began when I received a copy of *Banana Label Times*, the specialist newsletter for banana label collectors. I was particularly impressed by the following statement from Danish collector Thomas Anker Jorgensen, who owns twelve hundred different banana labels:

'In 1980, I left my parents and moved into a collective with many young people like myself. Often, we ate bananas. And for some reason we put the stickers on my loudspeaker. After a time, I moved and got a new speaker system and so put the banana stickers in a small glass frame. There were only about ten of them at that time. Through contacts in the USA and elsewhere my collection grew . . . I think that collecting *anything whatsoever*, any object or subject, helps a person to make some kind of order in a world that is increasingly complex. To put it another way: We are put into a world which we can hardly survey as a whole. You can hardly make a worthwhile estimate of reality. But you can see exactly what *is* with your banana label collection. From this collecting comes both satisfaction and perhaps something similar to peace of mind, which some people achieve through meditation. Collecting banana labels can indeed be a form of meditation.'

Quoting that passage might have been the end of the matter – except for one thing: the editor had also enclosed an *album*, with 256 blank spaces for banana labels. Well, they always say you should write from experience, and so . . .

Life changed in the following months. I can remember when Elaine and I went to a cocktail bar: she ordered a Yellow Bird – and I couldn't take my eyes off the banana as the barman chopped. He even remarked, 'Are you studying my chopping technique?' I smiled. I was desperate for him to turn the peel over. Then I caught a glimpse of a label: unfortunately, it was a Del Monte, which I already had. Believe me, if it had been a new label, I would have asked for that peel!

Another time, I can remember walking towards a market stall, because in the distance I had seen a glint of yellow . . . and the disappointment as I got closer and saw that it was a stall with yellow *flowers*. Not that the bananas I bought were always yellow: I was prepared to go for the greenest and unripest, inedible for days, simply for a label. (And it's important to stress that one has to *buy* the fruit – it's one of the rules. Banana label enthusiasts are ethical collectors, and will never steal labels.) Worst of all, some shops and stalls sold bananas *without* labels; here, a piece of terminology evolved between Elaine and myself – such bananas were called 'Pirates'.

One becomes adept at looking for, and excited by, minute variations. This is the very essence of banana label collecting. There are relatively few major players in the production and marketing of bananas worldwide, but these players have many different farms, so every basic label design comes in dozens, and sometimes *scores* of forms. Following the strategy of the Danish collector, I thought I would take advantage of overseas contacts: as Elaine is Canadian, the call for help – the apPEEL – went out to her friends and relatives. Her mother and father found me a number of Del Monte variations, distinguished by tiny differences in the typeface. Her friends, John and Karen Wood from Vancouver, did the same for Chiquita, sending me variations which bore the mysterious letters 'AH' and 'AK' in one corner. Her sister Janice found me several other Chiquita variations, and also wrote: 'I'm not sure I understand why your guy needs banana stickers, but that's his biz . . . but am *I* somehow contributing to his insanity by passing on these things?'

Banana Label Times: not just the name of a newsletter, but a description of my life.

Contact: *Banana Label Times*, PO Box 159, Old Town, FL 32680-0159, USA.
Tel: 352 542 9526 Fax: 352 542 3447

Barbed Wire Collecting

The barbs on barbed wire do many things. They cross their legs, wind like spaghetti, splice like a mariner's knot, coil like a spring, and curl like a lock of hair. If you were to take a length of fencing, and clench it tightly in your palms, the stigmata would be different for every manufacturer. It's easy to start wondering how many more types of prickle there can possibly be. Hence, the urge to search and to collect – and that's why there's a specialist magazine, *The Barbed Wire Collector*.

Contact: *The Barbed Wire Collector*, Box 290, McLean, TX 79057, USA.
Tel: 806 779 2225

Bathtub Racing

There are two sorts of bath racing – the water being either inside or outside the bath. In the Tin Bath World Championships, covered later in this book, the water is, or should be, outside, because the bath is used as a canoe. In the other kind, the water is, or should be, inside: one of five team members has to take a bath in public – among yipping dogs, ogling spectators and squealing children – while his four teammates pull the bath, which is on wheels, in a dash towards the finishing line. The tub must be full of water at the start, and have no less than ten gallons left at the finish.

'It's got to be hot water, or I'm not getting into it!' said one contestant at a recent championship. Well, the event *is* held in Alaska.

Contact: Rasmussen's Music Mart & Store, PO Box 2, Nome, Alaska 99762-0002, USA.
Tel: 907 443 2798 Fax: 907 443 5777

The Beale Cipher Association

The address below could be worth $20 million to you.

In 1880, in Virginia, a pamphlet was published on *The Unsolved Cipher of Thomas Jefferson Beale*. Its author claimed to have partially decoded a message left in a box by one Thomas Jefferson Beale. The decoded part said that if the rest of the message could be deciphered, it would give the location of a cache of gold and silver, buried somewhere in the Blue Ridge Mountains.

Well, it might all be a hoax; but enough people believe it to be true to have formed an association solely devoted to cracking the Beale cipher. Many members think that the cipher is related in some way to another, unknown document – it might be anything from the American Declaration of Independence to an obscure nineteenth-century novel – and if you can only find that document, you'll have the key. Thus, the hunt for the treasure often takes place in public libraries.

So, here is the promised address. And when you're making out your will, please remember who gave you this information.

Contact: Beale Cipher Association, c/o Michael Timmerman, 68E2 West 23rd. Street, Bayonne, NJ 07002, USA.
Tel: 201 339 0442

Bed Racing

Is bed racing the sport of choice for sexual athletes? It does involve mixed teams: six men push a woman, or six women push a man, on a bed on wheels. The object is to cover the course in Knaresborough, North Yorkshire, England in the fastest time; this includes going up a cobbled hill with a 1 in 4 gradient, and hurtling down the other side.

The teams also have to cross a river, so the bed has to be able to float. (What – you've never heard of a water bed?)

Contact: Steve Archer, 36 The Spinney, Knaresborough, North Yorkshire, HG5 OTD, UK.
Tel: 01423 868581

The Birdman Rally

Flying elephants, flying nuns; human seagulls, Eddie the Eagle; Buzz Lightyear, Peter Pan, the Red Baron; a 32ft Concorde, all four Ninja Turtles; whirling doughnuts and flapping ice creams; and a naked jumper called John. In spite of attracting these contestants over the years, the Bognor Birdman Rally is serious business. Every August, when there is a Sunday high tide around noon, men and women jump off a 30ft-high platform on Bognor Regis pier, attempting to defy gravity – and there is a £15,000 prize for anyone who can travel more than 100m before hitting the sea. Think that sounds impossible without strapping yourself to an autogiro? Consider that the previous 'impossible barrier' was 50m, which was broken by a German hang-glider pilot in 1984, who flew 57.8m and won £10,000.

He was narrowly ahead of a flying squirrel, Donald Duck and the Pope.

Contact: Arun District Council, Arun Civic Centre, Maltravers Road, Littlehampton, West Sussex BN17 5LF, UK.
Tel: 01903 716133 Fax: 01903 725254 Website: www.arun.gov.uk/arun-dc/
E-mail: info@arun.gov.uk

Black Sheep

Running my finger down a small ads column, I saw the following: "*Black Sheep* – a Seth/Jane Roberts fanzine, featuring world grid info, poetry, stories."

I was immediately intrigued: I had never heard of Seth, nor Jane Roberts, nor the world grid. I sent away for some back issues . . .

I discovered that the late Jane Roberts was a 'channeller', and 'Seth' one of the spirits she channelled, starting in 1963. Seth called himself 'The Black Sheep of the Universe', and the world grid he described may be thought of as a series of lines of energy, or ley lines (*see* Earth Mysteries) on the surface of the Earth. Where these lines intersect is a 'co-ordination point', which in turn may be thought of as an 'energy vortex' or a 'power place'.

'Some people have the ability to sense the locations of these points,' says *Black Sheep*'s editor, Madelon Rose Logue. 'There is an ever so minute alteration of gravity forces in these areas and a wavering effect, and a spinning sensation.' For those who can discern it, there is a difference in the air, too, as if it appears 'thicker'.

Upon reaching these locations, Madelon checks out the direction of the spin using a pendulum or coathanger dowsing rods, and then stands on a bathroom scale: because of the difference in gravity, at such spots she weighs less.

'There are a lot of vortices in the Los Angeles area,' she adds. 'I have located a few after hearing other people complain of headaches, dizziness or nausea in particular places.'

Though not everyone reacts adversely. One subscriber stood on a co-ordination point and announced: 'Hey, this is better than a cigarette!'

Contact: *The Black Sheep*, c/o Madelon Rose Logue, 3868 Centinela Avenue #12, Los Angeles, CA 90066-4431, USA.

The Blow Torch Collectors' Association

One British member of the Blow Torch Collectors' Association, known as 'Dave the Lamp' (after the British expression for a blow torch, namely blowlamp), owns over 900 blow torches, and admits that he gets a thrill out of cleaning off 60 years' worth of grime and soot, to discover hidden trademarks, and to reveal the fiery tool in its true beauty. 'When I display my lamps,' he writes in the Association's magazine, *The Torch*, 'I just sit there and watch all of the eccentrics walking by who *do not* collect blow lamps.'

Contact: The Blow Torch Collectors' Association, Ronald M. Carr, 3328 258th Avenue SE, Issaquah, WA 98029-9173, USA.
Tel: 206 557 0634 E-mail: swcv70e@prodigy.com
Or: *Blow Lamp News* c/o Les Adams, Stacombe Farm, Doccembe, Moretonhampstead, Devon, TQ13 8SS, UK.
E-mail: LES_GINA@classic.msn.com

The Bog Snorkelling World Championship

There are things I have done I wish I hadn't done; and things I haven't done, I wish I had; of course, there are things I have done, that I'm glad I've done; and then … Then there is the Bog Snorkelling World Championship.

Lying in the quadrant of things that I haven't done, and I'm glad I haven't done, is a sport as unlovely as its name implies. If you turn up for the event in August, held in Llanwrtyd Wells, Wales, you will find yourself diving into a channel 60 yards long, cut straight out of a peat bog. You will be required to swim two lengths as fast as possible, using a snorkel – in water so cold that most people get out after half a length, indeed so cold that, as soon as you *do* get out, the muscles in your arms and legs will go completely solid. And if you think of pure spring water as being as clear as a diamond, then the water here will be some other, darker arrangement of carbon molecules. You will have to be hosed down afterwards to get rid of the sediment.

What's more, you will be charged several pounds for the privilege of taking part.

Contact: Gordon Green, Neuadd Arms Hotel, Llanwrtyd Wells, Powys, LD5 4RB, UK.
Tel: 01591 610236

The Boomerang Society

The wind was too strong. When it moves the leaves, and only the leaves, then it's fine. But the branches as well? No.

I waited till the trees said yes and then I drew back my hand. With the sun behind me, I cast a long shadow ahead – like an Australian discobolus? Or a sort of falconer? Who knows? By then, I'd stopped looking down and I was watching only the spinning in the sky.

Dammit, too far back. It went over my head, to be lost in the sun. When the boomerang landed, it lay in the tall grass far away, like a teacher's tick.

The other man in the field, Sean Slade, was actually a teacher by profession. He also runs the British Boomerang Society. Did his return? Return his did. 'I like to see a big symmetrical circle,' said Sean. 'There's something very satisfying about that.' He remarked that boomerang is the perfect slob sport: you don't have to be athletic or macho – once you've mastered the throw and the catch, you stand still. 'And how many other sports can you play on your own?' he said.

When we returned to Sean's house, the real surprise was that many boomerangs are not, well, boomerang-shaped. There are thousands of types. I saw a 'water molecule', consisting of three circles, a big 'hydrogen' and two smaller 'oxygens'; a 'cat', to be tossed by the tail; a 'tomahawk'; a 'tennis racket'; and a 'gurkha knife'.

'I had one member of the society phoning me up,' he told me, 'and he said, "Have you ever thought of making them out of old LPs?" The ridged surface could have interesting effects on the airflow.'

He also spoke of the adjustments, the slight twists to the shape, that affect the aerodynamics. 'There are different approaches to tuning them,' he said, as a pile clattered down on his kitchen table. 'I put the wooden ones in the microwave for 10 to 15 seconds.'

Contact: British Boomerang Society, Sean Slade, 1 Berkeley Ave, Mapperley Park, Nottingham, NG3 5BU, UK. Tel: 01602 604992
United States Boomerang Association, Betsylew Miale-Gix, PO Box 182, Delaware, Ohio, 43015, USA.
Website: http://www.staff.uiuc.edu/~brazelto/USBAinfo.html
Boomerang Association of Australia, Bruce Carter, 21 Fran St., Glenroy, Melbourne, Victoria 3046, Australia. Tel: 03 9300 2374

Boomerang Association of Canada, John Cryderman, 136 Thames St., Chatham, Ontario N7L 2Y8, Canada.
Canadian Boomerang Society, Jim Bradley, PO Box 65695, Stoney Creek, Ontario L8G 4S1, Canada.
Boomerang Club of New Zealand, Earl Tutty, 17 Truscotts Rd, Heathcote, Christchurch 2, New Zealand.

Bottleshooting

I suppose the most appropriate firearm to shoot bottles with would be a *magnum* ... In Belgium, *flessenschieten*, or bottleshooting, is an organized sport, with weekly competitions. Marksmen shoot at bottles hanging by the neck from a distance of 40 to 58 metres.

Contact: Volkssportconfederatie, Warandelaan 10B bus 2, 8340 Sijsele, Belgium.
Tel/Fax: 050 35 84 62 Website: http://www.snv.be/vosco/ E-mail: VOSCO@snv.be

Bottlewalking

If a regular at the Swan Inn asks for ice, do not assume that he wants to chill his drink. The ice may be needed for his *palm*: to numb a small red circle there, stamped upon the skin as perfectly and as painfully as a rancher's brand. Such a customer would have been taking part in *bottlewalking*.

'Yes, it can hurt a bit sometimes,' I was told by Andy Morris, the landlord, and one of the pub's best bottlewalkers. He lifted the tongs from the ice-bucket and dropped an ice-cube into a customer's hand. 'But you tend to get better at bottlewalking when you've had a few beers. You can tolerate more pain.'

The rules are straightforward. First, a darts mat is laid on the floor, to form the bottlewalking surface. Then, a competitor crouches at one end, with his feet off the mat, holding an empty beer bottle in each palm. The next stage is to 'walk' the hands forward using the bottles as stilts, while ensuring that the feet stay off the mat. This means that the body has to go through a series of positions: the 'arch', the 'press-up', and finally, 'the rack', when the competitor is stretched to the limit. This much alone requires the strength of a gym instructor – Andy admitted that, after a night's bottlewalking, he often awakes the next day with pains across his neck and shoulders – but now comes the hard part.

The object of the game is to place one of the bottles as far away as possible from the starting-point and leave it there; but in doing this, no part of the body should touch the mat. Thus, when the competitor is at full stretch, he must immediately convert his two bottle-stilts into a single bottle-pogostick – and hop backwards all the way to the start. The pain and the pressure are therefore doubled, concentrated at the bottle-rim under the competitor's hand; and with every hop, he die-stamps his palm.

Yes, I did take part in a contest; but a combination of cowardice and pain led to a pitiful best of 31in ... compared to Andy, who achieved 88¾in, and a local farmer with an astonishing 93½in. Andy did try to go farther – but whenever he exceeded 90in, a bottle would wobble and fall. Sometimes *both* bottles collapsed underneath him and his entire body crashed onto the mat.

Just before the pub closed, Andy conceded defeat. 'I should never have tired myself out playing rugby yesterday,' he remarked. 'But he's never beaten me before – and I'll get him next time.'

Contact: Andy Morris, The Swan Inn, Swinbrook, Nr. Burford, Oxon, OX18 4DY, UK.
Tel: 01993 822165

Bricks 1: Brick Collecting

Life, the biologists say, has building-blocks. And building blocks are Henry Holt's life.

The event that changed the course – should we say the *damp*course? – of Henry's life, occurred twenty years ago. 'A factory was being knocked down opposite our house,' he told me. Walking past the demolition-site, he happened to look on the ground: he saw an old brick with his name upon it – HOLT, imprinted into the clay. Could the brickmaker be a relative? After research, Henry found out that this was not so. But in the kiln of his head a passion had started to be fired ...

On his front-room table, 79-year-old Henry and his wife Mary, 80, had spread out some of the collection for me to see. There were bricks with holes, bricks with lugs, bricks with manufacturers' names. The Holts have amassed over 5000 different specimens – one of the largest collections of bricks in the world. I mention the world, for I do not want you to think they are alone: inevitably, there is an International Brick Collectors' Association.

Henry and Mary reminisced about how they used to travel all around Lancashire, visiting a different demolition-site every Sunday. In some cases, they would watch a condemned property for years – like masonry vultures, hovering – just waiting for the arrival of the wrecking crew. 'But why?' I asked. 'What's the attraction?'

Henry just shrugged. 'We haven't got any children,' he said. 'What else can we do?'

Contact: Ken Jones, Treasurer, The International Brick Collectors' Association, 100 Manor Drive, Columbia, MO 65203, USA. Tel: 573 445 7171

Bricks 2: Brick Wall Enthusiasts

There are two walls of surpassing interest to tourists: the Wailing, and the Great Wall of China. But I was beside a brickwork garden boundary in the backstreets of Luton, England.

Terence Smith, my guide, had already explained the difference between the bricklaying methods known as *Flemish Bond* and *English Bond* – saying with a smile that, 'Flemish Bond is more common in England and English Bond is more common in Flanders.' Now he informed me that the bricks making a course in this ordinary garden wall were probably late nineteenth century; and he should know – because Terence is the Chairman of the British Brick Society, a group of over 250 fans of humanity's oldest manufactured building material. The society runs excursions to towns near and far simply to look at the walls.

'Brick is homely and welcoming,' said Terence. 'Other materials can be a bit aloof at times.'

Brick wall enthusiasts will tell you that, just as there are regional cheeses, so there are regional bricks – from the gault clays of Cambridgeshire with their creamy buff colour, to the weald clays of Sussex, with their iron-oxide red. Furthermore, the mortar and the bonding arrangement can have a profound effect upon the look of a wall. A light-toned mortar will make the bricks themselves appear lighter, while a recessed joint will cast a bold shadow. Then there are unusual uses of bricks to look out for – brick murals, for instance.

'When I was in the Netherlands,' said Terence, 'I was on a train that had just left the station at Harlingen – and suddenly I glimpsed a picture of Noah's Ark in coloured brick. So I got off at the next station and caught the next train going back. I just had to get a better look.'

He did remark, though, that a trip to the Netherlands can be rather confusing, because the Dutch have a tendency to call a brick a *steen*, which means a stone. 'So you're never really sure of the building material they're talking about,' he said.

Contact: The British Brick Society, c/o Brick Development Association,
Woodside House, Winkfield, Windsor, Berkshire, SL4 2DX, UK.
Tel: 01344 885651 Fax: 01344 890129 E-mail: brick@brick.org.uk

British Cultural Section
1-18: Introduction

As a resident of the United Kingdom, I sometimes encounter distinc-
tively British leisure activities, which require a knowledge of British
culture to appreciate: if you have never seen Bruce Forsyth, the King of
British TV game shows, then you are likely to be mystified by the antics
of the Bruce Forsyth Social Club. However, these activities deserve a
place in this book, and therefore I have grouped them all together as
entries in this section, with appropriate explanatory notes. Another
British angle is provided by UK-based teachers of unusual spare-time
skills, meetings with whom formed an important part of my early expe-
riences in unusual leisure. The teachers are listed here because of the
geographical bias, not because their skills are peculiarly British. For
similar reasons, this section includes the activity of Letterboxing and the
society Subterranea Britannica.

British Cultural Section 1:
The Alan Whicker Appreciation
Society

Alan Whicker is renowned as a television interviewer who travels the
globe, seeking out the rich and famous. Easily recognized by his mous-
tache and glasses, he has a distinctive vocal style, as well . . .

There are times when a word or two of explanation cannot be avoided.
'Look,' I said to the taxi driver, 'I'm going to put on a false moustache.'
    So I chatted away as I peeled off the backing-paper and stuck the
brush to my face. The bristles were jet-black, several shades darker
than my natural hair, and reminded me of those draught-excluders
that people put in door-jambs. Taking out a pocket-mirror, I checked

my upper lip. Hmmm. Lopsided. Still, not necessarily a bad thing – just as a bow-tie needs *some* imperfection to show it's not a ready-made on elastic, so a false moustache needs to show it's genuinely false. I changed the angle of the mirror. Yes, I was satisfied with the spectacles, too. As for the rest of me, that was smart yet casual – blazer, club tie, pressed grey trousers. 'We're here,' said the driver. He stopped at the pub.

Before long, other Whickers started to arrive, for their monthly lunchtime meeting. There were fifteen in all. One or two even had real whiskers and genuinely defective eyesight, but most took spectacles out of cases and then stood at the bar, spirit-gumming their facial hair. After that, they began to speak in that slightly staccato delivery, that stream of nasal alliteration, subtle innuendo and dreadful puns which is known as Whickerspeak, Whickeric, or Whickerese. Hence: 'Here, amongst the flotsam and jetsam of human existence, lapping the shores of the urban paradise . . .' And: 'Here, in a village at the foot of the Sussex Downs, not a stone's throw from rigor mortis . . .' I myself had a go, repeating phrases like 'a typical run-of-the-millionaire', using that special world-weariness of one who has seen the whole globe and found nothing but Shangri-Las.

Thus, we assumed our places at the table. As an aroma rose from tureens as large as swimming pools, as meat and vegetables went down like a Lear-jet landing under a setting sun, and as we tasted a dessert as rich as the Sultan of a small petroleum-producing protectorate, we tried to understand the essential appeal of television's most-travelled man. 'It's that suave staccato,' said one Whicker, doing it himself, 'it's his constant search for the improbable dream . . .'

Contact: John Ferdinando, 2 South Street, Ditchling, East Sussex, BN6 8UQ, UK.

British Cultural Section 2: Art from Within

You have heard of painting by numbers. You might call 'Art from Within' painting by random numbers. Paint *anyhow*: splash it, dab it, daub it. Whether your fancy is circles or squiggles, moons or horses' manes, emptiness or meaningfulness – the 'what' doesn't matter. Neither does the 'how'. If you're right-handed, why not hold the brush in your left? Or even paint with your eyes closed? Or, as I did, see whether your master-work is improved by crumpling and unfolding the paper while the paint's still wet. As Avril Wigham, who runs the class, says: 'Lack of technical ability could be an advantage.'

Contact: Avril Wigham, 21 Elms Road, London, SW4 9ER, UK.
Tel: 0171 622 9530

British Cultural Section 3: The Bed of Nails

It is six foot by two foot. It is a porcupine rectangle, it is where fakirs are horizontal, it is my oblong of pain. I had come to learn the technique of lying on the bed of nails.

In the room with me was Terry Cole, who describes himself as the Greatest One Man Circus on Earth. Amongst his achievements is the world record for balancing milk-crates on a chin: Terry has held twenty-five in a single pillar so weighty that his teeth were left shattered. As he let go of his lower lip, after showing me his shipwreck of a mouth, he said simply: 'It's the price I pay.'

I watched as Terry lowered himself onto the points – in my imagination, they seemed to gleam all the more, as if they were welcoming him.

'Is that comfortable?' I asked.

'Absolutely,' he answered and smiled; then he turned over and laid on his front.

'Doesn't that get a bit . . . awkward . . . around the crotch?' I asked.

'I suppose you could always wear a condom,' he replied. With that, he lifted himself off the bed, and offered me the opportunity of taking his place.

Every pain is specific. Kicking your toe is a different experience from a stinging in the eye. All I can say is that the bed of nails is unique and unpleasant: like a migraine of the back, or a toothache of the spine, or a rheumatism in your very pores. As I lay there, I realized the absurdity of this self-inflicted agony. Why was I doing it? I could only grin at my ridiculousness. Grin and bear it . . . the facial muscles employed in making a grimace are not so dissimilar from those for a grin . . .

I stayed for a few minutes. Yet Terry aims to go for the world record and spend 400 hours on the nails. To do that, you would need psychological preparation, you'd have to be completely involved with yourself, you'd have to forget your surroundings, and enter a semi-meditative state.

I left Terry's house feeling silliness mixed with self-esteem; thoughts of comedy, pain and pride. Beds are often where we are born, often where we die; and the nails? A bed in-between. But at the time, I felt like

---

saying to myself: yes, this is experience, this is what it's all about – as if, until I had lain on a bed of nails, I hadn't lived at all.

The points don't make an impression *only* on the skin.

Contact: Terry Cole, 6 Acacia Rd, Walthamstow, London, E17 8BW, UK.
Tel: 0181 518 6278 or: 0956 173539

British Cultural Section 4:
The Bruce Forsyth Social Club

Bruce Forsyth is the King of British game shows, noted for his brilliance as an all-round entertainer, his stream of catchphrases, and the fact that his hair is . . . well, let's just say that it probably has a different DNA-structure from the head beneath it.

I was on one knee in the Barbican Arms public house in Plymouth. The initiation was under way. Fifteen men formed a circle around me and began singing the song most sacred:

> Life is the name of the game
> And I want to play the game with you
> Life can be terribly tame
> If you don't play the game with two . . .
> *And I want to play the game with you!*

Whereupon the object they were holding – a cream-coloured square of carpet, attached to a strip of double-sided double-strength carpet-tape – was pressed down upon my head. At last I was given the official greeting into the organization: 'Nice to see you, to see you – NICE!' It was time for game number one.

The Bruce Forsyth Social Club was formed by Mike Colwill, a bank employee with an admiration for the all-round entertainer and king of the game shows. 'He's great with people,' he told me. The members meet every two months to play their own versions of Brucie games: putting the toupee on the landlord (a variation on putting the tail on the donkey); one-legged butt kicking (combining the athleticism of Long John Silver with the viciousness of Thai boxing); and hunt the carpet-tape. In every game, Mike is the perfect Bruce, putting his arms around the contestants' shoulders: 'Do you want to go first or second? First? Yes, get it over with.' Then, when a game is finished, he offers the appropriate commiserations to the runners-up, 'We're sorry to lose you, we really are.'

But let me say a little more about those wigs. Because of the generosity of a local carpet-fitter, the club is kept well-supplied with off-cuts, which are then trimmed to the size of a mortar-board. Any colour or design are acceptable – bright red, striped, even fluorescent – though if someone in a pub asks about the material used, there is an official club reply: 'They're real hair.'

Contact: Mike Colwill, 2 Cranbourne Ave, St Judes, Plymouth, PL4 8RT, UK.
Tel: 01752 661387

British Cultural Section 5: Carry On Appreciating

The series of 30 *Carry On* films defined a universe, a sex 'n' lavatories nether-world, in which life does not have a meaning – but a double-meaning. Consider the immortal dialogue from *Carry On Abroad*:

Babs (Asking for a drink): 'Have you got a large one?'
Sid: 'I've had no complaints so far.'

Or Bernard Bresslaw's dismissal of an Indian fakir in *Carry On Up the Khyber*: 'Fakir – Off!'
The *Carry On*s captured a part of the British soul on screen; and as long as the British are British, they're going to find this kind of sauce a source of amusement. Carl St John, the man who runs the appreciation society for the films, believes that the *Carry On*s were just about the best humour that Britain has ever produced. 'We've got members in the society who nowadays never go to the cinema or watch TV because they find nothing else entertaining,' he told me.

Contact: Carl St John, 27 Brookmead Way, Orpington, Kent, BR5 2BQ, UK.

British Cultural Section 6: Conkers

The game of conkers is part of growing up in Britain. Kids attach a nut from the horse-chestnut tree to a piece of string and then take turns to use it like a medieval mace and chain – attempting to smash an opponent's conker, which is held dangling as a target. The conker that smashes first is the loser.

If I talk of a sea of leaves, it is merely to mention the sea-mines. Remember, under horse-chestnut trees, kicking aside most of autumn's waves, looking only for the green and prickly shells? I wanted to relive it all.

Thus, in the Chequered Skipper pub in the village of Ashton, home to the World Conker Championships, I met John Hadman, the event's organizer. Soon we started a game . . . and I rediscovered one memory which nostalgia had filtered out: how painful it is when you miss and the conker continues its trajectory towards your own body. John smiled, and remarked that some competitors wear a crotch-protecting box, used in sports like cricket. 'And you can tell from the sound when they've been hit,' he said.

Contact: John Hadman, The Ashton Conker Club, 22 New Rd, Oundle, Peterborough, PE8 4LB, UK.
Tel: 01832 272735

British Cultural Section 7: The Eagle Society

The Eagle was a British boys' comic, published from 1950 to 1969 – its most famous character being Dan Dare, a spaceship pilot.

'One year, we recreated a cricket match that featured in a 1951 Dan Dare adventure,' said Howard Corn, one of the leading members of the *Eagle* Society, which keeps alive the memory of the famous comic. 'There is a scene where a UFO lands on a cricket pitch at Nether Wallop in Wiltshire, which is a real place. So we went down there one Sunday morning and had a match on the village green.'

'Does anyone,' I said, 'ever tell you, "Grow up"?'

'Well, I stopped reading the *Eagle* when I was about 15 – but then I came back to it in 1977,' said Howard, who is now in his fifties. 'At one time I was quite embarrassed about admitting I still liked it. I thought I was being childish. But then I discovered all these other people who liked the *Eagle* – professors, doctors and highbrow professional men. So I came out of the closet and said I love the *Eagle* and I'm never afraid to mention it now.'

Then he said: 'I've often thought to myself, that if ever I was terminally ill, lying in hospital, I would get my *Eagles* and I would sit and read them from start to finish. Every copy. I'd be highly delighted if I died with an *Eagle* in my hands.'

Contact: The Eagle Society, Keith Howard, 25a Station Rd, Harrow, Middlesex, HA1 2UA, UK.

British Cultural Section 8: The Eurovision Song Contest Fan Club

One night every year, the nations of Europe do battle against each other – with songs. The Eurovision Song Contest has, probably unjustly, a reputation for the trashiest pop music you can find – epitomized by the British entry in the early 70s 'Boom-Bang-a-Bang'.

'Just as other people like football, so we like Eurovision,' said Perry Robbins, a leading member of the Eurovision Network, the fan club for the Eurovision Song Contest. 'I wish people would give it a chance. The music's so varied – it's not all "Boom-Bang-a-Bang".' His fellow-enthusiast Keith Foord agreed – he admitted that he had been passionate about Eurovision since childhood when, on the night of the contest, he used to drape national flags across the lounge and follow the action on his own chalk scoreboard.

Perry and Keith made me realize that Eurovision music is, well, European, and cannot be dissociated from the history, conflicts and politics of the continent. Take ethnic tensions. One year, Turkish television decided to black out the Greek entry – and so the following year the Greeks responded with a charming chanson about a Turkish napalm attack carried out during the invasion of Cyprus.

Then there are the political bandwagon tunes. Fears about nuclear obliteration led to a Finnish entry entitled 'Don't Drop the Bomb On Me'. The thaw in relations between East and West produced the Norwegian song 'Glasnost', with a chorus about Reagan and Gorbachev.

Norway, as you may know, has a special place in the history of the contest – as the country that achieved the distinction of scoring zero ('*Nul Points*'). The disgrace prompted the Norwegians to hire a professor of linguistics to write lyrics that would smooth out the more unpleasant of the Scandinavian sounds – and when Norway eventually won the contest, the country went wild: flags waved, car horns honked and a national holiday was declared. 'But unfortunately, when the contest took place in Norway the following year,' said Perry, 'the Queen of Norway had her bag snatched.'

Contact: Joseph Currie, Eurovision Network, 1 Byres Road (4/3), Glasgow, G11 5RD, UK.
Or: Perry Robbins, 4 Parkin Street, Alfreton, Derbyshire, DE55 7JS, UK.

British Cultural Section 9:
Flower Communication

'When I was growing up,' said Ruth Rankin, 'I loved to make daisy chains. I can remember getting very upset when the grass was cut – because the mower cut the poor daisies' heads off. And to me, they were like my little friends.'

Ruth is an expert in 'flower communication' – which she defines as 'a method of accessing energies or "essences" in flowers'. In her workshops and one-to-one sessions she explores the effect that flowers have upon moods, emotions and creativity. 'A favourite of mine is pansies,' she told me. 'If you look at them, they're like little faces. Pansies are about facing the world and being open. They're to do with self-esteem. But every flower has its own signature, its own properties.' Daffodils for joy, Easter lily for removing guilt, field poppies for discovering strength within, and so on. 'I can also attune myself to the flower simply by holding the seeds,' she said.

Contact: Ruth Rankin, 20 Woodstock Grove, London, W12 8LE, UK.
Tel: 0181 740 4764

British Cultural Section 10:
Flying Trapeze Training

In an unsuccessful launch, the trapeze artist does not swing in an arc: often, the novice will end up being dragged across the floor still attached to his safety lines, like a marionette dangling on its strings. In my case, that wasn't the only humiliation. The friction of my clothes against the mat pulled down first my shorts, then my underpants. So it was perhaps wrong to use the marionette metaphor: after all, puppets are not usually anatomically correct.

Contact: The Circus Space, Coronet Street, Hackney, London, N1 6HD, UK.
Tel: 0171 613 4141

British Cultural Section 11: The George Formby Society

Nowadays, it's hard to realize how big a star George Formby once was. Famed as a ukulele player, he was Britain's highest-paid entertainer during the 1940s, earning £100,000 a year even in those times. Now, thirty years after his death, the 1,000 members of the George Formby Society continue to sing his songs and keep his memory alive.

Standing on the platform at Blackpool, waiting for the late train to Euston, the one thing that wasn't going to depart was the memory of my first ukulele lesson.

It's very easy to get hooked on the uke and its plink, plinkety-plunk. Sure, the fretboard was no longer in my hand, but mentally my fingers were still forming chord-shapes. Rather like amputees who want to scratch the empty air where a limb once grew . . . only such comparisons are too morbid for the song I'd learnt, 'When I'm Cleaning Windows'.

> Ladies' nighties I have spied,
> I've often seen what goes inside,
> When I'm cleaning windows . . .

Fifty years on, it's still worth a chuckle; though it does sound a little odd when you hear it performed by a boy as young as eight. You see, there is no age discrimination in the George Formby Society. I had attended their convention in the Winter Gardens, Blackpool – I had never seen so many ukuleles in my life.

A number of the members told me of the power of Formby's charisma; from the posters and photographs on display at the Winter Gardens, it was easy to see what they meant. It's in the face. The mouth, the buck teeth, the saucy wink – you can't take your eyes off Formby, even if you want to. He may have looked like a cross between Goofy and Olive Oyl, but he had the stamp of a star.

31

Contact: Peter Pollard, 42 Ullswater Avenue, Dewsbury, West Yorkshire
WF12 7PW, UK
Tel: 01924 462249
Website:http://freespace.virgin.net/peter.pollard/
E-mail: peter.pollard@virgin.net

British Cultural Section 12:
The Hattie Jacques
Appreciation Society

Hattie Jacques, who died in 1980, was a plump British actress perhaps best known for playing matronly figures in 14 Carry On *films (see* Carry On Appreciating*).*

'Do you see?' said Sue Todd, pointing at the TV screen. A video of her heroine, Hattie Jacques, was playing. 'She's got a mole on her face in exactly the same place as I have. And it's the same colour as well. I'll often say to my husband, "I've got two things in common with Hattie Jacques – my size and that mole." '

'Do you like her clothes?' I asked.

'Oh, I'd *love* to acquire some of Hattie's dresses – it may sound strange, because I know she's dead, but I'd wear Hattie's clothes.'

Sue added that if Hattie Jacques were still alive today, she wouldn't feel any need to slim. 'Hattie could make a joke about her size. But I am afraid that I am bothered about *my* size. I've been teased – and it *hurts*. Society puts so much pressure on women to stay slim. But if Hattie were here, I could say to people that Hattie's plump, and she's a brilliant star, and she's happy the way she is – so why shouldn't *I* be happy the way *I* am?'

Contact: Sue Todd, 34 Freemantle Avenue, Sutton Trust Estate, Hull, HU9 4RH, UK.
Tel: 01482 796991

British Cultural Section 13:
Hot SPICE

The Special Programme of Initiative, Challenge and Excitement (or SPICE) is a multi-activity leisure club, with many regional branches. The

emphasis is on adventure sports like canoeing, gliding and ballooning –
activities which do not quite fall within the scope of this book. However,
SPICE organizes a host of events, all year round – and fire is a feature of
the SPICE calendar. I am therefore including three 'Hot' SPICE activities:
fire-eating, fire-walking and the human torch. Obviously, these involve a
degree of risk – and under no circumstances should they be attempted
without the expert supervision provided by SPICE.

Fire-eating: You practise by putting an unlit 'firebrand' into the mouth –
for without dummy runs, you'd miss the target. As I didn't fancy a poke
in the eye with a burning stick, I had no intention of shirking on the
training. Then all I had to do was repeat the action with the firebrand
alight . . .

Well, there is more to it than that; but just in case there is someone out
there who is stupid enough to try it without expert supervision, I'm not
going to reveal all the secrets. I will merely say: I did it. I stuck a blazing
firebrand right into my mouth. True, I had qualms – millions of years of
genetic programming tell you it's not a very good idea to chew on naked
flames. But once you've overcome that fear, you get to like it. The ultimate acquired taste.

Fire-walking: Let me say that there are no tricks. No chemicals are
applied to the skin and you don't need thick, calloused soles. But one
factor looms large in the fire-walker's craft: self-belief. You have to be
absolutely convinced that the coals can be crossed without pain or harm.

The full psychological training takes several hours. You need to imagine that you have *already* completed the fire-walk, *already* conquered
the impossible, even though you have yet to attempt it. You have to feel
the elation of that experience and come up with some gesture, personal
to yourself, that expresses it – my gesture was to punch the air and shout:
'Yes!' We were told that when we were standing at the threshold of the
coals, we should repeat that gesture over and over again until we felt
ready to walk – and, when it came to walking, we should look up and say
'Cool moss, cool moss', as we strode. (One member of the class was from
Saudi Arabia, and he said 'Cool moss' in Arabic.)

So the entire class went outside where we faced a four-metre bed of
glowing coals. Quite simply, one by one, we walked across.

What did I feel? I can honestly say: nothing. I had no sensation of heat
whatsoever – and these were coals at nine hundred degrees centigrade.
All I can recall is the crunchiness of the bed underfoot. There was no
pain and I was totally unscathed. I couldn't understand it – but I'd done
it. 'Yes!'

Subsequently, I *have* heard attempts to explain fire-walking scientifically – it's supposed to be possible because of the low speed of
transference of heat from the coals to the body. But there is a problem

with this, which makes me think it's not the full explanation. At the workshop, a radio journalist came along to interview us for a feature; and she decided to walk on the coals herself. If the scientists have got it right, she should have done it easily. But she, unlike the rest of us, had not gone through several hours of mental preparation – *and she was the only person there who complained about burning her feet.*

The Human Torch: I had received by mail a notice of the precautions I should take: specifically, that under no circumstances should I wear any clothing made of artificial fibres. Although the clothes would be covered by outer garments and wouldn't be burnt, such would be the heat surrounding the body that nylon and polyester might melt. So, before setting out, I double-checked the label in my underpants. Well, you've got to be careful if you're going to set fire to yourself.

Obviously, we had to wear protective suits. I am under oath to keep the secret of precisely what the protection is, because the SPICE instructor doesn't want anyone to turn themselves into Baked Alaska without the help of an excellent chef (i.e. a SPICE instructor). But when that protection is on, a genuine gasolene fire is started on your back and the flames lick you with a thousand tongues. We did it in the evening, for a better effect: and when burning people go for a walk, it looks Satanic – the damned on a stroll out of hell. Other shapes suggest themselves: gigantic butterfly wings of fire, flapping in the night air; or flame-prickles, like a dead holly leaf, coinciding with a person's torso.

But the experience of being, rather than watching, a human torch, is not what you would expect. Inside the protective suit, you do feel *some* heat – as if you were standing too close to an electric fire – but that is only towards the end of the 40-second burn.

Because, you see, as an added safety-measure the protective suit is made sopping wet. So in reality, the experience was like sprawling on a wet fish counter.

Contact: SPICE UK, 13 Thorpe St, Old Trafford, Manchester, M16 9PR, UK.
Tel: 0161 8722213 Fax: 0161 8489465
Website: www.spiceuk.com

British Cultural Section 14: Indian Head Massage Training

At its gentlest, the thousand-year-old Indian tradition of head massage can be a simple laying-on of hands – think of the 'See no evil, speak no evil, hear no evil' monkeys and you will have a rough idea of where to touch someone's face. Other times, the going gets more energetic, with the scalp, shoulders, neck or skull receiving 'brain shaking', 'piano playing', or the dreaded 'windscreen wiper', which destroys all known hairstyles.

'Learning head massage will help your friends . . . and those who will become your friends,' says the head massage teacher Narendra Mehta. For the tranquillity inside a well-rubbed head has to be experienced to be believed. I have heard that in a state of relaxation a brain emits alpha rhythms, which can be detected on an electro-encephalograph machine; but a woman on the course I took became so relaxed under head massage that her brain went to the other end of the alphabet and produced the *zzzzz* of a full-blown snore.

Head massage has just one drawback, though: the snowstorm of dandruff which the technique rakes out of your scalp and deposits on your shoulders for all to see.

Contact: Narendra Mehta, 136 Holloway Rd, London, N7 8DD, UK.
Tel: 0171 609 3590

British Cultural Section 15: The Janet Ellis Fans

Janet Ellis is a former presenter of the British children's television programme, Blue Peter, *a magazine-style show which encourages children to make things, try out new experiences, raise money for charity and so on. The show has had numerous presenters since it began in 1958 and Janet was one of a team of three from 1983–7.*

It is not simply that he records her every television appearance, though naturally, he does that. No, what makes Nicholas Hall such a special fan is that when he goes to work, he leaves the VCR running, just *in case* Janet Ellis should appear. You see, Nicholas Hall stands at the core of a small, but very dedicated group of fans; he edits the specialist publication, *The Janet Ellis Fanzine*, aimed at those who follow the career of the former *Blue Peter* presenter.

You may be thinking that nobody would read a magazine about such a – with due respect – *minor* celebrity as Janet Ellis. You're probably wondering how this magazine can exist, because what on earth is there to say about her? She's never had a hit record, never appeared in a movie, never done a cheesecake photograph – though since leaving *Blue*

Peter she has featured prominently in a soap powder advertisement. She doesn't do *anything*, you would think, that fans could latch onto. But that is wrong. To prove the point, Nicholas showed me a file of correspondence, several inches thick, from fellow Janet-enthusiasts. My eyes were opened as soon as I started reading.

There were letters which analyzed her minutest mannerisms: 'She has a very characteristic way of drawing her lower lip into her mouth, extending her chin slightly and nodding to denote agreement.' There were letters testifying to her inspirational qualities: 'There is something about sitting back and concentrating on Janet Ellis. Just a picture of her is more than ample reason for all other matters to vanish and make you feel good enough to tackle anything.' And there were letters which talked of her 'supernatural sex appeal' and 'her radioactive attraction'. Sometimes there was just worship: 'I love everything about her: the flare of her nostrils, the curve of her bottom, even the delicate arch of her instep . . .'

Nicholas's own enthusiasm is unique because it did not even begin with *Blue Peter*. He first spotted Janet five years before she presented the show, when she was playing a bit-part in a 1978 episode of the crime-drama *The Sweeney*. When I visited Nicholas at his home in Poole, Dorset, he showed me the very clip that changed his life. It cannot last longer than a minute, but that was enough for him to be smitten. All those years ago, he waited till the credits came up to see the name: Janet Ellis. 'I honestly thought she was the most attractive woman I'd seen on TV.' He told me that his ultimate ambition is to own a tape of Janet's stint on the toddlers' programme *Jigsaw*. 'I'd pay £50 for a tape of old *Jigsaw* material,' he said.

The fanzine itself squeezes an impossible amount out of the Ellis phenomenon. Apart from a Janet-related crossword – where you might be asked the colour of the T-shirt she wore in that episode of *The Sweeney* – and articles on such subjects as Janet's problems with asthma, or the exclusive announcement of her latest pregnancy, particular attention is given to the clothes she wears. There is a top ten of her outfits (no. 8: grey jacket, black top, short black skirt, worn in the series *Parenting*, 'Multiple Births' episode), and in one case, a review of Janet's appearance in a nuclear power video, we can read an account of the likelihood of Armageddon, juxtaposed with details of her clothing. ('Could a Chernobyl-type accident happen in Britain?' she asks. She wears a black jacket, black top and white trousers. 'Do leaks from nuclear power stations cause leukaemia?' She wears black trousers, purple sweater and red scarf.)

Best of all are the readers' recollections of their heroine's appearances. Says one reader, recalling an episode of *Blue Peter*: 'Who can forget the spectacle of Janet in T-shirt and shorts crawling on her belly across the mud-flats of the River Exe as part of an endurance test. "It was quite fun, actually, once you were good and dirty," she assures viewers afterwards. Wotta Gal!' Another fan reminisces about a *Blue Peter* episode in which her fellow-presenter Peter Duncan plays the inventor of a lemon-tea footbath and Janet is in a creamy-pink Edwardian dress: 'From beneath her long dress she places one petite and naked foot into the bowlful of cold tea. For months after that particular edition of *Blue Peter* I dreamed of holding Janet's little foot in my hand and kissing those tantalising toes over and over.'

Like other minority groups, Janet-fans have to face society's lack of understanding, perhaps having to hide their recordings of *Blue Peter* in the middle of the tape, so that no-one finds them; or, in the case of a ship-yard worker, getting teased for rushing home for the broadcasts on Mondays and Thursdays.

The real question is: why do thirty-odd people regularly subscribe, with an additional hundred-and-twenty or so expressing occasional interest? Nicholas believes that Janet has a special 'natural' quality. 'You can imagine her coming into your home, patting the dog and sitting down,' he told me. Nonetheless, almost all the subscribers are men. What they seem to like is the way that Janet Ellis manages to be sexy within the supposedly demure world of children's television. Even within the constraints imposed by a wholesome show like *Blue Peter*, she was prepared to wear short skirts, plunging necklines, and tight T-shirts. She would show a lot of cleavage while tap-dancing and often she put on a low-cut bathing suit for some escapade involving water. Perhaps significantly, she is known as the *Blue Peter* girl who had a child out of wedlock – which led some Conservative MPs to demand that she be fired from the show for setting a bad example.

Whatever the secret of Janet's appeal, Nicholas believes he will be a fan for life. He admits that he does not intend to get married and, now in his thirties, he says that he is quite happy being single. He and Janet exchange Christmas cards, he sends her the first copy of every issue of the magazine – she owns up to being flattered by all the attention – and perhaps once a year, if she is at a public exhibition such as a car show, he has the ultimate thrill of meeting his idol face-to-face.

I asked him what that was like the first time: 'When I saw her,' he said, 'it was like she had an aura. She smiled directly at me and my mouth went dry. I had to walk away to compose myself.'

Contact: Nicholas Hall, 12 Alderney Avenue, Parkstone, Poole, Dorset, BH12 4LG, UK.
Tel: 01202 722798

British Cultural Section 16: Letterboxing

There are letterboxes under rocks, in holes in the ground, near land-marks, and occasionally in pubs.

As you will have guessed, these letterboxes have nothing to do with the mail. (Or perhaps you *won't* have guessed – given all the strange variations on philately in this book.) The boxes are hidden all over Dartmoor National Park – the first was planted in 1854 – with new ones being added continually, and some old ones being taken away. Each box contains a visitors' book and a rubber stamp: letterbox hunters follow cryptic clues to find the boxes, then use the stamp to record the find in their own books, and mark the visitors' book in the box with their own personal stamps. The object is to collect as many stamps as possible.

'Letterboxing is a great social leveller,' said Pat Clatworthy, who runs the Letterbox 100 Club which is open to anyone who has discovered at least 100 boxes. (She herself has notched up thousands.) 'You'll find a boy scout of nine sitting on a rock talking to a professional man like a doctor or a dentist about the location of a letterbox . . .'

Contact: Pat Clatworthy, Letterbox 100 Club, 1 Dryfield, Exminster, Exeter, EX6 8DJ, UK.
Tel: 01392 832768
(The club also publishes a catalogue of letterboxes, together with clues to locations.)

British Cultural Section 17: The Model Helicopter Flying School

I was standing in the middle of an abandoned airforce base in Shropshire and moving my thumb and forefinger a millimetre or two. Ten metres away, and a metre off the ground, an object bobbed in the air like a buoy, with every gust of wind a wave. My first task was to steady it, by sending out another wave, a *radiowave* – because my fingers were operating a transmitter and the object was a model helicopter. Sadly, all too often I peaked when I should have troughed and troughed when I should have peaked and was not averse to throwing in the odd *tsunami*. But then, flying a model helicopter demands considerable patience – which is why people book lessons with Radioflight, the UK's first model helicopter flying school.

As with a real aircraft, a novice never flies solo. A cable links the instructor's transmitter to the pupil's – which is known as the 'Buddy Box' system. This enables the instructor to override the pupil's radio signals, to avert a possible crash.

Yet there are moments when even a beginner gets it right. Then, there can be an extremely satisfying, almost uncanny sense of *resonance*: when operating the tail rotor you not only know which way the helicopter will turn, it somehow seems that *you* are turning, too.

Contact: Radioflight, 7 Knatchbull Way, Brabourne Lees, Ashford, Kent, TN25 6PY, UK.
Tel: 0410 190815

British Cultural Section 18: Subterranea Britannica

There was an electric light upon the walls, where centuries ago there would have been candlelight. What there was not, what there had never been, was a single ray of sunlight.

I was thirty feet underground in a mysterious and unnatural cave. Unnatural, because no geological process, no erosion, no seeping water-action could have given it such a shape: like an upright winebottle, with a neck that narrowed the higher it went. Mysterious, because when you are standing at its base and staring upwards you cannot help but ask yourself: who built it? And when? And why?

'Coming down here changed my life,' said Sylvia Beamon, who had accompanied me along the passageway that led to Royston Cave. It was a chance visit to the cave with her children in 1974 that started Sylvia's fascination with the achievements of the human mole. The experience led her to found Subterranea Britannica – a group which studies and explores the UK's man-made underground structures: sewers, drains, wells – anything from a prehistoric burial chamber to a nuclear fall-out shelter.

Sylvia's own belief is that Royston Cave was built by the Knights Templar, initially to store market goods and then turned into a chapel. Is she right? My own knowledge was just too meagre to judge. I only knew of one thing concerning the Knights Templar: were they not rumoured to possess the Holy Grail? And could the Grail *possibly* – just possibly – have been stored in this strange cave at Royston?

'Ah,' said Sylvia with a smile, 'You're flying a kite with that one . . .'

Contact: Malcolm and Barbara Tadd, 65 Trindles Rd, South Nutfield, Redhill, Surrey, RH1 4JL, UK.
Tel: 01737 823456

C

The Campbell's Soup Collector Club

In reply to my letter, the club said: 'We think the concept of your book is souper!'

Dedicated to the collection of Campbell's Soup advertising and memorabilia, the Campbell's Soup Collector Club was founded by David Young and his wife Micki, from Wauconda, Illinois, USA. Ten years ago, David took off on a shopping trip to search for red and white items to match the kitchen. He encountered a popcorn tin, decorated with Campbell's Soup Company advertising . . . which turned out to be the first of 600 Campbell-patterned items in David's home: hats, aprons, mugs – and of course, Campbell's Soup in the larder. 'We're a Campbell's family through and through,' commented David.

That could apply, *a fortiori*, to two of the club's 300 members – a brother and sister, who are actually called Jim and Janet Campbell. As children, they were dressed up as the Campbell company's 'Campbell Kids' for a fancy dress party; as adults, they have done the reverse of David Young – and *chosen their house decor to match their Campbell's memorabilia*. The upstairs is painted red and white to match the soup labels, and the large bathroom features a soup can shower stall. 'Every time I see something with Campbell's on it, I have to buy it,' said Janet.

Contact: The Campbell's Soup Collector Club, 414 Country Lane Ct., Wauconda, IL 60084, USA.
Tel/Fax: 847 487 4917 E-mail: Dyoung4641@AOL.com

The Canal Card Collectors' Circle

Much as I would like to describe these collectors as 'deltiologists with the emphasis on the delta', it would represent a diversion from, as it were, their true course: they do not collect postcards of *rivers* – the waterway has to be man-made for its postcard to have any appeal. Here is an extract from their newsletter:

'There are at present 3,341 cards on the list (of known postcards, featuring British canals, produced during the pre-colour-printing era) while the British waterways total at my estimate 3,819 miles. This gives an average of 1.1 miles per card, or 0.9 cards per mile, depending on how you look at it. The most represented canal is the Crinan, with 172 cards in 9 miles, or 19.9 per mile. The worst is the Ashby, with only one card in 30 miles, though there are some canals with no cards. I did once meet someone who claimed to have a card with a bit of the Hereford and Gloucester on it, but we don't have that one listed.'

Contact: Canal Card Collectors' Circle, c/o David Clough, 12 Wellstead Gardens, Westcliff-on-Sea, Essex, SS0 0AY, UK.

The Cane Collector's Chronicle

Perhaps one should call Ted Boothroyd 'the man with a millipede in his soul'; how else to describe a desire to accumulate over a thousand walking sticks?

'A stick like this would have been used by a nineteeth-century lawyer,' he commented, as he passed me the ivory handle, a representation of a fist clutching a scroll. The end of the scroll unscrewed, revealing a hidden chamber – at one time, it would have held several snorts of cocaine. 'Even today this little chamber has got a funny smell about it,' he remarked.

His favourite stick? One that bears the inscription on its collar: 'To Cassy from Doo – Easter 1913'.

'I've always been intrigued by that inscription,' he said. 'Was the stick an engagement present? Or a wedding present? It sounds so romantic. It seems a world away. I'd love to hear from someone who knows something about Cassy and Doo.' The stick is now in the possession of his granddaughter . . . who was named Cassy after it.

Contact: The Cane Collector's Chronicle (a specialist publication for walking-stick enthusiasts), c/o Linda Beeman, 2515 Fourth Avenue, # 405, Seattle, Washington 98121, USA.

The Cardboard Boat Racing World Championship

'We were edgy. The floor was all squishy. During the race you'll feel a nudge in your back and you'll think that another boat has hit you. But it's your own boat starting to buckle.'

Contact: Heber Springs Area Chamber of Commerce, 1001 West Main Street, Heber Springs, Arkansas 72543, USA.
Tel: 501 362 2444 Website: http://www.heber-springs.com

The Carnivorous Plant Society

'You get some people feeding them bits of beef and cheese,' said Dudley Watts, as his Venus Fly Trap's jaws closed around my finger.

It's an eerie sensation, being gripped by vegetable teeth, and it's not surprising that Darwin dubbed the Fly Trap 'the most wonderful plant in the world'. But although that particular killer bloom is very widely known to the public, most people are not aware that there are about 500 *other* types of carnivorous plant, with more being discovered every year.

Take the Portuguese dewy pine, whose leaves are long, red, tipped tentacles that exude a sticky solution for catching flying prey. 'Some of these sticky ones can became black with flies in the summer,' said Dudley, as we walked around his menagerie-cum-greenhouse.

Or take the bladderwort: on its stems are tiny bubble-like sacs, containing water under pressure, and on each bubble is a trapdoor mechanism, and a sensitive hair. Pity the poor insect that touches that bristle – the trapdoor is immediately flipped inwards, sucking in the water and the prey. Dudley remarked that he'd heard a recording of the sound made by the bladderwort's trapdoor: death comes with a pop.

Contact: The Carnivorous Plant Society, Derek Petrie, 100 Lambley Lane, Burton Joyce, Nottingham, NG14 5BL, UK.
E-mail: cps@clara.net

The Cast Iron Seat Collectors' Association

There's nothing like an in-joke to define an organization: 'The best seat I was able to buy that day was broken . . . #151 Broken, that is. It certainly made my day.'

(The #151 Broken being one of 2,200 known cast-iron seats used on horse-drawn farming implements between 1850 and 1900.)

Contact: Charolette Traxler, Cast Iron Seat Collectors' Association, RFD 2 Box 38, Le Center, MN 56057, USA.

Catamenia

Some people may be offended by this interest appearing in the book. Yet, if I look at the material it covers – history, folklore, art, collecting – it is on a par with many others. So here goes:

Harry Finley is a bachelor in his fifties who is fascinated by the history of women's sanitary protection. It all began when he was living in Germany, and realized from the ads in the magazines that some countries were very open about feminine hygiene, while others were ashamed. In time, he began to explore the history of the subject – such as whether tampons really originated with the ancient Egyptians – and established a Museum of Menstruation (MUM) in his basement, and an accompanying newsletter, *Catamenia*, which has now been replaced by a website. Yes, he does receive hate mail, and his family have all but disowned him, but Harry continues in his crusade.

For instance, in an issue of *Catamenia* he noted that: 'Pretty soon we'll display a contemporary Russian tampon at the museum, a Japanese tampon with an unusual delivery system and much else to do with tampons – patents, boxes and instructions.' He added that he had recently acquired two old dispensers for Kotex and Modess 'from an anonymous donor'. There was also a feature on some early advertising for sanitary protection (which proclaimed that it gave women 'freedom to play golf' and a photograph of a Hawaiian menstrual hut, known as a *hale p'ea*, one of many structures used by cultures around the world to segregate menstruating women.

'Women feel the effects of their own menstruation,' he continued, 'but who has seen a moving, menstruating uterus?' There followed a report from Medical Imaging International about creating moving images of a menstruating uterus using ultrasonography. 'MUM hopes to be able to show visitors a copy of this video in the near future.'

He finished the issue with an appeal: 'If you have created art related in some way to menstruation, show it on the MUM website.'

Contact: The Museum of Menstruation, PO Box 2398 Landover Hills Branch, Hyattsville, MD 20784-2398, USA.
Tel: 301 459 4450 Fax: 301 577 2913 Website: http://www.mum.org
E-mail: hfinley@mum.org

The Cave Radio and Electronics Group

It could be described as caving with callsigns; as static by stalactites; as microphones and miners' lamps. This is the world of the Cave Radio and Electronics Group – subterranean radio hams, potholers with aerials.

'Actually, it always strikes me as inappropriate to talk of "aerials" when you're underground,' said Mike Bedford, the group's chairman, as he and I stood outside the entrance to Kingsdale Master Cave, near Ingleton, North Yorkshire. Strictly speaking, he was right – 'antenna' being undoubtedly the more felicitous term, under the circumstances – but of course it takes a while to wrap one's brain around the very idea of Mike Bedford's group. 'Manhandling boxes of fragile electronic equipment down a cave might seem like an eccentric way of spending a weekend,' he commented. 'And certainly, we have been known to raise more than the odd eyebrow at field meetings.'

Nearby, two other members of the group examined a 'surface beacon': a grey metal box that emitted electronic chirrups, like a synthesized grasshopper. The beacon was a stand-in, a dummy radio operative, because there were no volunteers who were prepared to stay behind and send messages from the surface: everyone in the group wanted to be underground, to receive transmissions. I asked the beacon's constructor, Rob Gill, exactly why this activity held a fascination. 'Mainstream amateur radio is something you tend to lose interest in after a while,' he said.

'And this is more of a challenge because radio waves do not travel easily through rock,' said another member, David Gibson.

Of the various solutions to this problem that do not involve dynamite, the one under consideration on that day was so-called *earth-current signalling*. This meant hammering two copper rods into the ground, some 100 metres apart, at surface level, and connecting them by an electrical cable: a *single* cable – though the earth itself would be a conductor, completing the circuit.

'When a signal is sent into this system by the surface beacon it should in theory be possible to receive it underground,' said Rob. He remarked that communication via earth-currents had been known for a long time – it pre-dated conventional radio. 'But it's never found any major applications,' he said, 'apart from very briefly in the First World War, to send messages from trench to trench. We want to try it out in caves.'

So, our party approached the cave's mouth, and one by one, it swallowed us. I might even say that the cave salivated – only, the last thing I want to suggest is that the water inside was warm and spittle-like. The water was as cold as the cave was dark, and by no means shallow. Soon, it was over the top of my boots, right down inside the leather, stealing the feeling from the toes. As we went further, the level grew higher: to the thighs, to the crotch, to the waist – sometimes, to the chest. Worse, certain passages had to be negotiated with the body bent double.

It was the hell of Jonah: *epiglottic* darkness, with a boulder ever ready to trip you up, like a gigantic, slippery molar.

A quarter of a mile in, two hundred feet below the surface, we reached a dry shelf. Here, we sat, and Rob took his prototype receiver out of its watertight box. We listened . . . and heard nothing. We listened again.

'The signal is quite weak,' said Rob. To make matters worse, the background sound of the running water was quite loud. 'But if you put your ear right against the loudspeaker . . .'

Now, there is a scene in old Western movies – the one where an Indian scout puts his ear against the track and listens for an oncoming train. I mention it because the surface beacon was producing that familiar train rhythm, diddly-di-diddly-di-diddly-di. But the sound was so quiet that one must talk in terms of listening on the Trans-Siberian Railway – with one's ear down by the sleepers in Moscow and the train having just departed from the Vladivostok terminus, six thousand miles away.

'Is it worth all the misery just to listen to *that*?' I asked Mike.

He was unequivocal: it *was* worth it, because one day the group's endeavours could lead to the development of radio equipment which might be used in cave rescue. 'This could save lives,' he said.

Well, maybe so. I would not decry such aims. But David, joining in the conversation, took the line that cave electronics was an interesting hobby in its own right, regardless of any contribution it would make to cave rescue, and that there was no 'group policy', demanding a humanitarian aspect to the experiments.

'There's one member,' he said, 'who's built an electronic bat-detector, which converts the animals' ultrasonic squeaks into audible tones. There are members who are into the electronic aspects of cave photography. Or cave detection. In a sense, the group doesn't exist – there are just the experiments performed at the field meetings.'

By then, my feet were so numb that I had only one thought: the experiment of that particular day was not just reproducing the trench communications of the First World War – it would probably give me the trench foot of that era as well.

Contact: Cave Radio and Electronics Group, BCM BCRA, London, WC1N 3XX, UK.
Website: www.sat.dundee.ac.uk/~arb/creg/
E-mail: gibson@mcrosolv.demon.co.uk
Or: Speleonics: c/o Frank Reid, PO Box 5283, Bloomington, IN 47407-5283, USA.

Cereal Hobbyists

I am a serial hobbyist – and the homophone exists, as well: collectors of cereal boxes, and associated 'Free inside!' gifts and 'Send away three box tops!' special offers. And here I must declare that, in my life as a serial hobbyist, I would rank the cereal hobbyist magazine *The Freakie Magnet* as one of the most impressive specialist publications I've ever seen. Consider the quality of the research in just one issue, concentrating on parodies of cereal boxes in popular culture:

** The oldest known parody of a cereal reveals itself as Wheedies, on the cover of a 1955 issue of a *MAD*-like comic, *PANIC*. Free in the package was one Cadillac ashtray.

** In 1958, another magazine called *CRACKED* lampooned several cereal boxes in one cover, including Rice Krispies, whose elves were re-named WHAM, BLAM and POW, and whose free gift panel promised everything: cowboy suits, horses, a trip to the moon, a trip to the sun, the Empire State Building, Elvis, a submarine, a complete outdoor movie (with cars), etc, etc.

** A gum company in 1960 put out a series of cards called Foney Ads, which included Kill-Logs, showing cereal with bugs in it. In Canada a different set was released called Baloney Ads, which featured Smelloggs Worn Flakes.

** Another gum company released parody stickers in 1967 – featuring All-Brain, Cheapios and Alpain; while a cloth patch company put out Blind Mice Crispies.

** To top it all, *The Freakie Magnet* went to the trouble of producing its *own* full-colour cereal parody stickers. (Fancy a bowlful of Quap?)

What is it that drives such enthusiasm? A letter to the magazine states: 'Cereal box promotions bring out the fun youthful remembrances of childhood. Nothing compares to the rush of nostalgia that a collector experiences when he or she acquires a cereal box from childhood.'

Unfortunately, cereal box collectors won't let their *own* children have the likes of a plastic sabre-toothed tiger, or the cut-out coupon for a *Casper the Friendly Ghost* pen set: gifts and boxes are just wasted on kids. The sad irony is that the children of cereal box collectors will be the very ones denied the nostalgia of the cereal box experience.

The Freakie Magnet, Kevin Meisner, 8 Oakwood Drive, Gales Ferry, CT 06335, USA.
Website: http://members.aol.com/FREAKIEMAG/index2.htm
E-mail: freakiemag@aol.com

Chariot Racing

If I look at the *reality* of this sport, it is merely a type of horse racing; yet if someone were to say to you, 'My hobby is chariot racing . . .'

I think you'll understand why it's in these pages. The revival in modern times dates back to the 1930s, in the Star Valley region of western Wyoming. Competition among the drivers of horse-drawn milk-trucks to be the first to reach the creamery evolved into a sporting event – and as a variation in winter, bobsleighs were attached to the horses. As the races became more competitive, lighter cutter sledges were used; then, when the snow melted, and the desire to compete was as solid as ever, someone hit upon the idea of attaching wheels to the sledges.

As it says on the soundtrack of the sport's promotional video: 'It's as old as the pharoahs, as young as the American West.'

Contact: World Cutter & Chariot Racing Association, c/o J. Victor Adams, 2632 South 4300 W, Ogden, Utah 84401, USA.
Tel: 801 731 8021

The Checker Cab Club

'I was sitting at a T-Junction, and this guy came running over and said, "Can you take me downtown", or whatever, and I had to say, "Sorry, this is not a cab". And saying that while you're driving a cab, you might as well swear at someone or tell them they're stupid because they get really incensed. They say, "What do you mean, this isn't a cab?" '

That was the inevitable problem when Colin Peck pursued his hobby of driving an American Checker Cab while living in the USA. But Colin is an Englishman – and when he moved back to his home country, he shipped the cab with him. 'Here, you get more stares, more people rubbernecking, than if you were driving a Ferrari or a Rolls Royce,' he said.

Contact: Checker Cab Club, Alan Pritchard, 1 Curbar Rd, Great Barr, Birmingham, B42 2AT, UK.
Tel: 0121 6082737
Or: The Big Apple Taxi and Checker Club, c/o Mike Angelich, 77 North Street, Huntington Station, New York 11746, USA.
Or: The Checker Car Club of America, 10530 West Alabama Avenue, Sun City, Arizona 85351-3544, USA.

The Cheirological Society

'I just happen to have a couple of hand-prints of mass murderers,' he said. Christopher Jones opened a ring binder containing dozens and dozens of pictures of hands, as if an entire tribe of 1950s Hollywood-style North American Indians were saying 'How!' one after another. 'Here,' he said, when he reached the page.

They were unusual mitts, right enough. The palms were too large, suggesting an ape, or perhaps some ancestor of *Homo sapiens*, not a man; one finger was so abnormal it looked like a crooked chimneystack.

Years ago, people believed in physiognomy: that it was possible to relate behaviour, and in particular criminal tendencies, to the narrowness of the brow or the closeness of the eyes. Is it perhaps *the hand* that reveals a man's character? When the knuckle-dusters are off, can we still identify the man who wore them? The Cheirological Society says yes. Furthermore, they would only need sight of an empty hand to know the policeman who swings the baton, the judge who wields the gavel and the jailer who turns the key.

Taking its name from the Greek word *cheir*, meaning hand, the society was formed as long ago as 1889, with the intention of studying and teaching the link between hand and person. Yet cheirologists are second to none in opposing palmistry. 'I went to a palmist for a joke,' said Christopher, the society's current secretary, 'and I ended up reading *her* hands.' Cheirology examines the whole hand, not just the palm; and, more importantly, cheirologists do *not* predict the future. 'Palmistry comes out of the Middle Ages,' said Christopher, 'when life was short and people were looking for immediate signs. Like an "M" in the palm is supposed to represent money, marriage and good fortune.' I checked my own palm. There was an 'M' there. 'But everyone has one of those,' he said.

Now you will probably agree that, up to point, a hand will tell you something about a person: a building labourer is unlikely to have the hands of a violinist. Yet can analysis really go any further? In spite of cheirology's dismissal of the palmist, do they belong in the same booth?

There is some evidence to indicate that the hand *can* be used for medical diagnosis. A good example concerns Down's Syndrome, in which there is a so-called simian line, or single crease on the palm. Sufferers also have distinctive hand shapes and unusual fingerprint patterns. If genetic disorders are mirrored in the hand then so might be genetic components of personality. Yet cheirology goes beyond this. It claims that in the hand are not only the moles of nature but also the calluses of nurture. How can that be?

'The lines in the hand aren't static,' said Christopher. 'Broken lines can join up. Or lines can diminish and lose definition.' He brought forth another of his ring binders and showed me two hand-prints belonging to the same woman, but at different times in her life. At the time of the first print, she was having problems with her husband. When the second print was taken, a few months later, she had found happiness with a new man. The two prints were entirely different.

Then it came to the real test: Christopher carried out an analysis of *my* hand. I have to say he was uncannily accurate. I suppose he could have gleaned a lot about me from our conversation – I would like to see a more rigorous test – but he made me believe that cheirology shouldn't be, shall we say, dismissed out of hand. The key to my character? The whorls on my fingertips. Most people have a couple – I have five. People with those extra whorls have a strong unconventional streak; and I've certainly done one or two things off the beaten track.

What's more, he pointed to a feature called a 'writer's fork'. Just think: if it hadn't been for those snake-tongue lines on my palm, you wouldn't be reading this now.

Contact: Christopher Jones, The Cheirological Society, 37 Florence Park Road, Oxford, OX4 3PW, UK.
Tel: 01865 715087

The Cherry Pit Spitting Championships

The organizers hold a 'Pit Spit Clinic' to help people work on their spitting techniques. Well, you'll need training if you're thinking of taking on Rick 'Pellet Gun' Krause. (Krause has not only won the Cherry Pit Spitting Championship a record ten times since its inception at the Tree-Mendus Fruit Farm in 1973, but also holds the record spit of 72ft 7½in.)

Contact: Herb Teichman (Contest Founder), Tree-Mendus Fruit Farm, 9351 E. Eureka Rd, Eau Claire, MI 49111, USA.
Tel: 616 782 7101
Or: Lynne Sage (Publicity Manager)
Tel: 517 625 7253 Fax: 517 625 5588

The Chess on Stamps Study Unit

A 1980 stamp from Djibouti depicts the chess match between Samisch and Romanovsky in the International Tournament held in Moscow in 1925. It took one of the members of the Chess on Stamps Study Unit – a group dedicated to collecting all philatelic material relating to the game – to discover that, unfortunately, the position shown is not taken from the match. At no time was the white rook on h6 as seen on the stamp.

Furthermore, the black king never left the eighth rank, but according to the stamp, this rank is empty. The only detail in the stamp that seems to be consistent with the game is that the black queen on e4 is checking the white king on h1.

Contact: Chess on Stamps Study Unit, Anne N. Kasonic, 7624 County Road 153, Interlaken, NY 14847, USA.
E-mail: akasonic@epix.net

The Chopper Club

If ever a bicycle was the counterpart to a pair of trousers, it was the Chopper. Launched in 1970, when flares turned legs into a pair of triangles, the Rayleigh Chopper did much the same to the cycle-frame, with a rear wheel substantially larger than the front. If you add its other eccentricities – high-rise handlebars, a stretched saddle and a T-shaped gear stick – then you have the icon-bike of the times.

It was horrific in more than a visual sense, too: by the time the Chopper was ousted by the BMX in the early 80s, it had earned a reputation for terrible handling and poor brakes. Why, then, is there a modern-day club for Chopper enthusiasts? Some of the 350 members are undoubtedly in it for nostalgia, to recapture their youth; others to recapture the youth they never had – for the Chopper was a childhood status-symbol, a rich kid's bike. As one member writes in the club's newsletter:

'Why do I ride a Rayleigh Chopper? It's maybe because I never had one as a kid. My mum was convinced they were jerrybuilt deathtraps and my dad as a rule never paid more than £70 for his cars. But the buried desire never went away. So when I found a secondhand Chopper for sale, my wallet was out in nanoseconds . . . Ride one, and heads turn, people point and smile and you spend as much time chatting to strangers about Choppers as you do actually riding.'

Contact: The Chopper Club, 32 The Meads, Edgware, Middlesex, HA8 9HA, UK.

Churdling the Spurdle

No-one can explain to me the meaning of 'to churdle'; and 'spurdle' is pretty mysterious, too. However, in the sixteenth century, in the village of Chardstock in Devon, England, Churdling the Spurdle was a game played in celebration of the harvest: the villagers would race against each other, wearing pigs' bladders filled with blood around their necks.

The game was forgotten for centuries, and might have been lost forever – but in 1989, a local historical researcher found a reference to the game in a diary; and in conjunction with the local pub, the George Inn, he decided to revive it – the main difference being that, in modern times, balloons replaced bladders, and red jelly replaced blood. Contestants raced around the village, downing a pint of beer as fast as possible at three different stopping-points, and hoping that their balloons wouldn't burst. (Many did.)

That was 1989. The game has disappeared again – but the landlord at the George has plans to revive Churdling the Spurdle on a regular basis, probably starting in harvest-time 1998. 'You'll be the first to receive an invitation,' he told me.

Contact: Mr Watkins, The George Inn, Chardstock, Nr Axminster, Devon, EX13 7BX, UK.
Tel: 01460 220241

The Circular Chess Society

Here is a chess-problem to solve. During a game, a pawn is captured – and placed in the *middle* of the board. Not to one side, not in the box, but in the very centre, next to other captured pieces, an ashtray and a pint of beer. Yet the expressions on the players' faces, and the presence of the two-faced chess-clock, indicate that a serious contest is in progress. Can you explain why the players are untroubled by the objects in the centre?

If you're stuck, it's because you have made the assumption that the chessboard has to be *square*. At the Tap and Spile pub in Lincoln, headquarters of the Circular Chess Society, the board is a 2ft-diameter *circle*: reviving a medieval version of chess, the playing area might be compared to a running-track, with four active 'lanes', each of sixteen cells, and a large 'void' in the middle.

'You need a different thought-process altogether when you're playing circular chess,' I was informed by a member of the society. On the one hand, the influence of the rooks is magnified: they can now travel 15 cells in a single move – the entire 360 degrees of the board. On the other hand, the influence of the bishops is reduced: the big 'X' formed by the crossing of the corner-to-corner diagonals has vanished – on a circular board, the maximum diagonal is just four cells. 'And in normal chess, when attacking the enemy, it's just A against B,' he said, 'whereas with this, it's more like a real theatre of war, with attacks on two flanks. You can go round behind the enemy and take him.'

As I soon discovered by being checkmated. I could only drown my sorrows in a pint. A remark from a Tap and Spile regular did offer me hope, though: 'Don't worry,' he said, 'when you've had a few drinks, the board starts to look square.'

Contact: The Circular Chess Society, 11 North Parade, Lincoln, LN1 1LB, UK.
Tel: 01522 887666
(See also the entry on Variant Chess.)

Clog Dancing

'So we rolled back the proggy mat and we danced on the lino next to her sink.'

If you manage to find a proggy mat – a carpet made from sacking and rags – you'll probably be visiting a pensioner's house in a working-class district of Tyneside in England. I heard a lot about trips to see sixty-, seventy- and eighty-year-olds at the Maidenhead Festival of Clog Dance; collectors of rare clog dance styles know that dead heels don't click – and that they'd better make some notes before the Grim Reaper takes to the floor. Hence, at sixty-three, Mrs Ivy Sands, owner of the opening sentence's mat, was asked to give a performance; something she hadn't done since the age of nine.

'It took her two years to remember all the steps,' I was told by a collector, 'and then we had to write them all down. Here, have this, free of charge.' He handed me a booklet marked *Mrs Ivy Sands' Double Hornpipe*. 'We have notation for well over a hundred dances in triple time hornpipe rhythm alone,' he added. I turned the pages and saw instructions like click heel, tip tap, step, shuffle, hop.

Clogs, as you will know, are shoes with wooden soles; but they are, above all, *working* shoes, still worn in some heavy industries, and out of the mimicry of the rhythms of machines, the first dances emerged. It is said that if you listen carefully to the tapping of a heel, you'll hear the grinding of a mill, or the chugging of a boat, or the shuttling of a loom. From these beginnings in the workplace the clog dance has travelled. There is apparently a gumboot version in Uganda; and in a French-speaking Irish community in Quebec there is believed to be a caller who calls in an Irish brogue to dancers who can't understand.

As the Festival proceeded, there was some of the trickiest dancing I have ever witnessed. When Pat Tracey – known as Britain's best dancer – tapped along to the tune of 'Oh Susanna', you could almost hear the words in her heels:

> Don't you cry for me
> I'm going to Alabama
> With a banjo on my knee.

For to every syllable of that lyric, she fitted a decisive click. Then along came a French Canadian who danced such a difficult hornpipe that the MC remarked: 'You've seen it done – so now you know it's possible.'

Surrounded by children, and a few brave adults, I joined a clog-class for beginners. I shuffled and I tapped and sometimes I was in rhythm. Then I heard a woman of my own skill-standard whisper behind me: 'Forget beginners – is there a remedial class?' At the first coffee-break, she and I escaped – you couldn't see our heels for dust; or should that be, our wooden heels for sawdust?

Contact: Chris Brady, Flat 31 Felbridge Court, 311 High Street, Harlington, Middlesex, UB3 5EP, UK.
Tel: 0181 897 1700

The Cluck-Off

In England, when people imitate a rooster, they go cockadoodledoo; in Holland, kukeleku; in France, coquerico; and in Spain, quiquiriqui; but in Wayne County, Nebraska, USA, people sound pretty much like the real thing. At least they do in July, when the National Cluck-Off Contest is held, to find the best chicken impersonator in the land. (And probably, the world.)

Contact: The Wayne Chicken Show, Box 262, Wayne, Nebraska 68787, USA.
Tel: 402 375 2240 Fax: 402 375 2246

The Cookie Cutter Collectors' Club

Why do people have unusual hobbies? The origin often lies in events of childhood. Consider the following statement from Ruth Capper, the Secretary and former President of the Cookie Cutter Collectors' Club:

'My love of cookie cutters started when small, as my grandmother and mother always baked. I can still remember taking a big ginger cookie to the spring house, removing the slate from the milk crock, and dipping the cookie into the cream. My favourite shapes are gingerbread people and sheep.'

Contact: Ruth Capper, 1167 Teal Road S.W., Dellroy, Ohio 44620, USA.

The Coo-ee Calling Championship

'Coo-eeeeeeeeeeeeeeeeeeeee!' Enough 'e's? Admittedly, this section would come across better in a talking book.

The Coo-ee Calling Championship, which is held every October in Gilgandra, Australia, derives from an event of October 1915, when a contingent of 34 men set out from Gilgandra on a recruitment march, using the Aboriginal word for help, *Coo-ee*, to enlist volunteers for the war effort. By the time they reached Sydney, the marchers had enlisted 263 men. A re-enactment took place in 1987, which led to the establishment of the first Coo-ee Calling Championships.

The calling is done on one side of the Castlereagh River. The judges are positioned on the far side of the river, 500 metres away. Each contestant calls 'Coo-eeeeee', and is judged on various criteria, including decibel level and clarity.

In other words: message received, loud and clear.

Contact: Gilgandra Visitors' Centre, Coo-ee March Memorial Park, Newell Highway, PO Box 23, Gilgandra, NSW 2827, Australia.
Tel: 02 6847 2045 Fax: 02 6847 1292

Cow Observers Worldwide

The Minotaur was half-man, half-bull; but what do you call a creature that is half-woman, half-cow? The answer is Mrs Merriel Starret – or, as she prefers to be known, Mrs Moo.

Now in her 60s, Mrs Moo, of Phoenix, Arizona, is so obsessed by cows that she actually strives to look like one, by dressing in black-and-white Friesian-style clothing. Her house is the same: apart from the thousands of bovine ornaments and mooing knick-knacks (including a mooing toilet-seat), there is that black-and-white pattern throughout – on the curtains, on the walls, on the furniture. The only deviation from the colour-scheme is the carpet . . . which is light-green, suggestive of grass.

Mrs Moo may represent the most extreme form of cow-enthusiast, but she is not alone – she is the honorary president of Cow Observers Worldwide (C.O.W.), a group of 500 cow-lovers, who subscribe to a quarterly magazine, *The Moosletter*. Here, you can read about the latest cow-merchandise, from cow dolls to car horns that go moo. 'I've got one of those horns in my car,' says the editor, Carol Peiffer. 'It's great, because I no longer have to moo out of the car window whenever I pass a herd.'

Contact: *The Moosletter*, Cowtree Collector, 240 Wahl Avenue, Evans City, PA 16033, USA.
Website: http://www.cow.net/moosletter
E-mail: stormy@nauticom.net

The Cribbage Board Collectors' Society

Cribbage boards have been drilled into almost every object imaginable – bowling pins, bowling balls, swordfish jaws, park benches, toilet seats. Their holes can go in circles, squares, straight lines, zig-zags. They may feature scenes from the state of Wyoming, or be in the shape of the number 29. So it's hardly surprising, really, that I am able to give you the following address:

Contact: The Cribbage Board Collectors' Society, c/o Bette L. Bemis, Box 170, Carolina, RI 02812, USA.

The Crop Watcher

A few years ago, when crop circles were exposed as the work of hoaxers, media interest fell away. Ironically, the study of crop circle hoaxers is *itself* of interest to some people – and in particular, to the readers of the magazine *The Crop Watcher*.

'In 1991, I founded *The Crop Watcher* to publish all the evidence which other research groups hid from their followers, for example the arrests of hoaxers and eyewitness accounts of hoaxing,' I was told by the editor Paul Fuller. 'My current view is that 99 per cent of crop circles in the UK are man-made and that one per cent represent whirlwind-produced ground traces.'

It contrasts strikingly with the attitude of another researcher I met, also in 1991, as we stood in a cornfield, looking at 360 degrees of flat-tened wheat. 'There can be no doubt,' he said, 'that these circles are caused by the landing gear of a spacecraft.'

Note: Do not enter a cornfield to examine a circle without asking the farmer's permission.

Contact: *The Crop Watcher*, Paul Fuller, 3 Selborne Court, Tavistock Close, Romsey, Hampshire, S051 7TY, UK.

Crown Point

There
  are
    even
      some
        p
       e
    o
   p
    l
      e
     w
   h
  o
   c
    o
     l
     l
   e
  c
   t
   l i g h t
       n
        i
         n
        g
          R O D S!

('Crown Point' *is a specialist magazine for collectors of all lightning protection items.*)

Contact: *Crown Point*, c/o Rod Krupka, 2615 Echo Lane, Ortonville, MI 48462, USA.
Tel: 248 627 6351

The Cryptogram Association

Though I can summarize and describe, I can never give you the *experience* of a hobby. Except in this case.

Below is a cipher, in which every letter of the alphabet represents another letter: decode it, and you'll find a statement loosely on the theme of city living. You will not find the answer in this book. The only clue is that the word with the * is a proper name. So go ahead:

OB ISZDPH *GQG EFBE KZE NZUZPJ SQQO ZE EQ EOFNN
AKFA BQT YFP'A EKQTA FA AKD YFA VZAKQTA JDAAZPJ F
OQTAKITN QI KFZS.

Enjoy that? Then you should consider joining the American Cryptogram Association. (A worldwide group, despite the title.) The members create problems in cipher systems for the other members to solve, for the sheer fun of it. But be warned: the cipher I have given is of the easiest kind. As a member told me: 'I prefer the polyalphabetic ciphers in which one letter can stand for *more* than one other letter.'

Contact: ACA Treasurer, RR3, Box 987, Meredith, NH 03253-9401, USA.
Website: http://www.und.nodak.edu/org/crypto/crypto/

Cryptozoology

Do elephants exist? Of course. Do pink elephants exist? Of course not. Do pygmy elephants exist?

I'll terminate the paragraph there, make a gap in my words, for the only answer is no answer. It boils down to whether you can trust explorers. They do claim to have seen pygmy elephants. They say these creatures have tusks and trunks, are neither dwarfs, nor babies, nor normal elephants shrunk in the wash. Pygmy elephants, it is said, are an undiscovered species, and if you cannot afford to travel to Africa to see one, they do have another habitat – the pages of the journal of the International Society of Cryptozoology. I assure you its writers have not been influenced by *The Adventures of Babar*.

Cryptozoology. Let me give you a definition: 'The scientific study of hidden animals, that is of still unknown animal forms about which only testimonial and circumstantial evidence is available, or material evidence considered insufficient by some.' Obvious examples are the Loch Ness Monster and the Abominable Snowman. Less well-known is Mokele-

Mbembe, the dinosaur which is reputed to inhabit the swamplands of the Congo.

'I actually think that's one of the most likely to exist,' said Dr Karl Shuker, one of the leading British cryptozoologists, when I spoke to him about Mokele-Mbembe. 'That part of Africa has been totally unchanged for millions of years. There's hundreds of square miles of lagoons and impenetrable jungle. It's like an island that is cut off from the rest of the continent.' According to eyewitnesses, the dinosaur is about the size of a non-pygmy elephant, with a long serpentine neck. Are there photographs?

'There are some blurred photographs,' said Dr Shuker. Ah, blurred. 'But photographs are never satisfactory evidence even when they're very clear. There are many faked pictures. And the fakes are getting better.'

I have a suspicion that some of you are thinking that Mokele-Mbembe is about as likely to exist as King Kong. But hold on.

'Yes, Miss, it is a strange fish. I have been trawling for over thirty years, but I have never seen its like.' Words spoken by a trawler captain when his nets brought up the first coelacanth. That was over fifty years ago, but as recently as 1986, the Society published a list of over a hundred unknown animal forms – and since that time, three on the list have been confirmed by specimens and the case for several others strengthened by evidence. The most spectacular of the recent discoveries is the Onza, a long-legged puma-like beast, rumoured to exist in Mexico for five centuries.

The fact is, many species have been discovered throughout the twentieth century and are still being discovered. 'As recently as 1990,' said Dr Shuker, 'a new species of marmoset was discovered near Sao Paulo – near a centre of population! And the creature had orange, red and yellow fur! How could people have missed it?'

Contact: International Society of Cryptozoology, PO Box 43070, Tucson, Arizona 85733, USA.

Cultural Entomology Digest

If an entomologist met an etymologist at a party, would they talk about those phrases derived from the names and behaviour of insects? For example, 'social butterfly', 'don't bug me', and 'sent away with a flea in his ear'.

The exploration of the links between insects and language is just one aspect of Cultural Entomology – which may be defined as the study of insect allusions in literature, music, art, religion or any other sphere of human activity. *The Cultural Entomology Digest* is a magazine devoted to this very subject. Among its contents you might find pieces on: 'The Dragon Fly Wing used as a Noseplug Ornament'; 'British Museum Beeswax Treasures'; and 'The Role of Lice in the Old Testament'.

So whether you're an entomologist or an etymologist or neither, think of this the next time you're ordering a cocktail – and make yours a 'Bee's Kiss' or a 'Stinger'.

Contact: Cultural Entomology Digest, Dexter Sear, PO Box 796, Kalaheo, HI 96741, USA.
Website: http://www.insects.org
E-mail: dexter@insects.org

D

The Dawn Duellists' Society

In Craigmillar Castle, a 15th-century stronghold three miles south-east of Edinburgh, I put on my outfit: breeches, a silver and black waistcoat, a frilly jabot and a pink knee-length coat. Topped off with a tricorn hat, I looked like a cross between a town crier and the lyric from 'Lucy in the Sky with Diamonds'. This, I am afraid, was the best the fancy-dress shop could offer me; otherwise, I would have been down to a straight choice between Spiderman and Frankenstein's Monster.

I was worried that the two men with me in the castle's tower, Paul Macdonald and Manuel Hegelich, would take one look at my costume and think that I was sending them up – because they were busy changing into *historically accurate* 18th-century clothes: leather boots, baggy breeches, billowy shirts and gauntlets. Though if I *had* accidentally slighted them, I suppose that could have provided a *raison d'être* for the afternoon: being duellists, they really needed to be insulted to get going.

'Let me show you the salute with that hat,' said Paul. He took the tricorn and placed it on his own head; he also selected a rapier from the various swords that were propped against the stone wall. Then, he demonstrated the niceties that two late-18th-century gentlemen would have displayed before attempting to kill one another.

'Duelling has its own rules and codes of honour,' he remarked, returning the hat to me. 'It's not a free-for-all. It's all very civilized. It's an art form.' Even the insults that often provoked a duel had a certain style. Two men might look at each other across an inn and then exchange words along the lines of:

'Sir, I've noticed that you've been staring at me.'

'I have eyes.'

'That's the fault of the crows that have not pecked them out.'

Anyway, with some reason assumed to exist for a score to be settled in blood, Paul and Manuel prepared to do each other damage. Or rather, *pretend* damage: the wit may be sharp, but the sword must be blunt – that is the essence of the Dawn Duellists' Society.

The society was established in 1994 by Paul, who works as a professional swordmaker. (Tourists to Edinburgh can acquire a copy of Mel Gibson's *Braveheart* sword from him for just £300.) Though accomplished at modern fencing, Paul likes the greater freedom of duelling:

modern fencing means simply moving forwards and backwards, but in duels there is the 'Errol Flynn factor', and the participants can move anywhere. In an environment such as Craigmillar Castle, this can mean cut-and-thrust up and down stone staircases, or being trapped against a wall. And, true to the society's name, the members sometimes fight at 4am, attended by seconds.

'But we're not at all like the German duelling societies,' said Manuel, himself a German national. 'The duelling scene in Germany is a bit right wing and crazy,' he told me. 'People are obsessed with getting cheek scars. You even hear of people putting hairs from horses' tails in their wounds to get a more prominent scar.'

For the Dawn Duellists it would be virtually impossible to acquire scars. They are prepared to compromise the historical accuracy of their dress for safety, by wearing modern protective headgear, as well as fencing jackets under their period clothes. Nonetheless, they strive to replicate the techniques that unprotected duellists would have adopted. By consulting treatises written by 18th-century fencing masters, they have learnt to adopt a stance in which the head is held further back than in modern fencing, simply because it was unprotected.

So I watched, as Paul and Manuel went ... well, not hammer and tongs at each other, but rapier and dagger; the horn-handled dagger, held in the left hand, being used for parrying, because according to the code of duelling, it is generally considered rather unsporting to *strike* with the dagger.

Then Paul caught Manuel off guard, and thrust into the German's breastbone: a scoring attack, under the rules by which the society determines the outcome of a duel. (Five such hits mean death.) The two men paused for a moment and Paul showed me the major target areas. The armpit, for example. 'Catch it, and then draw the blade back and you've severed an artery. Your opponent will bleed to death,' he said. 'Then there's the main artery on the inside of the groin. Slice that, and he's not got long to go . . .'

Well, it was soon time to put my groin and my armpit on the line. I took up my rapier and dagger, put on the mask and squared up to Paul. He had the skill and experience – but I had a trick up my sleeve . . . my pink sleeve. I was inspired by the thought that my outfit might be used to play Prince Charming in a British pantomime, and I recalled the traditions of the genre.

'Behind you!' I said.

He turned his head and I ran him through.

Contact: The Dawn Duellists' Society, c/o Paul Macdonald, 2F1, 11 Edina Place, Edinburgh, EH7 5RN, UK.
Tel: 0131 661 6457

63

The Decimal Time Society

Time itself went out of fashion.

At least, the way of telling it did. I can still remember the steeple-jacks at work on the face of Big Ben. And how someone brought out a new version of 'Rock Around the Clock'. There was a bit that used to go 'Nine, ten, eleven o'clock, twelve o'clock rock' and it was changed to 'Nine, zero, one o'clock, two o'clock rock'. I didn't think the new lyrics fitted as well as the old. I guess that's what you'd call a sign of the times.

As I understand it, the new system was based upon the work of a man called Mike Pinder, who in the early 1990s established the Decimal Time Society. It was difficult to escape his logic: we'd already decimalised everything else, so why not have a ten-hour day and an 100-minute hour? Mind you, it wasn't just the clocks he had in his sights; it was the whole calendar – so that's how we got the ten-day week. No more Mondays and Tuesdays; we had Oneday and Twoday instead. Getting rid of Sunday caused a hoo-hah, I can tell you. 'God created the world in six days and rested on the seventh' – all that stuff. In the end, the government gave the different religious groups their own special days – so that days zero and five were for the Muslims, one and six for the Jews, two and seven for the Christians and so on.

Our lives certainly changed. There was no such thing as the week-end anymore. (Funnily enough, people still talk about a 'dirty weekend' – though it's come to mean any assignation.) Anyway, once we were rid of the seven-day week, we all started working five days on, five days off. That had some consequences. Firms started to have two hierarchies: a first half of the week team and a second half of the week team. In theatres, every play had two casts. And it was then that we introduced two leagues for every major sport. For a while, young-sters used to call someone a 'twenty-five-hour man' – which meant that he was not only old-fashioned, believing in the old twenty-four-hour day, but also stupid because he didn't even know how many hours the old day had.

And me? I sit here writing my memoirs. I look at the top of the page and see it says Wednesday. Old diaries are worth a bit of money now because quite a lot of people – for example, yours truly – like to use them as notebooks.

Contact: Mike Pinder, The Decimal Time Society, 6 Hamble Close, Warsash, Hampshire, S03 9GT, UK.

Decoy Duck Carving

In the village of Farrington Gurney, not far from Bristol, is the UK's only school of Decoy Duck Carving. It is here that you will learn how to make a mallard out of sugar pine, or if you prefer, a red-breasted merganser out of Bornean jelutong. I went along, ready to make anything that wouldn't sink in the bath.

And then the Stanley knife slipped. Sophie Ridges, who runs the school, fetched the first aid box and applied a sticking plaster to stop my finger staining the wood – blood does not run off a decoy duck's back.

The school was founded by Sophie's late husband, Bob, who took a course on duck carving in the USA. Originally, the Americans used art to attract life: poor old Donald or Daffy would waddle along, thinking he'd found a quacking pal, only to see a shotgun barrel poking out of the reeds. Nowadays, with stricter controls on hunting, decoys are carved as a sport in their own right – for there is a world championship, in which entrants strive for total duck realism. The painting of these models is virtually a matter of applying DNA on a brush: one competitor has described decoy art as 'mixing paints with infinite subtlety to achieve black which is not black, but a soft feather tone which identifies the crimson sparkle of the chest'.

'At the championships, you hear people saying, "He's really got the *jizz* there",' said Sophie, 'jizz' meaning the spiritual essence of a flapping, swimming bird. Sophie's husband once achieved this, with a wooden mallard: he was carrying the bird under his arm and a stranger came up to him and asked, 'Is it injured?'

Contact: World Championship Wildfowl Carving Competition, Ward Museum of Wildfowl Art, c/o Jane Rollins, Events Coordinator, 909 South Schumaker Drive, Salisbury, MD 21804, USA.
Tel: 410 742 4988 Ext 106
Or: The Decoy Gallery, Hollow Marsh, Farrington Gurney, Bristol, BS18 5TX, UK.
Tel: 01761 452075

The Dental History Society

School history lessons used to be about kings and queens; the type of history I have been studying is more concerned with crowns – *dental* crowns. Specifically, I have been looking at the magazine *Dental Historian*. The cover illustration is of beautifully decorated dental probes

– silver gilt, with fleurs-de-lis. And many are the subjects this journal explores: '150 Years of Anaesthesia', 'Dentists in Seventeenth-century Holland', 'The History of Dentistry in Western Painting', etc. To find out more, I went to the publishers of the magazine, the Society for the History of Dentistry – a club for those intrigued by the evolution of drills, extraction equipment, amalgams and the rest of the armoury used in the battle against decay. Some of the members actually collect dentists' chairs.

My appointment – I think we should call it that – was with Julia Marsh, the society's secretary. She also happens to be the curator of the museum of the British Dental Association, and so she took me on a tour of the exhibits. We stopped at an array of X-ray equipment and a spittoon that looked like a font. Then it was on to 'anaesthesia corner', with its many machines devoted to numbness; followed by a display of dentures, including the black ones made for habitual chewers of betel nuts; and finishing at the cabinet of probes, rootscrews and other instruments of torture. I asked Julia whether working amongst all this equipment had changed her attitude towards dental hygiene. 'I floss now – I didn't before,' she said. 'I've seen too many journals describing the nasty things that can happen if you don't care for your teeth.' She claimed that she wasn't frightened of dentists. 'They've never hurt me,' she said. 'Not even when they did my root canal work.' And we began discussing the history of the toothbrush.

Contact: The Society for the History of Dentistry, 64 Wimpole Street, London, W1M 8AL, UK.
Tel: 0171 935 0875

Dicks of America

My name may be Stephen, but I'm a Dick.

You can be a Dick, too. Because the Dicks of America can perform a painless operation known as an 'Addadicktome', which allows them to add a dick to your name. Who are these Dicks?

'United we Dicks must stand!' proclaims their brochure. 'It's the only way we can change the image of our name. Imagine a world where Dick wasn't a name used in vain. Perhaps together we can popularize the use of another name for that purpose – like Mike. "Hey, up yours, Mikehead!" '

Founded in 1986, with the aim of making Dick the most prestigious name in America, if not the world, the Dicks' newsletter *Dickin' Around* not only carries reports about Dicks in the news, such as sportsmen and congressmen, but also lively letters, such as the following:

66

'I've been a Dick for nearly 48 years long. That makes me a long dick. And, at 6ft 1 inch, 208 lbs, I'm a rather big dick. So there you have it. I'm a big long Dick.'

Yep, I'd say you are.

Contact: Dicks of America, PO Box 600782, San Diego, CA 92160, USA. Website: www.dofa.com

The Disinfected Mail Study Circle

It is said that the art of letter-writing is dead. There was a time when it was believed that the art of letter-writing was *death*: that correspondence was a carrier of cholera, as well as plague, leprosy and other diseases. The handling of this problem by the postal authorities of the world has created a small enclave in postal history – which fascinates the 150 members of the Disinfected Mail Study Circle.

'I've collected stamps since I was a small boy,' said Denis Vandervelde, the Circle's founder, 'and in 1971, I was at a postal history auction. A lot came up of two Italian letters which had been certified as disinfected. I was intrigued. So I bought them.' That was the beginning of his explorations in the history of mail disinfection, taking in the study of wax seals, handstamps, labels and manuscript notes which attest that the mail is safe to receive.

Denis explained that since 1493, when there was an outbreak of plague in the South Casscano district of Venice, postal authorities have used a variety of methods to disinfect letters, including dipping in vinegar, fumigation with sulphur, perfuming it with sweet-smelling herbs and baking over charcoal fires. Each of these techniques leaves a distinctive stain or discoloration, and thereby creates a unique philatelic item. 'I've got a letter in my collection which was left too close to the charcoal,' said Denis, 'and it's singed beyond recognition.' He also showed me a brown-stained letter from Naples which had been dowsed in vinegar at its destination, Portugal. The contents noted that: 'The plague is still confined to the village of Noja, where it originally broke out.'

In addition, this letter had been slit at Naples, to allow extra fumigant to enter; and the history of slitting or puncturing the mail, so as to allow fumigants in, or pestilential vapours out, forms another aspect of the Circle's work. In a recent issue of the Circle's journal, Denis has analysed in detail the distribution of punctures in a wrapper of 1831 sent from the Royal and Imperial Military Hospital at Pettau (now called Ptuj, Slovenia) to Stochach in Baden. He noted that it has more than 20 punch-holes, in four rows – probably made by a device called a rastel, which resembled a pair of spiked tongs – and he has measured the distance between each of the holes. ('The top row has holes 44, 60 and 32mm apart; the second row, 22mm below, has holes 39, 46 and 39mm apart.' And so on.)

I asked Denis whether any of these techniques to disinfect mail in fact *worked*. 'No, they didn't,' he said. It is now known that the diseases the authorities were disinfecting against – principally, plague, cholera, typhus and leprosy – could not be conveyed on dry paper. Indeed, a photograph in the Circle's journal records 'An End to the Disinfection of Leper Mail in 1968', as an American postal clerk places a sack of mail in an oven for the last time. 'Actually, smallpox *can* be transmitted by mail,' he added. 'Though until the twentieth century, nobody bothered disinfecting against that.'

Contact: Mr V. Denis Vandervelde, 25 Sinclair Grove, London, NW11 9JH, UK.

The Dock Pudding World Championship

If there were a World Championship for the cheekiest usage of the words 'World Championship', the Dock Pudding World Championship would win outright. The 'World' in this case is not the globe, not the continent of Europe, not England, not Yorkshire – but one *small corner* of Yorkshire. Specifically, the Calder Valley, around Hebden Bridge, Heptonstall and Mytholmroyd, where the green and slimy speciality known as dock pudding is eaten. This breakfast and supper dish is made from the weed *Polygonum Bistorta*, which is found growing along canals.

About two dozen people enter the World Championship every May. 'If we had any more,' I was told by one of the organizers, 'the judges would be sick.'

Contact: Mytholmroyd Community Centre, Elphaborough, Mytholmroyd, Hebden Bridge, W. Yorks, HX7 5DY, UK. Tel: 01422 883023

Dog Sled Racing

Really, you need to be in Alaska. But the lack of snow in England isn't a big problem. All you do is put wheels on your sled, harness together ten Siberian Huskies, and say . . .

Well, actually dog-sled racers don't say 'mush'. That was one of the myths to be shattered when I met an enthusiastic sledder and her dogs at Thetford Forest in Norfolk. The real commands are 'Haw' and 'Gee' which mean left and right and 'Okay' which means . . .

We were hurtling forward through the forest. Though the driver was in control, harnessing the pack-urges of the huskies, I had a contribution to make, being required to shift my weight at corners. I must tell you that dog-sled racing without the snow is not exactly comfortable – as we went over the forest's ruts, it was like resting my bottom on a pneumatic drill.

And incidentally, sled-dogs have a unique talent, which I couldn't help but notice from my position in the sled: the ability to eliminate waste-matter on the move.

Contact: Mrs P. Evans, The Siberian Husky Club of Great Britain, The Old Post Office, 3 High Street, Lamport, Northampton, NN6 9HB, UK.
Or: The International Federation of Sleddog Sports, Glenda Walling, 7118 N. Beehive Rd, Pocatello, ID 83201, USA.
Tel: 208 232 5130 Fax: 208 234 1608
Website: http://www.worldsport.com/sports/sleddog/home.html

Doorknob Collecting

When a leading doorknob collector died, his wife honoured his interests forever – with a carving of one of his favourite knob designs on the family cemetery monument.

Contact: The Antique Doorknob Collectors of America, PO Box 126, Eola, Illinois, 60519-0126, USA.
Tel: 630 357 2381 Fax: 630 357 2391

Down the Slot

One day, the penny dropped. It dropped from my teeth.

While looking through some old scrapbooks put together by my late father, Bob Jarvis, I came across an undated cutting about a pub game, believed to be unique in the world, played at the Blacksmith's Arms in Rotherhithe Street, in the London Docklands. In the game, the cutting said, a coin is gripped in the mouth – the object being to drop the coin into a moneybox-sized slot in the pub's floor.

Was the game still played? Did the pub exist any longer? Had it changed its name? And is an interest in unusual leisure activities passed on in the genes? These were my thoughts as I set off on a pub crawl in the name of research.

A street of pints later – and Rotherhithe Street happens to be one of the longest streets in the whole of London – I walked through the entrance of the mock-Tudor establishment that is the modern-day Blacksmith's Arms. Set into the floor in the rear section of the bar was a brass plate with a slot. I asked whether anyone in the pub could explain the game to me.

'It's an old docker's game,' said Sibbo, one of the regulars, who by chance had recently refitted the brass plate. He explained that Down the Slot had been played at the Blacksmith's Arms for as long as anyone could remember. Though the game isn't as popular nowadays, years ago dockers would place bets on their teeth-eye co-ordination: if one docker successfully dropped the coin down the slot, and no-one else did so, then that docker would take all the money that had built up in a kitty. 'You used to get kitties of sixty, seventy, eighty pounds,' said Sibbo – for Down the Slot is a perfect example of a game that's much harder than it looks.

To demonstrate, Sibbo literally put his money where his mouth was: he stood over the slot, and dropped a coin from his teeth – but it merely bounced off the brass. My aim was no better.

'Smaller people have more chance,' Sibbo said. 'They're closer to the slot.'

Contact: The Blacksmith's Arms, 257 Rotherhithe St, London, SE16, UK. Tel: 0171 237 1349

Dowsing

It was saying yes, no, yes, no, and I hadn't even asked a question. There's nothing that goes up and down quite like a novice's V-rod.

Walking about the room with a dowsing tool alive in my hands, maybe I should have been astonished, but I am afraid I was not. I attributed no magic to the V-rod. It was just an unstable structure: two lengths of plastic, each straining like an archer's bow, meeting at a single point. Something has to give. But people who *are* serious about dowsing say that when it 'gives', the rod can be used to answer questions: not just the traditional 'Is there water here?' but any kind of query for which a yes/no is required. In fact, dowsers say that you don't really need the V-rod, or even that other popular tool, a pair of L-rods. 'You can dowse with anything,' I was informed by the British Society of Dowsers. 'You can put a button on a piece of string and still get results.'

The interplay of these two propositions – that you can dowse with anything and that you can ask a host of questions – defines the activity of the society. One member even uses her *arm* to dowse, dangling it like a pendulum, and depending on whether it swings to and fro or in a circle, she gets her answer. If she doesn't do that, she uses the blink method – one quick blink after asking a question means yes. These forms of dowsing are very convenient in supermarkets, I understand: the woman goes up the aisles, swinging her arm and blinking, asking whether this food or that contains additives.

Note: There are many dowsing groups throughout the world. Here are three major English-speaking dowsing societies:

Contact: The British Society of Dowsers, Sycamore Barn, Hastingleigh, Ashford, Kent, TN25 5HW, UK.
Tel/Fax: 01233 750253
Or: The American Society of Dowsers, PO Box 24, Danville, VT 05828, USA.
Website: http://newhampshire.com/dowsers.org/
E-mail: ASD@Dowsers.org
The Canadian Society of Dowsers, RR2 Sharbot Lake, Ontario, Canada KOH 2PO.

The Dozenal Society

According to the schoolboy joke, the word 'smiles' is the longest in the English language because there is a mile between first and last letters; and over seventy years ago, when Arthur Whillock was at school, his geography teacher gave a certain sort of smile – a smirk – which burrowed deep into the boy's brain, leaving a conviction about the importance of miles and other traditional measures.

'I can see his face now,' said Arthur, aged 84, when I visited him at his home in Oxfordshire. 'There was a proposal going round at the time that Britain should adopt the metric system – and my teacher obviously didn't agree with it. He said to the class, "When they set up the metric system, they measured the earth twice and got a different answer each time." And he said it with such a smirk. I've never forgotten it.'

Arthur Whillock is the man who runs the Dozenal Society, a group founded in 1959, which is not merely opposed to metrication, but in the longer term would like to strike at the foundation of the metric system by changing the very way we *count*: in a dozenal world, the base of our numbers would not be ten, but twelve. (So that, for instance, the number written '111' would represent not one hundred plus one ten plus one, but rather, one gross plus one dozen plus one, or 157 in our current notation.)

The membership of the Dozenal Society may not be large – there are about 60 members in the UK, though the American sister-organization has a membership of several hundred – but Arthur was keen to emphasize the reasonableness of the dozenal cause. He remarked that, over the centuries, many mathematicians and philosophers have acknowledged that it would be preferable to base our counting upon the number twelve. The most obvious advantage is divisibility – the fraction one-third can be expressed exactly in base twelve (as 0.4, or four-twelfths) whereas in base ten, there is the 'inaccurate' recurring decimal, 0.3333 . . .

'I'm a practical man and the advantages of feet and inches struck me most forcefully when I was working as an engineer in hydraulics research,' he said. 'If you were working out flow rates and forces, you would get whole numbers for things like 60ths and 24ths. Then the department was metricated and we'd finish up with rows of figures. Metricists believe that they're being so scientific – but the truth is the reverse. Scientific facts start out as ratios, and ratios can be more accurately expressed in feet and inches.'

Aside from the mathematical and scientific benefits, Arthur believes that traditional measures have evolved to meet bodily needs: it cannot be a coincidence, he told me, that so many cultures, from ancient Crete to modern Japan, have adopted a unit of measurement roughly equivalent to an English foot. 'The point is, a distance of a foot is the maximum that can be seen comfortably at arm's length without moving the head,' he said. 'A longer scale would require two looks to avoid loss of proper accuracy, while a shorter one would require more frequent movements of the scale itself. I think that there is considerable resentment among ordinary people towards metrication – but they don't realize why they're objecting. But imperial measures are ergonomically sound, unlike the metre which was developed without reference to human dimensions.'

Arthur's interest in traditional measuring systems has led to his acquiring a collection of rulers from around the world, from the Greek Heraklion to the Cantonese Chik. Once, when he visited Japan to discuss an engineering project, he told his hosts that the only souvenir he wanted to buy was the traditional Japanese ruler, a Shaku. 'They were astonished to think that an Englishman should know about such things. Then they explained that they were terribly sorry, but the Shaku was no longer authorized for use. So I told them yes, I knew that, but I also knew that the dry-goods Shaku was still legal. They gasped.' Their parting gift to Arthur was a stainless-steel metre rule, which was also marked with three Shakus. 'I had a bit of a job getting it through Customs this end,' he remarked. 'They thought I'd got a sword.'

Yet does not this concern with tradition sit rather uneasily with the Dozenal Society's extreme radicalism – namely, its plan to change the way we count? Furthermore, is there not a human-based origin for the decimal system in the number of our fingers?

Arthur calmly informed me that counting to ten is not the only way to use our hands: in certain parts of Northern Iran, there is a tradition of counting to twelve on the fingers of *one* hand, using the thumb as a pointer and counting on the fingers' twelve segments.

'Our numbers have changed before – think of the transition from Roman numerals to Arabic,' he said. 'And I feel that if there were recognized symbols for ten and eleven then dozenal counting would evolve.' His own preferred symbols are an upside down 2 and 3 – and he has altered his typewriter so that it can type these. (Many American dozenalists, though, use * and #.)

Is not the Dozenal Society fighting a lost cause? Is not the world destined to go metric? 'Alas – probably, yes,' said Arthur. 'But as long as the USA sticks to imperial, there's always hope. I think it's very important to keep our history alive.' Then he added, 'I think my old geography teacher would approve.'

Contact: Arthur Whillock, The Dozenal Society, Walnut Bank, Underhill, Moulsford, Oxford, OX10 9JH, UK. Or: A. Denny: 0181 947 9200. Or: R. Carnaghan: 01923 241548.
Website: http://users.aol.com/dozenal/
Or: The Dozenal Society of America, c/o Jay Sciffman, 377 Pine Street 1F, Philadelphia, PA 19107, USA.
E-mail: marior@armanda.dorsai.org

The Dracula Society

'I should make it clear that we've got a rule that prohibits our members from dressing up as the Count,' I was told by founder member Bernard Davies, when I attended the Dracula Society's Annual General Meeting. He referred to 'an embarrassing incident' on British television, which led to the prohibition. 'Media people just love us to dress up and put in fangs,' he said.

In spite of this, the society does own one item of clothing of special significance: the actual cloak of Dracula. At least, it owns the one worn by Christopher Lee in all of the Hammer horror films. At the society's little museum – which includes exhibits of assorted stakes, rubber masks of Bela Lugosi and bottles of red liquid marked *Dracula Elixir from Romania*, – I had the privilege of trying on that cloak. I was amazed by the weight. The museum's unofficial curator, Robert James Leake, told me that the cloak was made heavier in certain places, 'so that it would billow just right'. So now you know.

The Dracula Society is a group for all those with a serious interest in Gothic horror; its members range from skinheads in Alice Cooper T-shirts to silver-haired pensioners. One of its aims is to promote discussion about Bram Stoker's masterpiece. 'Pre-Stoker, the returning dead had always been treated in a Byronesque, romantic manner,' Bernard Davies told me. Stoker's treatment, though, was totally anti-romantic. 'Dracula was a filthy, stinking creature,' said Mr Davies. 'He had halitosis. Stoker told vampirism like it was.'

Like it was? But aren't we talking about fiction? I pressed Mr Davies on the point – do vampires really exist? 'I have an open mind on the subject,' he told me. 'I firmly believe that there are more things in heaven and earth – I certainly don't pooh-pooh the idea of vampires.'

Getting a bit worried, I asked Bruce Wightman, another founder member, whether he had ever met anyone who genuinely believed in the undead. 'Yes, there was one woman who was a member for a short while,' he told me. 'She used to frighten her room-mate by getting up in the middle of the night. She'd be wearing only her nightdress, and she'd throw open the bedroom window and shout, "Take me Dracula, I'm yours." Of course, she didn't really want Dracula – she wanted Christopher Lee in his underpants.'

One of the society's activities is organizing tours of Transylvania. Long-standing member Peter Swindell remarked: 'When we return from the tours of Transylvania, we say to everyone back home in England that the Romanians still believe in vampires because they string up garlic outside their houses. What we don't tell people is that the Romanians also string up carrots and cabbages. It's simply their vegetables drying out.'

Contact: The Dracula Society, c/o Julia Kruk, 213 Wulfstan Street, East Acton, London, W12 0AB, UK.
(See also the entry on the Vampire Research Society, for more on the existence of vampires.)

Dragonlore

The fat of a dragon dried in the sun is good against creeping ulcers.

The medical use of dragons is something you discover in the pages of

The Dragon Chronicle, The International Journal of Dragonlore. Oh you've never seen a dragon? Not so difficult. I could even show you one breathing fire: as it notes in the *Chronicle*, there is the constellation Draco, the Dragon, which lies between Arthur's Chariot (part of Ursa Major) and Polaris. The fire? There is a meteor shower called the Draconids – and if you trace the path of these shooting stars back across the sky in perfectly straight, imaginary lines, they seem to emanate from the dragon's head, and with a little more imagination, from the dragon's mouth.

The editor of the *Chronicle* told me in a letter: 'For as long as I can remember, I have always had an interest in dragons. When I was a boy, I had a secret friend, a very old and wise dragon called Canute – and I would fantasize that I was a dragon-boy, travelling to distant realms with dragon companions, young nephews of Canute.'

His letter concluded: 'Dragons are wild, rebellious, non-conformist, mystical, wise, mysterious, magical and highly symbolic. I think the dragon represents something for everyone and that there is a dragon in all of us, just waiting to get out.'

It's a wonder, really, that the paper wasn't scorched.

Contact: *The Dragon Chronicle*, Dragon's Head Press, PO Box 3369, London, SW6 6JN, UK.
Website: http://www.stalkerlab.ch/dragon/index.html
E-mail: dragonet@vtx.ch

The Dr Pepper Club

Ever had Dr Pepper in burger form? Amongst the material sent to me by the Dr Pepper Club – whose members study the history and memorabilia of the Dr Pepper drinks company – was the following recipe for Dr Pepper Spoonburgers:

    1 pound ground beef (lean)
    1 tablespoon shortening
    1 clove garlic (minced)
    1 medium onion (chopped)
    1 teaspoon salt
    ¾ cup Dr Pepper
    1 can tomato paste (6 oz)
    1 tablespoon Worcestershire sauce
    Few drops of Tabasco to taste

Brown meat in shortening, breaking into small pieces. Add garlic, onion and salt. Cook 5 minutes. Add remaining ingredients. Simmer about 20 minutes or until thick. Spoon onto toasted hamburger buns. Makes 8 burgers.

Contact: The Dr Pepper Club, 3100 Monticello, Suite 890, Dallas, TX 75205, USA.

Dry Stone Walling

A dry stone wall is a structure in which skill replaces mortar: nothing bonds the pieces, except the way they are placed. It's often called a three-dimensional jigsaw puzzle, though really the comparison is inappropriate – the parts of the wall are not pre-cut and, except by chance, do not slot snugly together. The other characteristic is the material used: naturally occurring stone, unshaped except by hammer-blows, lacking altogether the geometry and uniformity of bricks.

There are people who enjoy building such walls as a hobby; there are even people who do dry stone walling as a *sport*, competing against their fellow wallers to build the most attractive stretch in a given time. 'You can get a better feel of the stones without gloves,' I was told by one waller, 'but you don't realize how much of your fingertips you've worn away, until someone hands you a mug of hot tea and you take it without using the handle.'

Contact: The Dry Stone Walling Association of Great Britain, YFC Centre, National Agricultural Centre, Stoneleigh Park, Warwickshire, CV8 2LG, UK.
Tel/Fax: 0121 378 0493

Dung-Throwing 1: Buffalo Chips

There is an old joke: 'What's brown and sounds like a bell?' The answer of course is dung. But what is brown and reminds you of a Bill? Why, buffalo dung.

I might have said 'What is brown and lands in a bowl?' – because that's the essence of the annual Buffalo Chip Throwing Contest, held in Luverne, Minnesota. The targets are two toilet bowls, one ten feet away, and the other fifteen feet away: one point for a chip thrown into the first toilet bowl, two points for a chip in the second. Teams of three compete, with three chips per team member.

And I'll bet not even the winners have a chip on their shoulders!

Contact: Luverne Area Chamber of Commerce, 102 East Main, Luverne, Minnesota 56156-1831, USA.
Tel: 507 283 4061

Dung-Throwing 2: The Cow Chip Throwing World Championship

The idea of throwing a cow-dung discus does not in itself revolt me. It's the fact that some 'professional chip throwers' lick their fingers between throws. (The world record, set in 1979, is 182ft 3in.)

Contact: Beaver County Chamber of Commerce, PO Box 878, Beaver, OK 73932, USA.
Tel: 405 625 4726
(Note: A similar event – Le Concours International de Lancer de Bousats – takes place in Le Perrier, France. See entry on Ningle Jumping for contact information.)

Dung-Throwing 3: The Moose Drop Toss Game

The moose gets its name from its actions at one end of its alimentary canal – because *moos*, in Algonquian, means 'he strips off', referring to the creature's habit of stripping off tree bark and eating it. Moving to the other end, we go from the name to a game. Every July, in the town of Talkeetna, they play the Moose Drop Toss Game, to raise funds for the local historical society. Each contestant pays a dollar and receives 10 moose droppings, which he then pitches at a flat target board, marked into scoring sectors worth different amounts of points. The droppings are then retrieved, and the points tallied; the contestant with the highest tally splits the cash pot with the historical society.

But you know, the thing I dislike about this game is not the idea of handling the droppings, but the target: it bears a painting of a moose, and the scoring sectors are different parts of the animal's body. Poor moose. Even a painting has a right to dignity.

Contact: Talkeetna Historical Society Museum, PO Box 76, Talkeetna, AK 99676, USA.
Tel: 907 733 2487 Fax: 907 733 2484

E

Earth Mysteries

There is a type of musical composition known as the 'list song'. Cole Porter's 'You're the Top' is one of the finest: 'You're the Nile, You're the Tower of Pisa, You're the smile on the Mona Lisa . . .' Love for Porter is a pot-pourri – hard to define, easy to list; and I feel it's much the same for the subject of earth mysteries. This is a complex, many-sided passion, involving archaeology, folklore, dowsing, astronomy, various New Age concerns, investigations into earth energies, explorations of unexplained phenomena and lots more besides. To investigate the subject further, I went on a field trip with the members of the London Earth Mysteries Circle, to the prehistoric hill-fort of Old Sarum, in Wiltshire.

As I sat on top of this ancient mound, I chatted to the Circle's organizer, Rob Stephenson, and he told me of a typical interest: strange lights in the sky. 'People see Will-o-the-Wisps and such like,' he said, 'and they tend to appear above stone circles and other ancient sites. Now why is this?'

He advanced a theory: that as the moon's gravitation pulls the sea up, it also lifts the land – leading to the chafing of rock against rock. Couldn't this generate electricity? Might not electricity lead to sparks and lights in the sky? Maybe ancient man worshipped natural fireworks? And perhaps that's why stone circles appear on the Earth's fault lines, where land-masses rub and electricity is most likely to occur.

It might all be true . . . or it might not. Like the moon's influence on the tides, one's belief can ebb and flow. But I do not dismiss the hypothesis – not when Rob can tell me about a standing stone in Gloucester, known as the 'Tingle Stone', which, when touched, actually gives an electric shock.

Then there's the case of ley lines. We were at Old Sarum because of a line linking this hill-fort to Salisbury Cathedral and to Stonehenge. Leys are alleged to be straight lines in the Earth just sizzling with energy, which coincide with the alignment of ancient monuments; some Circle members detect ley lines with dowsing rods. A man and a woman, both dowsers, joined in the discussion: 'We were once in a field at the crossing of two leys,' said the woman, 'and we looked up in the sky and saw some Canada geese. We realized that their flight path coincided exactly with one of the leys. Then, when the geese got to the point of intersection, they shot off in the direction of the other ley.' The man rubbed his beard and added: 'What's more, there was a horse in the same field that seemed to know about the lines, too.'

Or perhaps I should say that *was* the case of ley lines. The most modern research dumps the views of leys as energy lines. It is now thought that ancient monuments are aligned because of the cultural belief that the spirits of the dead moved in straight lines. This was prompted by the discovery of such features as the medieval Dutch *dood-wegen* (death roads) which run straight into cemeteries, and similar roads for conducting the bodies of Viking chieftains.

So there you have it: the briefest of introductions to a vast field. If it's clear as mud to you ... well, what more could you expect from *earth mysteries*?

Note: There are many earth mysteries groups, publications, and websites, but the following is an excellent initial contact, being the world's longest-running earth mysteries magazine:

Contact: The Ley Hunter, PO Box 258, Cheltenham, Gloucester, GL53 OHR, UK.
Tel: 0402 998208 Website: http://www.leyhunter.com
E-mail: leyhunter@compuserve.com

The Electronic Voice Phenomenon and Transcommunication Society

'My son died in 1992,' said Judith Chisholm, 'and I had to find him.'

What might be called 'the usual channels' followed: mediums, spiritualist churches, seances. There *were* manifestations – raps on the table and so forth – but all left her sceptical. Then one evening, Judith decided to take a pocket tape recorder along to a seance. She switched it on. 'I was the only woman there that evening,' she said. 'And when I played the tape back, I was astonished. I heard another woman's voice, and she whispered my name ...'

She played me the tape. There *does* seem to be a woman's voice, who *does* seem to say, 'Judith'.

Judith Chisholm isn't the first to encounter spirit voices on tape – it is estimated that five million examples of the 'electronic voice phenomenon' (EVP) have been recorded. To this must be added the related phenomenon of transcommunication, in which spirits use other electronic methods to communicate with the living: pictures on televisions, fax messages, telephone calls and computer print-outs.

'The important thing about EVP,' said Judith, 'is that the voices are on tape for all to hear, thus proving they are real and not hallucinations.' It was this very fact which led Judith to found the Electronic Voice Phenomenon and Transcommunication Society. Some of the experiences of the members are worth recording in these pages:

One member's wife was in hospital with a broken ankle, and when he visited her, he took a tape recorder along, and set it running. He discovered afterwards a male voice on the tape which said: 'Which leg is it, lady?'

The same member owns two Siamese cats which were squabbling while his tape recorder was on. When he played back the tape, voices had been dubbed onto their yowls. One said, 'Scratch my back!' The reply on a rising crescendo said, 'No I won't!'

A member called George Bonner was sitting down recording, when he somehow managed to slip off the sofa; a voice on the tape said, 'Bonner looks quite ridiculous!'

Judith herself was recording when she happened to drop a bottle. A spirit voice, with a definite Irish accent, said, 'That was an amazing escape. You nearly broke the bottle!'

Most importantly, Judith believes she heard her late son speak snatches of sentences, two years after he died at the age of 36 – on one occasion he said the words, 'Laugh at us!'

'I know it's his voice, it has his intonation,' she told me. 'He had a tooth missing, and you can hear the slight whistle.' She added: 'I now know that death isn't the end.'

What is undeniable is that there is *something* on these tapes. I have heard it with my own ears, and anyone else is welcome to do the same. If there is a criticism of EVP research, it is that the voices are often indistinct – and that not everyone hears the same thing as the researchers. When I played EVP tapes to my partner, she couldn't make out the words of the messages at all – not even when I told her what they were supposed to be. Are researchers perhaps picking up bits and pieces of radio broadcasts, and other sonic odds and ends, and then interpreting them to mean what they want them to mean?

I don't know. But there is one final point I wish to make. When I met Judith, I tape-recorded the interview. I asked her whether she thought there would be any examples of EVP on the tape. She replied that if the spirits wanted to make their presence known, they would. Well, I played back the tape. At the moment when she makes that comment, there is just a *hint* of stray noise. It's not a voice, just a little tap. Did I knock the microphone with my sleeve? I'm not sure . . .

Contact: Judith Chisholm, 'An Teac na Pôl', Rossnagreena, Glengarriff, County Cork, Republic of Ireland.

Or: The American Association for Electronic Voice Phenomena, 816 Midship Court, Annapolis, MD 21401, USA.
Tel: 410 573 0873

The Engine Shed Society

Walking along the abandoned railtrack from Alnwick to Alnwick Station, you find just the stone edging of an old turntable pit amidst the undergrowth, its shed long gone and the pit itself having been filled in: although the members of the Engine Shed Society are fascinated by working, modern engine sheds – the 'houses' for railway locomotives – *anything* that bears the traces of an earlier generation of shed will be of interest. (As their magazine notes: at Lower Darwen, the shed's site is heavily overgrown but bits of flooring and a few bricks can be seen here and there; at Sutton Oak, the old shed is used as a supermarket, but its smoke vents are still *in situ* and can be seen from the railway bridge at Baxters Lane; at Lostock Hall, the floors and pits are easily visible, as are the holes in which the boilerwasher's hydrants were located.)

Contact: Major John Jarvis, Engine Shed Society (UL), The Laurels, Fire Beacon Lane, Bowd, Sidmouth, Devon, EX10 0NE, UK.

E.N.I.G.M.A.

The group's two founder-members will be referred to as C and M; that sets the atmosphere.

So, C, M and I – I being me, not a cover – sat at the table in an upstairs room. The radio was on, receiving nothing but static; until, at the precise time C and M had predicted, the English folk tune 'The Lincolnshire Poacher' broke through. When the music died, a woman's voice read a series of numbers, in groups of five, with each group repeated: 65742 65742 94475 94475 55434 55434 . . . etc. My first experience of a *numbers station*.

'I've been interested in radio since the 1970s, and it's something I've always been mystified by,' said C. 'I'd heard these numbers, and I didn't really know what they were, and there didn't seem to be anywhere to go to find out about them. Though I did come across some *ridiculous* explanations – anything from communications with UFOs to depth soundings in German rivers. One woman even wrote to the BBC about the numbers and was told that they were snowfall figures for the Pyrenees.'

'I first heard a numbers station at Christmas in 1963, when I got a radio receiver as a present,' said M. 'Since then I've always been curious about them.'

'What did you think they were?' I asked.

'Spies,' said M. 'Right from the start they sounded like spies.'

C and M are the founders of E.N.I.G.M.A., the European Numbers Information Gathering and Monitoring Association; though the word 'European' is something of a misnomer, because E.N.I.G.M.A. is the only such group in the *world*.

At least, the only such group outside the professional intelligence services – because M's early intuition that the numbers are coded instructions for spies is almost certainly correct. In some cases, it is even possible to correlate political tensions in a certain part of the world with increased activity by numbers stations – such as during the collapse of the Berlin Wall, or during the siege of Moscow, when Boris Yeltsin climbed on a tank.

'Every numbers station has its own characteristics,' said M. 'One station plays "Don't Cry For Me Argentina", and then uses a peculiar combination of single and double digits, such as 4-4-24. Another broadcasts 23 hours a day in Czech, and the numbers are read by a woman in an electronically sampled voice. There is one which broadcasts on a 17-day cycle and another which broadcasts just a couple of times a year.'

'Then there is a station,' said C, 'which is extremely accurate about timing. It comes on the air at *exactly* twenty minutes past the hour, and it's accurate to the very second – so they must take a great deal of pride in their work. Others are sloppy and come on late.'

'And actually, not all the stations use numbers,' said M. 'One of my favourites is the Tyrolean Music Station, which has a sinister Germanic voice reading out mysterious messages, interspersed with accordian music and yodelling.' He fetched a tape of this station – in which the broadcaster makes statements such as 'Our hen is about to lay one egg', 'The big 26 is 24', and 'The sunshine is fading'. It sounded so obviously spy-like as to be taken for a parody. Furthermore, the station was amateurish in the extreme: there were buzzes from speaker leads, clicks from switches and, M remarked, the broadcaster would sometimes cough and sneeze on air.

'It's hardly James Bond,' I remarked.

'This is the *real* world,' said C.

The beauty of the numbers stations is that they can be picked up by ordinary people, and so are the perfect cover for an agent – what could be more innocuous than a small 'world band radio'? At the same time, the messages cannot be understood unless the listener knows the codes; which may lead you to wonder: what is the *point* of listening to the numbers stations when their messages are incomprehensible?

'Espionage is a dark world,' said M, 'and there you are, in your bedroom, listening on primitive equipment, and suddenly you are *part* of that world.' He admitted that there was not the slightest chance of cracking the stations' codes, but one of the keenest pleasures was pitting wits against the security agencies and discovering at least *some* of the significance of a message.

For example, over a period of time, M has noticed that a particular station broadcasts some numbers on a more powerful transmitter than others – which would imply that those numbers are intended to be picked up by agents situated a long way from the European home base. By monitoring how many numbers of each type are sent, it is possible to get an idea of how much espionage activity is taking place in Europe, and how much further afield. The ultimate compliment to E.N.I.G.M.A. is that there are intelligence agencies who actually subscribe to the group's newsletter, to read about these discoveries.

'One East European embassy openly subscribes,' said C. 'Others are not so open, but they've made silly mistakes to give their identities away. And one intelligence agency even sent us a worried letter – they were concerned that their subscription had run out.'

Contact: E.N.I.G.M.A., c/o B.R.C. 17-21 Chapel Street, Bradford, West Yorkshire, BD1 5DT, UK.
Fax: 01274 779004 E-mail: enigma.box@centrenet.co.uk

The Ephemera Society

What is ephemera? Or should that be are? There is confusion about the grammar, the pronunciation (epheemera? ephmmera?) and the scope of the term. Ephemera is defined by the Ephemera Society, whose members collect it, as 'the minor transient documents of everyday life'. It includes admission tickets, reward notices, advertising and price tags – everything from an eighteenth-century receipt for the purchase of horse manure, to a handbill for a stage show from the 1890s, with its 'startling disrobing scenes'.

Talking of disrobing scenes, ephemera also includes the cards which prostitutes leave in present-day London phonebooths. Maurice Rickards, a distinguished graphic designer and founder of the Ephemera Society, showed me some examples from this part of his collection. 'My very respectable friends take great pleasure in bringing me handfuls of these cards,' he said, as we looked at the pictures of basques, fishnets, and whips, and the promises of 'spanking fun' with sexy eighteen-year-olds.

Maurice remarked that it was some time before he realized that 'TV' on the cards did not stand for television.

Contact: The Membership Secretary, Ephemera Society, c/o 146 Portobello Road, London, W11 2DZ, UK.
Or: The Membership Secretary, Ephemera Society, PO Box 95, Cazenovia, New York 13035, USA.

Eraser Carver's Quarterly

'Your job is to carve every colour, shape, size and kind of eraser that you can lay your hands on! Carve each one in turn to see how the different types feel as you carve. With the standard deskset-type pink eraser you'll find as wide a variation of consistency as anywhere. Some cut clean and easy while others are crumbly and a drag on your carving tool. Some are soft as butter and others as hard as linoleum. All are worthy of experimentation and for every knuckleheaded know-it-all who will tell you that ink erasers or pink pearls or art gums are not suitable for carving, I'll introduce you to a carver who not only gets results from erasers such as these but actually prefers them!'

(The words of Mick Mather, editor of *Eraser Carver's Quarterly*, the only publication in the world devoted to the hobby of making rubber stamps out of erasers.)

Contact: Mick Mather, *Eraser Carver's Quarterly*, PO Box 222, Clay, NY 13041-0222, USA.
Tel: 315 635 1477

The Etch-A-Sketch Club

Of the 39,000 members of a society intended for children, the International Etch-A-Sketch Club, it is estimated that ten per cent are adults. There are even professional artists who have worked with the drawing toy: Jeff Gagliardi, from Colorado, has twiddled the Etch-A-Sketch knobs to produce versions of both the *Mona Lisa* and Michelangelo's Sistine Chapel creation scene, while Jeff Gosline of San Diego specializes in murals, consisting of multi-screen displays, bringing together 36 or 72 separate Etch-A-Sketches. 'Drawing with an Etch-A-Sketch is spiritual in a way,' he says. 'Your drawing is just going to be erased. You know it won't be permanent. But how permanent is anything?'

Contact: The Etch-A-Sketch Club, The Ohio Art Company, One Toy Street, Bryan, Ohio 43506, USA.

Exotica Enthusiasts

There are record collectors . . . and there are collectors of recorded *exotica*: works so bad that you have to laugh, or so strange that the only appropriate response is '*What*?'

There are two specialist magazines on this subject: *Cool and Strange Music Magazine* and *Cannot Become Obsolete*. In these publications you might find a review of *The Way of the Wolf*, a CD by Charles Manson . . . yes, *that* Charles Manson. Or, an old record, found at a flea market, *Music to Strip By* by Bob Freeman and his Orchestra, featuring 'a bonus free G-string'. (Comments the editor of *Cannot Become Obsolete*: 'This is one of the few times where I am glad that the original free bonus was not included when I bought the record.')

Flicking through the pages, you will find articles on the likes of *Greatest Hits* by Eilert Pilarm, a Swedish garbageman who impersonates Elvis; *The Coming War with Russia*, a recording of a sermon by a Baptist fundamentalist, warning of the apocalypse; and *Keep Fit, Be Happy #2*, a 1950s exercise record by Bonnie Pruden with Otto Cesana. *What?* An old exercise record – what could be more lame? But as the reviewer remarks: 'There is one gem on this album which has a big brassy sound with some really out-of-this-world voiceovers by Ms Pruden. I get a small, somewhat perverse thrill when I hear her say "In . . . Out . . . In . . . Out . . ." with those trumpets blaring in the background.'

> Contact: *Cool and Strange Music Magazine*, PO Box 8501, Everett, WA 98201, USA.
> Website: http://members.aol.com/coolstrge/coolpage.html
> E-mail: coolstrge@aol.com
> And: *Cannot Become Obsolete*, PO Box 1232, Lorton, VA 22199-1232, USA.
> E-mail: itsvern@ibm.net

Experimental Musical Instruments

The toilet seat guitar; the flower pot-o-phone; the 'electric xylophone' of tuned fire alarms; even the smell-organ, which releases perfumes in music-like sequences – all these and more have been featured in the magazine *Experimental Musical Instruments*, whose editorial policy is to publish articles about 'The design, construction and enjoyment of unusual sound sources.' Consider some observations from its readers:

'I've discovered that the water tanks from broken humidifiers make excellent resonators for stringed instruments. The hard plastic walls work well as sound boards and the tanks come with built-in sound holes and carrying handles.'

'I have a series of recordings I made of the peculiar rhythms and inner voices available from close miking old upholstered spring rocking chairs. The springs give the feeling of a printing press or a typewriter or a rusty cuckoo clock. You can vary your tempo, depending on how fast you rock, and the older the chair, the more interesting the rhythms will be.'

'The great challenge in making the car horn organ was finding twenty-five auto-horns at just the right pitches.'

'Although I can't fix a toilet to save my life, the hardware store has developed more pull for me than the music store. I always bring a couple of mallets and a violin bow with me – I get to hear things I've never seen before. All hardware items must be admired for their sonic properties – pitchforks, egg beaters, crowbars, fireplace grates, shovels, anvils, rebars (the structural reinforcement rods used in poured concrete), trash cans – they're all waiting to be played.'

'I am paying more attention to the sounds produced by dragging chairs across the floor.'

'Has anyone tried listening to sanded-down CDs?'

Contact: *Experimental Musical Instruments*, PO Box 784, Nicasio, CA 94946, USA.
Tel/Fax: 415 662 2182 Website: http://www.windworld.com/emi
E-mail : emi@windworld.com

The Extra Miler Club

'Thank you for your recent inquiry about the Extra Miler Club. We are pleased that you share our interest in visiting all the 3,141 jurisdictions* of the United States. Our goal is to encourage our members in pursuit of their travel goals, whether they "collect counties" or strive to visit all the state capitals, all the National Parks, or just have their photo taken at each of the state "WELCOME" signs.'

(* 'Jurisdiction' refers to all the counties, plus certain incorporated cities such as Virginia, Maryland, and Missouri, and the political sub-divisions of Alaska.)

Contact: Extra Miler Club, PO Box 61771, Boulder City, Nevada 89006-1771, USA.
Tel: 702 294 2617 E-mail: carsonhere@juno.com

F

The Fairy Appreciation Society

Mitzi Huxley, otherwise known as the Fairy Queen, the founder of the Fairy Appreciation Society, sent me the following advice in a poem:

Fairy Spell by Mitzi Huxley:

To ask a fairy for a wish
Just say the word Hokus-Tish
When the Moon is full and round
Place a small pebble on the ground
(Better if it's near a fairy mound)
Then while on pointed toe thrice turn around
Be very careful not to make a sound . . .

The membership is divided between those who are interested in the folk-lore/literature of fairies, and those who, like Mitzi, have some belief (or half-belief) in the *existence* of fairies and similar nature spirits. As one member writes in the society's journal: 'When I was a child, I was told that the white fluffy seeds of a dandelion were in fact fairies in disguise doing their summer dance. Other children would try to catch them in order to get their wishes granted. However, I believed, and still believe, that the fairies had/have no desire to be crushed by human hands. Instead I still try, whenever I see one trapped in a spider's web or such-like, to gently free it. It still makes me smile when I see them dancing through the air. Well you never know . . .'

Contact: Mitzi Huxley, Dodwell Cottage, Coffinswell, South Devon, TQ12 4SW, UK.

Fence Post Collecting

You do get the occasional revisionist movie, which attempts to tell the 'true' story of the Wild West; whether the *truly* true story would be a box office smash is debatable. According to Gerald Huebert, such a movie should focus on one hero: the fence post.

'History has failed to mention the role of the fence post in civilizing the old West,' says Gerald, who has a collection of over 400 posts, ranging in height from 3 feet to 16 feet, and weighing from 2 pounds to 200 pounds. 'Contrary to popular belief, the old West wasn't tamed by the Colt .45 or the Winchester .73; it was actually barbed wire that changed the West. And where would barbed wire be without the fence post and the staple? On the ground, of course. Fences define the American landscape.'

For Gerald, the real fascination of fence posts lies in the part *underneath* the soil: some posts are screwed into the ground, some have flared anchors, while others are so sophisticated they might be mistaken for a mole trap. 'Collecting fence posts,' says Gerald, 'is an exciting lifestyle and an adventuresome sport.'

Note: Although fence post collecting doesn't have a separate society of its own yet, the hobby is catered for by the Hawkeye Barb Wire Collectors' Association, whose newsletter is called The Fence Post.

Contact: Gerald Huebert, Hawkeye Barb Wire Collectors' Association, 129 1100th St., Portsmouth, IA 51565-3000, USA.

Fictional Languages

If language is the dress of thought, then some people hope to be couturiers. Consider, for instance, the language *Valrast* – an entirely fictional tongue, which its creator describes as loosely based upon Spanish/Latin, although, as he remarks, 'much of its vocabulary is drawn from those strange areas of netherworld inside my head'. Here is a snatch of Valrast, taken from an old issue of a specialist newsletter for fictional-language enthusiasts, *The Glossopoeic Quarterly*:

'... hin Nareth jos oshu Olpa Sekel hin smol ve ketil hon jos tur em olpa.'

This translates as:

'... and Nareth saw the three Fallen, and drawing his sword, he slew them.'

(There is an explanatory note that Nareth is the Chosen Warrior, and the three are the Fallen Sons of Heaven – because the language's creator is also working out a mythology for the speakers of this language, which he has loosely based upon the history of the Byzantine empire.)

Like other languages, Valrast has a grammar. The rule for plurals is that you should add an 'e' at the end of the word unless it already ends in a vowel, in which case you would drop that vowel and add the e. There is also a correct way of stressing syllables: in Valrast, the accent is usually

---

90

placed on the first syllable, except when there are more than two syllables. Hence, we have: tir-an-EM, TOL-tra, tren-O-sa, Ler-e-TU and MI-reth. However, like any good language, there are exceptions to rules: stress patterns will tend to differ for words which are influenced by other fictional languages, like *Pezhüzhüm*.

What is the point of all this?

There is a role for invented languages in certain works of fiction – Tolkien is the obvious exemplar; more recently, *Star Trek* has given birth to the language of Klingon. (Which has in turn led to the emergence of two 'academies' to promote the language: the Klingon Language Institute and the Interstellar Language School.)

But would *you* have the sticking-power to invent a vocabulary of several thousand words? Would *you* work out detailed phonetics, as for Pezhüzhüm, which has a 'kw' sound lying somewhere between the sound at the start of 'queen' and the sound at the end of 'loch'? Especially when no-one but *you* can understand the language?

There is also the problem of what others would think. The editor of *The Glossopoeic Quarterly*, Steven Deyo, admits that he's become cautious about having people in the vicinity while he tries out various sound-system pronunciations. One of his languages is *Bzhaghitakh*, which has six or more levels of two-tone aspirants – a kind of mixture of guttural Arabic and tonal Chinese. 'Years ago,' he says, 'my sister once came into my room while I was practising toned vocalics for certain letters. She said I was weird.'

Contact: Steven Mark Deyo, 1165 Bidwell Street, West St. Paul, MN 55118-2231, USA.
E-mail: frodo@deyo.com
(Note: *The Glossopoeic Quarterly* no longer exists as a print publication, but will re-emerge as a website and internet discussion group. Currently, the subscribers form a 'correspondence special interest group'.)
Or: The Linguistics and Science Fiction Network. (They publish a newsletter covering various fictional languages, such as Elvish, Kesh, and Panglish.) Suzette Haden Elgin, Ozark Center For Language Studies, PO Box 1137, Huntsville, AR 72740-1137, USA.
Tel: 501 559 2273 E-mail: ocls@ipa.net
Or: Interstellar Language School. (*Star Trek* fans who have published the New Testament and other works in Klingon.) c/o Ken Traft, 6629 Park Avenue, S. Richmond, MN 55423-2538, USA.
Tel: 612 869 7694 Website: http://www.geocities.com/Athens/8853
E-mail: ktraft@classic.msn.com
Or: The Klingon Language Institute. (This takes a more scholarly approach to the Klingon language than the Interstellar Language School.

Their projects include restoring the complete works of Shakespeare to 'their original Klingon'.)
PO Box 634, Flourtown, PA 19031-0634, USA.
Website: http://www.kli.org

Filk Music

It is said to have got its name because 'o' is next to 'i': a typist, preparing the schedule of events for a science fiction convention of the 1960s, hit a wrong key – and instead of typing 'Folk Music', typed 'Filk Music' instead. The name stuck, to describe science fiction-inspired folk music, with a strong lyrical base. I asked Judith Hayman, a leading Canadian filker, about some of the themes that filk music covers.

'Of course, you get a lot of songs about space flight, or about making contact with aliens,' she said. 'But you might also get a song about computers – there's one called "Calm Down, It's Only Ones and Zeros". And I've written a piece about organ transplants called "Waltz for Organs and Guitar".' At a filk convention, she even heard a song about geology called 'It's not Gneiss'. 'And a lot of filk music has a sense of optimism to it – the idea that there's some *hope* out there and we can actually achieve something.' As an example, she played me a track called 'The Phoenix', about a spaceship, with the lines:

> My wings are made of tungsten
> My flesh of glass and steel . . .

The song was melodic, and I didn't dislike it, but it takes a while getting used to lyrics in which 'tungsten' is mentioned, rather than the normal 'I love you, baby'.

'Well, you do get a lot of scientific terms in filk,' said Judith. 'I've heard someone sing the Periodic Table.' Though filk music has its own love songs – such as 'Silver Metal Lover', about the amours of androids, or 'A Modern Romance', about two answerphones who engineer the romance of their owners.

And yes, there is a filk song called 'Send in the Clones' . . .

Contact: Judith Hayman, 98-145 Rice Avenue, Hamilton, ON, L9C 6RC Canada.
E-mail: hayman@bserv.com
Or: *From C to C* (a filk fanzine) published by Peggi Warner-Lalonde, E-mail: peggi@idirect.com
Or: OVFF (Ohio Valley Filk Fest – a major annual filk convention), E-mail:

DianaHuey@aol.com
Three important websites, which will give additional filk contacts are:
FilKONtario: http://www.bserv.com/community/fkoa.htm
Interfilk: http://www.lovesong.com/interfilk
Hayman family page: http://www.bserv.com/users/hayman.htm

Finch Sport

'Tje tje tie – trurrrrrr – sis ke wie wie wie' – yes, that's fine. 'Rin tin tin tin – blubblubblur – sis ke wie' – okay too. 'Tje tje tje – deeuw – deeuw – deeuw – sis ke weeuw' – most definitely not. 'Tji tji tji – trurrrrr – wie' – no, that won't do either.

Not gibberish, but birdsong. The sounds were transcribed directly from the rulebook for the Belgian activity known as *de vinkensport*, or finch sport, and the criterion for acceptability was that a snatch of birdsong MUST end on a two-syllable sequence, finishing with the sound 'wie'. In this hobby, which has been around since the 14th century, a line of enthusiasts sit in front of a line of birdcages, with every cage containing a finch: the number of valid tweets given by each bird is tallied and the bird that achieves the greatest score in an hour wins the contest.

Amazingly, there is a *weekly newspaper* for finch sport enthusiasts, just as in Italy you will find newspapers devoted to soccer. In its pages, you might read that at a competition in Ardooie, 98 birds took part, with Bianca coming first, scoring 401 tweets.

She narrowly beat Elvis, who could manage only 400.

Contact: Nationaal Volkssportmuseum over de Vinkensport, Hazestraat 4-8750 Hulste, Prov. West-Vlaanderen, Belgium.

Finger Tug of War

After the post had arrived, I looked dubiously at the roll of adhesive tape on my desk: being a ring, several inches in diameter, with a tape width of about half an inch, it was the closest object I possessed to the equipment used in the German game of finger tug of war. (I had heard that day from the Bavarian Tourist Board with the dates of the 1998 contests – there are three separate championships in August, May and June.) The idea is that both you and your opponent should take hold of the ring, place the outside edge of your foot against the corresponding edge of your opponent's foot, and then tug . . .

Contact: Bavarian Tourist Board, Prinzregentenstraße 18/IV, D-80538, München, Germany.
Tel:++49 89 21 23 97-0 Fax:++49 89 29 35 82

The Fire Service Preservation Group

There is a world of difference between 'extinguishing a passion' and 'extinguishing: a passion'. Somehow, I combined elements of both when I dressed up in a fireman's uniform: looking nothing like the well-done beefcake you get in those firemen calendars – said to represent women's number one fantasy man – while paying homage to the hobby of role-playing as a fireman. In two ways, I poured on cold water . . .

(I should make it clear that fire service enthusiasts – as represented by the Fire Service Preservation Group, or by the readership of *Fire Apparatus Journal* – do much more than simply wear firemen's uniforms. Many enthusiasts own fire trucks and other fire-fighting appliances, which they display at fire shows for the general public.)

Contact: Andrew Scott, Treasurer, Fire Service Preservation Group, 50 Old Slade Lane, Iver, Bucks, SLO 9DR, UK.
Or: *Fire Apparatus Journal*, PO Box 141295, Staten Island, NY 10314-1295, USA.
Tel: 718 448 5009 Fax: 718 981 2359

The Flashlight Collectors

Buzz Lightyear, Frankenstein's monster, Ninja Turtles and Coca-Cola bottles – all come in a form that sends out a beam of light, and all are to be found in toy shops. This leads to the following piece of advice, taken from a newsletter for flashlight collectors:

'The next time you're frustrated and need a flashlight fix; when you get that craving that only buying a flashlight will resolve; march yourself down to Toys-R-Us. It's cheap therapy.'

Contact: Flashlight Collectors, PO Box 4095, Tustin, CA 92781, USA.
Tel: 714 730 1252 Fax: 714 505 4067
E-mail: flashlights@worldnet.att.net

The Flat Earth Society

Some years ago, I met a man who took a perverse delight in arguing that the Earth was flat.

If you suggested to him that the Earth must be round because ships disappear over the horizon, he would tell you that that doesn't prove anything – for by the laws of perspective, a far-away object gets smaller and smaller, and eventually vanishes. What about photographs from space? Inadmissible as evidence, he would reply: the Earth's atmosphere has a refractive index, which distorts light and which could certainly account for the apparent curvature. Ah, but then surely circumnavigation is the trump card. . . ? But no, he wouldn't have that, either. The Earth could be a disk, with the North Pole at the centre and the South Pole distributed around the circumference – you would then travel in circles, just as you would on a sphere, and a ridge of ice would stop you from falling off the edge. This man claimed never to have lost a debate on the shape of the Earth. The point was, though, he didn't actually *believe* the Earth was flat.

But there are people who do.

Contact: The Flat Earth Society, Box 2533, Lancaster, California 93539-2533, USA.
Tel: 805 727 1635

Float Pen Collectors

A row of black ants march over the word ANTS. An almost transparent cloud floats over the Golden Gate bridge. A tipped bottle of ketchup pours a red line over a pile of French fries – and then mysteriously, the ketchup is sucked back into the bottle: time can run backwards in the float pen world.

You've all seen float pens: souvenir ball-points that contain a transparent chamber, filled with fluid, in which an object moves – anything from a gondola on the Grand Canal in Venice to Batman's fist punching the Joker – as the pen is tilted. You are much less likely to have seen *Float About*, a specialist publication for float pen collectors. Edited by Diana Andra, who has a collection of some 2,500 such pens, *Float About* is distinguished by its fascinating insights into 'The Psychology of a Float Pen Collector'. I'll let the editor of the publication speak for herself:

'I think we would all agree that there is something "soothing" or "relaxing" about items that float in water. But the object (in a float pen)

95

is not floating freely in a lake or ocean. The object is confined in a very small space and unable to get out of the water. When was the last time you found yourself in that situation? Let's see . . . suspended in water . . . in a completely confined space? It's a place each and every one of us have in common . . . the womb! Wow . . . that was a trip I did not want to take. I must have been channelling Freud. I think it's definitely time for a coffee break.'

Perhaps the deep-seated reasons for float pen collecting will never be fully understood. But *Float About* has published a useful breakdown of the emotional dynamics of the hobby, which I am reproducing because I am sure it would apply to many other branches of collecting, too:

The HUNT — The never ending quest for float pens.
SUCCESS — The joy of finding a pen that isn't already in the collection.
BARTER — The amazement! (You mean for just $3 I can take this home with me?) And the excitement of trading duplicates with other collectors.
DISPLAY — The fascination of organizing and displaying our trophies.
GROWTH — The contentment we experience as our collection grows.
HUNGER — The seemingly insatiable desire to own even more float pens.
Which leads us back to the HUNT and we relive the loop all over again. Life is good.

Contact: *Float About Newsletter*, Diana Andra, 1676 Millsboro Road East, Mansfield, Ohio 44906-3374, USA.
Tel: 419 529 8876 Fax: 419 529 3354 (continue transmission over outgoing message) Website: http://www.turn2001.com
E-mail: turn2001@richnet.net

Flounder Tramping

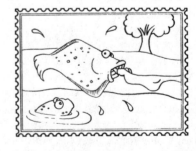

There are two containers into which you can pack all the fishing equipment you'll need. They are called your left and your right shoes.

We shall never know the name of the first man to wade across a river and realize that he'd trodden on something – his breakfast. But it is only in the tiny Scottish village of Palnackie that fishing with the feet has evolved into a competitive sport, the World Flounder Tramping Championship. It began over twenty years ago, with a bet made in a pub: a small group of trampers had a wager amongst themselves for a bottle of whiskey – the prize would go to whomsoever caught the largest flounder in the River Urr.

Now, the mudflats of the Urr are ideally suited to tramping. The flounder, a flatfish somewhat like a plaice, leaves the Solway Firth for the Urr's shallow estuary, and when the tide goes out, it lies on the bottom and buries itself in the mud. There, as it waits for the tide's return, it is vulnerable . . .

On the day of the championship, two hundred of us waded in waist-high, even chest-high. We foraged with our naked toes. For me, a first-time tramper, the Urr was not a pleasant place. Every so often, someone would jump halfway out of the water and cry 'Bloody crabs!' thereby putting you in fear for your toes. And the water is impenetrably murky. Your feet often brush against *something*, but what? Is it a strand of seaweed or ugh! – the fin of a fish? Imagine being stroked in the dark. The instinct is to lift the foot as fast as an Olympic sprinter.

It was hardly surprising I caught nothing, whereas the winner, a local man, tramped on a fish weighing 2lb 7oz. The correct technique, he told me, is to walk slowly until you detect a wriggling: then, if you can, try to get a good sound hold on the middle of the fish, reach down into the water, feel for the head, and hook a thumb into its gills. The fish is then brought to the surface and dropped in a bag – and it must be alive at the weigh-in: dead, it doesn't count.

The latter restriction dates back to the early 1980s, when there were suspicions of cheating: rumours that a prize-winning flounder had been caught not in the river, but on a fishmonger's slab.

Contact: Harry Ellis, 2 Glen Road, Palnackie, Dumfries and Galloway, DG7 IPH, UK.
Tel: 01556 600244

The Flying Nun Fan Club

'Sometimes people pigeon-hole you,' I was told by Jeff Michael, the President of the Flying Nun Fan Club – a group which holds theme parties based upon the 1960s TV show, at which the members don the Nun's headgear. 'They say that you have no life. But I'm not obsessed, this is just a part of what I do for my own enjoyment. I'm a songwriter and a cabaret performer first.' Though Jeff *has* written a song called 'I Want to Fly', which includes the lyric:

'I want to fly like Mary Poppins / Well, it looks like so much fun / I want to zoom on a broom like / The Witch of the West / I want to fly like the Flying Nun.'

Starring Sally Field, *The Flying Nun* told the story of Sister Bertrille (Field), a nun who weighed only 90 pounds. With such a light body, the huge hat worn by the nuns of her order functioned as a kite-cum-hang-glider – and when the wind blew, she soared aloft, leading to dialogue like:

1st Nun: (Pointing at the sky) What is it? A pelican?
2nd Nun: No, it's Sister Bertrille.

'From an early age, I've loved characters who could fly,' said Jeff. 'I loved Superman and Peter Pan. But what I really like about *The Flying Nun* is its optimism: in every episode, there's trouble, but it works out all right in the end.'

For instance, there was the Christmas episode, featuring an ailing old nun, who wanted to see snow, but the weather just wouldn' play its part. So the Flying Nun put dry ice in the clouds and sure enough, it snowed. The old nun told Sister Bertrille that she had a very special gift. 'What, that I can fly?' said Bertrille. 'No,' said the old nun. 'Making people happy . . .'

And Jeff would agree with that.

Contact: The Flying Nun Fan Club, c/o Jeff Michael, PO Box 481, Brentwood, NY 11717, USA.

Freedom For Feet

'There will come a time when the pointed shoe is consigned to the museum, like whalebone stays,' said Donald Campbell. 'We don't wear hats that crack our skulls, do we? So why do we try to make our feet fit our shoes, rather than make shoes that fit our feet?'

I might describe Donald Campbell as seeking 'animal rights for little piggies'. In 1988, he founded Freedom For Feet, a pressure group that would like to see a Government Health Warning on every shoebox containing pointed footwear. In the longer term, he hopes to persuade manufacturers to produce foot-shaped shoes, that splay out at the toes.

'I have to avert my eyes from the obscene objects on display in shoeshops,' said Donald, now retired, the former Director of Works at the University of Hull. 'Particularly when women's shoes are concerned. Both men and women suffer with their shoes, but the special horrors are reserved for women – principally, the high heel.'

'What do you think of *my* shoes?' I asked. From the moment I had stood upon the doormat at his home in Hull, and during the short walk through the hallway to his lounge, I had felt I was being judged. As with most people's footwear, there was a *degree* of narrowing towards the toe.

'I've seen worse,' he commented.

Donald admitted that the liberation of the lower extremities had been a theme of his life for as long as he could remember. 'As a boy, I yearned for the prehensile toes of a monkey,' he said. 'And I can recall going on holiday with my parents to Cornwall – when I took a perverse interest in climbing limpet-encrusted rocks in my bare feet.'

As the years passed, scrutinizing the footwear of people in the street became a virtual obsession for Donald. He felt the deepest sympathy for badly-shod feet, he was shocked by the cruelty that ordinary men and women inflicted upon their toes. He has even expressed his feelings in verse, such as his *Lines to a pretty girl seen walking uncomfortably in the street in tight pointed shoes and high heels*:

> You take great care of your hair, Claire,
> And your face you religiously tend
> You pamper your skin, it's impeccably fair
> As if bathed in the milk of an ass.
> But when we come to your feet, lass,
> They're punished as though they offend;
> You torture them both like a couple of spies
> And shut them away, in your shame, from our eyes.

On one occasion, he visited the National Gallery purely to study the feet in the historical portraits. 'I learned a lot about artists' feelings towards feet – though I aroused the suspicions of the Gallery staff,' he said. 'Basically, artists hate feet. They arrange for them to be outside the frame or hidden behind a convenient flowerpot. Rodin may have made a beautiful sculpture of entwined hands – but he never thought of doing the same for feet.'

Freedom For Feet is Donald's response to society's foot-phobia: he airs his views at public lectures ('Can the rise and fall of civilization be correlated with the size of the gap between first and second toe?'), he lobbies shoe-manufacturers (who give him, he admits, 'polite brush-offs') and he makes approaches to the Foot Health Council. ('Every year the Council has a foot health week, and I try, as it were, to get a toe in.')

Thus far, he has recruited four supporters, including a cobbler who produces hand-made foot-shaped shoes. Donald showed off the cobbler's work: polished black . . . *objects* . . . that have at last given freedom to Donald's feet. Shoes so wide at the toes as to suggest the webbed feet of a duck. 'But why shouldn't we have webbed feet?' said Donald.

Is not Freedom For Feet a lost cause? Will not fashionable society dig in its heels to retain the pointed shoe? Donald is undeterred. 'How did the slave trade get put out of business?' he said. In the meantime, he has declared 25 October 'Freedom For Feet Day', because this is the Saint's Day for the two patron saints of shoemakers, Crispin and Crispianus – and he proceeded to read me another of his verses, the *Jingle for St Crispin's Day*:

> It's Crispin's Day today and so
> Bend the knee and bend the elbow
> Bend the elbow, bend the knee
> Today's the day our feet are free!

Contact: Freedom For Feet, 163 Westbourne Avenue, Hull, HU5 3JA, UK.
Tel: 01482 343588

The Friends of Alferd E. Packer

Not Alfred, but Alferd. I could have written *sic* after his name . . . and even added an extra 'k' to that Latinism for good measure. For the facts are:

In February 1874, Alferd E. Packer led five gold prospectors into the San Juan Mountains in Colorado. In April, he arrived alone and well-nourished at the Los Pinos Indian Agency near Saguache. In August, the remains of the prospectors were found (minus some fillets) at a campsite near Lake City. The judge in passing sentence is reputed to have said: 'Alferd Packer, you voracious son of a bitch, there were seven Dimmycrats in Hinsdale County, and you ate five of them. I sentence you to hang by the neck until you are dead, dead, dead.'

Today, the Friends of Alferd E. Packer meet occasionally to feed on such appropriate items as steak tartare and lady fingers . . .

Contact: The Friends of Alferd E. Packer, John Wesley McCune, Chaplain, 603 3rd Street N.E., Washington D.C. 20002, USA.

The Friends of the Chimneys

'I understand,' my letter began, 'that you are interested in 19th and early 20th century brick chimney stacks, built to serve steam engine power facilities in various industrial applications.' Specific, I'll grant them that; but don't all old tall industrial chimneys look the same?

'Well, it's like anything,' I was told over the phone by one of the members, James Douet. 'If you're interested in them, they look different.

If you're not interested, they look the same. And the point about the *old* ones, is that the bigger they were, the more air they sucked through, which powered up the fire.' By contrast, in modern ones the height doesn't matter, because the heat of the furnace is electrically controlled from below. 'The modern ones are just exhaust pipes, not chimneys,' he said, dismissively.

Contact: Amics de les Xemeneies (The Friends of the Chimneys), Señor Carlos Pereira Castro – arquitecte, Llull 96 1er. 1a, 08005, Barcelona, Spain.

The Friends of the Museum of Bad Art

'Thank you for your interest in our illustrious institution. It is only due to the support of patrons such as you that we are able to continue in our mission to bring the worst of art to the widest of audiences.' – Marie Jackson, Director of Aesthetic Interpretation, Museum of Bad Art.

Organized under the slogan 'Art Too Bad To Be Ignored', the Museum of Bad Art displays such *mess*terpieces as: *Leading the Parade*, described as 'A work of mystery set in a garden in which the plant life is distinctly more animated than the human form'; *Rocky Road*, 'An enormous work oozing the warmth of mustard and chocolate'; and *Pauline Resting*, a reclining nude wearing boots – 'the underarm hair was probably done after the fact with magic marker'.

Contact: Museum of Bad Art, 580 High Street, Dedham, MA 02026, USA.
Mailing Address: 10 Vogel Street, Boston, MA 02132, USA.
Tel: 617 325 8224 Website: http://www.glyphs.com/moba/
E-mail: moba@world.std.com

Frog Jumping

Daniel Webster was a frog who could out-jump any other in the gold rush town of Angels Camp, California. He was a fictional frog, the star of Mark Twain's story, *The Celebrated Jumping Frog of Calaveras County*, published in 1865.

The Pride of San Joaquin was a frog who

could out-jump any other in the gold rush town of Angels Camp, California. He was a real frog, who took part in the first Jumping Frog Jubilee, inspired by Twain's story, in 1928.

Rosie the Ribbiter was a frog who could out-jump any other in the gold rush town of Angels Camp, California. *Ever.* In the contest, in which a total of three hops make up the official jump, she achieved a world record distance of 21ft 5¾in in 1986.

And the humans? Yes, frog jockeys can coax their charges to the best leap, either by words or tickles.

Contact: Calaveras County Fair and Jumping Frog Jubilee, PO Box 489, Angels Camp, CA 95222, USA.

The Frog Pond

Boasting a newsletter called *Ribbit, Ribbit*, and holding events such as a Spring Frog *Hop*pening at a restaurant called the Yellow Brick Toad, the members of Frog Pond, the International Frog Collectors' Club, are fascinated by anything in the shape of a frog: jewellery, pencils, puzzles, cookie jars, key-chains, etc.

Though there *is* one member who admits that her hobby is 'Toad Dressing'. It all started when her children decided to dress a live toad in a costume. 'It was so comical that I never forgot it,' she said. Soon, she was dressing toads herself and taking photographs: one issue of *Ribbit, Ribbit* featured a toad dressed as Santa Claus. This member admits that she puts a lot of thought into the costumes that she makes herself, often shopping all over town for just the right fabric. (After the photo session the toad is released. She wants to affirm that the toads are not harmed by the experience – she admits to having 'a real affection for the creatures'.)

Contact: The Frog Pond, PO Box 193, Beech Grove, IN 46107, USA.

The 'From Parts Unknown' Society

This is a society for fans of one type of wrestling: masked wrestling. As one member proclaims: 'It is perfectly logical for masked athletes to compete in professional sport. How much cooler would tennis, curling, ping-pong and bowling be if masks were an accepted part of the traditional dress?'

In *The Rasslin' Magazine From Parts Unknown*, you can read about the history of masked wrestling – apparently, the first ever appearance of a masked wrestler was in 1873, when a man entered a Parisian tournament as, simply, 'The Masked Wrestler'. Then there are reviews of masked-wrestler toys – the new models of Ultimo Dragon and Atlantis Mysterioso. Plus reports from the ring, concerning the likes of the Japanese wrestler Koji Kanemoto, himself a former masked wrestler, who is now a mask-hater – if he unmasks an opponent, he tears the whole mask to shreds, and even pulls off the scraps around the other wrestler's neck. In a recent match, he ripped El Samurai's new black hood to pieces, forcing him to work the match unmasked. 'WHAT A BASTARD!' says the magazine.

Is it all tongue-in-masked-cheek? A celebration of the gorgonzola element in an already-cheesy sport? Not entirely. There is something touching about it, too. I'll leave you with this statement from one of the members:

'Despite the 18 or 19 years gone by, I will never forget the feeling of first seeing Mil Mascaras, the Man of a Thousand Masks, on television. Saturday morning – my father interrupts whatever Shogun Warrior vs Micronaut battle I'm concocting with action figures, and energetically calls me over to the TV. It was a WWF broadcast, and then there he was ... He entered the ring in a vivid green and gold robe and vest, shining like all heaven. My dad's enthusiasm, wanting to share with his kid a sight that impressed him, was probably identical to that of fathers in Japan and Mexico. After all, children everywhere want superheroes to be real. Their fathers did when *they* were young, too. Masked wrestling contests are like brief comic book panels, superheroes in action, the closest thing to Shazam vs Black Adam or Hulk vs Thing you could get in real life.'

Contact: The 'From Parts Unknown' Society, Unknown Publications, PO Box 3061, New Bedford, MA 02741, USA.
E-mail: bluedemon@earthlink.net

G

G.I. Joe/Action Man Enthusiasts

When Chris Malbon was twelve, his mother decided that he was too old for toys. So, one day, she gave him some money to buy comics – something she did not normally do. While her son was out of the house, she gathered the toys together; when he returned, there was a bonfire in the yard. 'All my toys were burnt – and I wasn't given any choice. I was gutted,' he said, still recalling the incident at the age of thirty-seven.

Actually, not all the toys had gone. His Action Man soldiers (the British name for the American toy G.I. Joe) happened to be stored in a separate place and so survived . . . for a while. But at the age of fifteen, he came home from school to discover that his mother had simply given them away. 'She said that there wasn't space for them. I know I hadn't played with Action Man for years – but that wasn't the point, the toys were *mine*. If something is yours, it's wrong to take it away.'

Chris admitted that these two incidents in childhood may possibly explain why, as an adult, he has become a G.I. Joe/Action Man collector. 'Though I'm no psychologist,' he added. And if his parents' house had insufficient space to be a barracks for the twelve-inch fighting figurine, this does not apply to his own home in Birmingham. Here, a whole room is devoted to the toy – it is like a reference library or a wine cellar, but instead of books or bottles, there are soldiers, sailors, marines, astronauts, deep-sea divers, polar explorers: manifestations of machismo in miniature.

'But I want to stress that I never *ever* play with the toys – some of these figures haven't moved in a couple of years. I just enjoy collecting them and all the equipment. It's a quality toy.' To demonstrate the workmanship, he fetched, the Gemini space capsule and slid back the entrance panel. 'That's beautiful, isn't it? I never had this as a kid, but my parents did buy me the astronaut's outfit and I took it to school to show it off. Then a week later, another boy turned up with the capsule. At the time, I was a bit miffed.'

Since he became a collector, Chris has acquired considerable knowledge of the history of Action Man. The original G.I. Joe first appeared in 1964, and Chris can easily recount its subsequent development: how painted hair gave way to realistic hair; how the Vietnam War led to a drop in sales; how G.I. Joe changed from a soldier to a general adventurer. And then there was the case of the diver doll. 'There were complaints about that doll being supplied in the nude – so they put shorts on him.' The prudishness is especially strange since a quick look at an

104

undressed G.I. Joe or Action Man will reveal that he lacks one or two of the items of equipment possessed by a real man. Chris also pointed out that the anatomy is inaccurate in another way – there is a misplaced thumbnail. 'It was originally a production error,' he commented, 'but it's been kept, along with the facial scar, as a trademark.'

Contact: The G.I. Joe Collectors' Club, 225 Cattle Baron Parc Drive, Fort Worth, Texas 76108, USA.
Website: www.mastercollector.com
Or: The Action Soldier Collectors' Club, 30 New Street, Deiniolen, Gwynedd, North Wales, LL55 3LH.
Or: The Action Man Enthusiasts' UK Club, White Lodge Stables, Main Street, Whissendine, Leicestershire, LE15 7ES, UK.

The Gay and Lesbian History on Stamps Club

The criterion for inclusion of a hobby in this book is specificity, or even *super*-specificity. Stamp-collecting as a whole would be too broad an interest, but certain philatelic specialist societies *do* find their way into these pages – such as the Gay and Lesbian History on Stamps Club.

The members' collecting interests are in fact slightly wider than stamps which depict notable gay men and women, and events significant in the history of gay culture – they also collect stamps of flora and fauna scientifically proven to have homosexual behaviour. For instance, recent research by primatologists indicates that the Bonobo, a species of ape, uses homosexuality to improve its social life. So, as the club's journal remarks: 'Be sure to include stamps of Bonobos in your collection!'

Contact: GLHSC, PO Box 515981, Dallas, TX 75251-5981, USA.

Ghostbusting!

The sound was soft, but real – a drawn-out groan, repeated every so often, like the creaking of a ship's timbers. The gooseflesh began bubbling along my arms and legs. The noise was coming from the tunnel. We had all been warned – what else can one expect when hunting the walking dead?

It was 3am at Fort Amherst in Kent. Hours earlier, I had arrived with thirteen members of the Association for the Scientific Study of Anomalous Phenomena, or ASSAP, a group of paranormal investigators who hold all-night vigils in haunted locations.

Only weeks before, an ambulance had been called to the fort because a man in his twenties had fainted, believing he'd seen a ghost. On the night of the stake-out, one of the fort's managers, Richard Wozencroft, told us that he himself had had no unusual experiences, but . . .

He mentioned that in one part of the fort, an old mezzanine floor had been removed and visitors had reported hearing footsteps above them, in mid-air, as if feet were still walking upon the boards. 'Some of my staff refuse to go into the tunnels at night,' he said, the moon shining, as he led us into those very passageways.

The word 'warren' is inadequate for Fort Amherst. There always seems to be another turning. Hewn from the chalk by Napoleonic prisoners of war, the tunnel walls have weathered over the years into a joyless grey-green – and the atmosphere belongs to Gothic literature. Fingers of cold air stroke your cheek; footsteps echo; you cast long shadows. There are many alcoves – I did not allow my eyes to dwell upon their depths.

We split into groups and stationed ourselves in different parts of the fort. Monitoring equipment was set up – video cameras and temperature sensors – but once that was done, we simply had to wait. To pass the time, we chatted about the paranormal; in the environment of Amherst, it was easy for ASSAP members to recount experiences that sent a tingling up and down my spine. David Thomas, a long-standing ASSAP member, said that he first became interested in ghosts when he was thirteen. He was about to climb the stairs in his parents' house when he was aware of a *presence* behind him. He turned – to see a man in top hat and tails. The young David ran screaming up the stairs. The man vanished. Since then, David claims to have had 'glimpses of this, glimpses of that'. When I pressed him for details, he mentioned the family's cat. 'After the cat died, we went to a new house,' he said. 'Then one year we went on holiday, and when we came back, the neighbours said that it was cruel of us to leave a cat behind. We wondered what cat they meant.' The neighbours described the deceased pet. They had seen it inside the house, looking out of the window.

Other investigators told of occurrences at previous all-night vigils. Strange bangs; a hint of perfume, as if a spectral woman was walking around; the time when a door of a castle rattled; or when an investigator, listening through headphones, heard a low voice say 'Hellooooo'.

Hours passed and after many changes of station, I found myself in an annexe which was a mock-up of a World War II headquarters. Two of us were on look-out duties here – along with the wax effigies in battledress, which every now and then I checked to see that they hadn't moved.

Beyond, was an open doorway leading to the tunnels. Mr Wozencroft had told us that, a few months earlier, an electrician had been in this annexe when he was scared out of his life. While working on a rewiring job, the electrician was barged aside by *something*. He caught a glimpse of a black shape – it went out of the doorway and into the tunnels, where it disappeared. The electrician ran out and refused to finish the work. In this very place, at 3am, my colleague said: 'What's that noise?'

It was the groaning I have mentioned. I went cold. He said he would investigate. I didn't stop him; I didn't join him, however. He returned after a few seconds. 'It's okay,' he said. 'It's one of the ASSAP members. He's fallen asleep in a chair and is snoring his head off.'

Contact: Dr Hugh Pincott, ASSAP, 20 Paul Street, Frome, Somerset, BA11 1DX, UK.
Tel: 01373 451777 Website: http://ds.dial.pipex.com/assap/
Or: *Ghost Trackers' Newsletter*, Ghost Research Society, PO Box 205, Oak Lawn, IL 60454-0205, USA.
Tel: 708 425 5163 Fax: 708 425 3969 E-mail: DKaczmarek@aol.com

The Giant Vegetable Championships

The categories include the heaviest celery and the longest runner bean.

Contact: Baytree Nurseries & Garden Centre, High Road, Weston, Spalding, Lincs, PE12 6JU, UK.
Tel: 01406 370242 Fax: 01406 371665

Giants and Little People

It strikes me that you could put yourself in the right mood with a magnifying glass. You just look at the world through the lens – and try to imagine that the reason everything is larger is that you have got *smaller*. Though some people find themselves thinking along these lines without optical aids.

'... I'm pretty happy with my current height of 5ft 10in,' says Bob Nelson, 'but I'll often wake up in the morning and think about what it would be like if I'd shrunk to 6ins tall. I mean, how would you react if you suddenly saw your cat as bigger than a house?', But that isn't the only possibility he imagines. 'Or what if you were 60ft tall, so that you saw an elephant as small as a mouse? Or suppose, someone suddenly became the size of an eight-year-old child? Suppose I woke up and found I had gone from 5ft 10ins to 4ft 2ins ...'

He describes a world in which his clothes are now far too big; where light switches and doorknobs are higher than before; where he has to go on tiptoe to reach things; where 12-year-olds tower over him like basketball stars. 'Or, what if you actually *are* an eight-year-old child, but you're over 6ft tall – how would you convince a bus-driver that you have the right to travel half-fare? We're so used to seeing our world from an everyday perspective – it's exciting to see it from a different and bizarre viewpoint.'

For a while, Bob even produced a specialist newsletter, *Giants and Little People*, and sent out a readership survey form to the 25 subscribers that included the questions: 'How tall are you?' and 'How tall or short would you like to be?' Though the newsletter has now closed, its work continues as a website and as a column in another newsletter, *Raccoon Times*, and Bob exchanges letters and e-mails on the theme of size-changing with anyone who cares to write. His main aim is to explore literature, movies and TV shows in which people are scaled up or down. The classic example is, of course, *Gulliver's Travels*, but the theme is also covered in movies such as *The Incredible Shrinking Man* and in various television commercials – most famously, the ones featuring the Jolly Green Giant. And nowadays, Bob does admit that personal circumstances might be a *factor* in his fascination with altering human dimensions.

'I weigh 280lb,' he says. 'And I'd like to be thinner. So, yes, that's probably part of the reason for being interested in changing my size.'

Contact: Bob Nelson, 75 Hale St, Apt. #1, Beverly, MA 01915, USA.
Website: http://www.angelfire.com/ma/giantandtinypeople
E-mail: rac_cooney@hotmail.com OR rac_cooney@yahoo.com

The Gird 'n' Cleek Championships

I had better begin with a translation. 'Gird' is the Scots word for hoop; the 'n' you will know from rock 'n' roll; and 'cleek', another Scots word, turns the whole expression into something which might be referred to as 'rod 'n' roll' – for in the sport of gird 'n' cleek, you have to roll a hoop which is attached to a rod while racing around a running track. In the words of a rhyme:

> We'll have a go wi' Gird 'n' Cleek
> They say it's easy when it yer peak.

Which means, I suppose, it's difficult if you aren't. At the world championships, held every summer in the village of Parton in south-west Scotland, the gird is about 2ft 6ins across, made of iron, and the cleek is attached to it by a loop – as if the gird were threaded through the eye of an enormous needle. You *can* find girds with separate cleeks, but the attachment of the two requires more skill, for the cleek can interfere with the roll of the gird, acting as a brake and causing it to topple over.

Well, I practised and practised, till my hands turned orange-brown from the cleek's rust. The trick is to keep pushing as you hold the gird in its starting position: this means that a smooth transition occurs when you actually start running.

Not surprisingly, I came last in my heat, and watched a local man become world champion. But I was pleased that I managed to get my gird to roll smoothly *some* of the time; a gird in full roll makes a wonderful noise – like a metalworker's lathe, or how a bee would sound if its wings were made of steel.

Contact: George McCulloch, 4 Carney's Corner, Gatehouse of Fleet, Dumfries and Galloway, DG7 2HW, UK.
Tel: 01557 814030

Glass Music World

Every musical instrument has its verb. You *strum* a guitar; *beat* a drum: and *pluck*, *blow* and *bow* respectively a harp, a horn and a violin. And you stroke. . . ?

You stroke a *glass* instrument, the instrument of choice for the readership of the magazine, *Glass Music World*. ('Now serving glass music enthusiasts in 14 countries around the globe.') Mostly, the readers are concerned with playing the glass harmonica, an instrument invented by Benjamin Franklin, in which a series of graduated glasses is attached to a spindle: the glasses revolve by means of a foot treadle, and the performer strokes the rims to produce notes. But the readers are passionate about *any* vitreous performance, such as the one in Frederick Fellini's film *E La Nave Va* or *And the Ship Sails On*:

A group of passengers gather in a ship's galley, where they find a table full of wine glasses awaiting distribution for the next meal – so one of them wets a finger and starts playing a simple melody on the glasses, a second joins in, while a third performer taps champagne flutes with spoons and a fourth adds harmonies by blowing on water-tuned bottles. Though the magazine comments that the result is a spritely and imaginative piece of music, it notes that the performance is obviously not taking place in real time, since in several instances the glass players manage to get two different tones from the same goblet. What's more, the goblets are free standing – 'and as any glass player knows, if you don't hold a glass down while stroking its rim it will most certainly fall over.'

Contact: Glass Music International, c/o Mrs Elizabeth Glancy Brunelli, Harbor Point, 40 Westwind Road, Apt. 505, Boston, MA 02125, USA.

Globe in Transit

I have always had a fondness for the French expression *eminence grise*, meaning literally a 'grey eminence', an influential person wielding power behind the scenes. It is conceivable that an eminence grise might be at work in the pop music industry – one does read newspaper reports about chart-rigging, hyping of songs, manufactured groups and the like; but it was not until I met Daniel Transit that I realized the eminence grise of the pop world might actually be grey in colour. You see, the modern-day believer in extra-terrestrials doesn't believe in little *green* men . . .

'Do you honestly mean to tell me,' I said to Daniel, 'that the music of the Carpenters was written under the influence of aliens?'

'Yes,' he said, with utter calm. 'There's a line in "Close to You" which talks about "On the day that you were born, the *angels* got together and decided to create a dream come true".'

'And you think "the angels" is a reference to aliens?'

'Yes. Plus they did that song "Calling Occupants of Interplanetary Craft".'

For Daniel, that is the clincher; but then, he finds clinchers in the work of most, if not all, pop artistes. Our conversation consisted of my naming singers at random, and Daniel instantly giving me evidence that an otherworldly being should get co-writer's credits for their songs. Such as:

'Okay . . .' I said, 'Bob Dylan.'

'Well, there's the song "Mr Tambourine Man", which includes the line, "Take me on a trip upon your magic swirling ship".'

'Couldn't that be a drug reference?'

'But ships don't usually swirl unless they're spaceships.'

110

'What about singers from the Rock 'n' Roll era?'

'Rock 'n' Roll began with Bill Haley and the *Comets*. And then there's Jerry Lee Lewis's "Great Balls of Fire". That could have been inspired by seeing fireballs in the sky. And Elvis's father Vernon said that at the time of his birth there was a blue light over Elvis's home. Plus Elvis told Natalie Wood that a supernatural force had taken him over and made him what he'd become.'

'Okay, the big one – the Beatles.' Here, his reply was extensive.

'In the song "I am the Walrus" there are references to beings that are called The Eggmen. They're also described as "pretty little policemen all in a row", and they "run like pigs from a gun" and "fly like Lucy in the sky". Alien beings have been described as having egg-shaped heads and being small in size. They've also been reported to be wearing uniforms – sometimes blue. And to be able to move very fast. They also fly about the sky in spacecraft. And there is the line "I am you and you are me and we are all together". Some writers such as Whitley Strieber have written that aliens seem to have a group mind, and are reported as looking very much alike, as if they have all come from the same mould.'

Daniel believes that in some way – perhaps by the subtle routes of telepathy, beamed messages and mind-control, perhaps by direct close-encounter contact – aliens are using rock stars to pass information to the general public. The evidence for this is sifted over in Daniel's publication *Globe in Transit*, devoted to the study of alien influence in pop music, and from which he takes his nom-de-plume Daniel Transit. But what inspired his research in this area?

It began as a general interest in UFOs, in 1982, after Daniel saw strange lights in the sky in the King's Cross area of London. 'They were much faster than an aircraft,' he told me. 'And moving in a zig-zag path. I saw them on two separate occasions. The first time, it was an orange-red light, and then the second time there were three white lights moving independently. But both times they were zig-zagging and very fast. And nothing we know of could do that.' The connection between ET and CD, as it were, didn't happen for another three years. The moment of insight occurred as a result of attending a concert given by Toyah Wilcox – at which the stage-scenery featured a number of transparent blue cones. 'And I subsequently read a piece in *Flying Saucer Review* which said that cones were an important part of many UFOs.'

Our conversation continued: Elton John, Led Zeppelin, Queen – and of course, David Bowie, who unlike many rock stars, uses *overt* alien references. For Daniel, those zig-zags in the night sky led directly to *Ziggy Stardust*.

'In Bowie's song, "Moonage Daydream", he even says, "I'm a space invader". And there's a lyric about a pink monkey bird – which could be an alien creature.'

'But I once saw a TV documentary about Bowie,' I commented, 'which showed him cutting words out of a magazine and just sticking them together to make up lyrics he liked the sound of.'

'There are just too many connections between pop music and aliens for it *all* to be coincidence,' said Daniel.

Contact: *Globe in Transit*, 11 Wharton Street, London, WC1X 9PX, UK.

The Gnome Club

Liz Spera, who runs the Gnome Club: 'There are people who believe gnomes are mythical beings or a part of folklore, and then there are others who really do believe gnomes exist. There are individuals who claim they have met and spoken to gnomes. They say that you can also learn ways to invite gnomes into your life and make friends with these marvellous beings.'

Contact: The International Gnome Club, Liz Spera, 22841 Kings Ct., Hayward, CA 94541-4326, USA.
Tel: 510 889 9978 Fax: 510 889 0343 E-mail: GNOMEGNET@aol.com

Goldpanning

In the World Goldpanning Championships, contestants receive a sack of sand containing a certain number of flakes of gold – perhaps one, perhaps ten. The winner is the fastest to identify the exact number of flakes in his sack – and a flake might be smaller than the period punctuation you're now going to see.

Contact: Michael Gossage, The Goldpanners' Association, 12 Pikepurse Lane, Richmond, North Yorks, DL10 4PS, UK.
Tel: 01748 822515
Or: Vince Thurkettle (Secretary) Tel: 01953 498721

The Golliwog Collector Club

Soft, black, cuddly, it's a pussy cat . . . no it isn't. Not only is it *not* a pussy cat, it's got *nothing* in common with the initials 'PC'. The golliwog – the toy condemned as a disgraceful racial stereotype, with staring eyes, red lips and frizzy hair – is now feted as a desirable collectable by the members of The International Golliwog Collector Club. Is this a hobby that's best left out of the book?

As I open the pages of the club's newsletter, I feel a frisson of excitement deriving from the sheer *naughtiness* of this hobby in today's world: some golliwog items are *so* stereotyped, *so* inappropriate, that it's difficult to avoid a cackle. (For instance, a 1934 piece of sheet music, *The Dancing Golliwog*, featuring three golliwogs, two seated on each end playing their banjos, with a dancing golly in the centre. Or, the most non-PC item I've ever encountered, an old postcard 'Golliwog Harpoons a Seal'.)

But should one comment *honi soit qui mal y pense*? The 400 members of the club point out that in the original golliwog stories of British author Florence Kate Upton, beginning with *The Adventures of the Two Dutch Dolls* in 1895, the golly was a lovable character and, if anything, the story taught a lesson that one shouldn't fear people who look different from oneself: the Dutch dolls are initially scared of the golly, but are soon walking with him arm-in-arm. Later stories cover surprisingly modern themes such as pacifism and vegetarianism. Most extraordinary of all is the story set in the African jungle in which the golly is tied up and held by African natives who *don't regard him as black*.

So, I've made my decision, and the club is listed in these pages. And if I find myself banned from libraries, as golliwog stories have been? Well, if the task of this book is to render the essence of an unusual hobby, I suppose a library ban would be the most perfect rendering of all.

Contact: I.G.C.C., PO Box 612, Woodstock, NY 12498, USA.
Website: http://www.teddybears.com/golli.html
E-mail: OhGolli@aol.com

The Grassy Knoll Gazette

There was a line from a song on the envelope, both words and sheet music. 'Who killed JFK, MLK, RFK, MJK?' the song asked, and answered itself: 'Not LHO; not JER; not SBS; not EMK, not any way.' (MJK – by the way – is Mary Jo Kopechne. You should be able to work out the rest for yourself.) The magazine inside, *The Grassy Knoll Gazette*, proclaimed its editorial policy: CONSPIRACY IS NOT A DIRTY WORD.

Maybe that message is aimed at you and me, reader; maybe both of us think that conspiracy theory is an attempt to make life more meaningful than it really is. And yet, and yet, and yet . . .

Talking of aiming, Sirhan Bishara Sirhan was 48 inches in front of his target when he killed Robert Kennedy ... with a shot fired from less than two inches behind the candidate's right ear.

Contact: *The Grassy Knoll Gazette*, Cutler Designs, Box 1465, Manchester, MA 01944, USA.

(The Association for) Gravestone Studies

Andrew Marvell famously wrote: 'The grave's a fine and private place. But none, I think, do there embrace.' Though two people did come pretty close – by getting married among the gravestones of a Massachusetts cemetery. 'Our guests thought it a little odd at first,' commented the groom, 'but it turned out quite lovely.'

The couple are members of a society of gravestone enthusiasts, the Association for Gravestone Studies. Join, and you'll learn techniques of reading weathered epitaphs, such as the 'mirror technique', which involves reflecting sunlight at an angle over the gravestone to highlight the carving with shadows, or the 'wetting and brushing' technique, in which the dirt on the surface is moved into the letters while the rest of the surface starts to lighten. You'll also be able to attend lectures on subjects such as 'The Graveyard in Art' or 'Fear of Cemeteries – Is There Really a Need?'

And returning to the theme of love and cemeteries: why not give your partner a piece of graveyard jewellery as a gift? The association sells attractive pewter earrings, whose designs are reproductions of tombstones. (Choose from a skull or an angel.)

Contact: The Association for Gravestone Studies, 278 Main Street, Suite 207, Greenfield, MA 01301, USA.
Tel: 413 772 0836 Website: www.berkshire.net/ags
E-mail: ags@berkshire.net

Groundtastic

I am within a centimetre of betraying my principles. I guess that's the height of a soccer boot stud, and could be taken as the distance separating the pitch from the action. A fanzine for the world's most popular sport has no place in these pages; but what about a fanzine for soccer *grounds*?

Groundtastic, which is just such a fanzine, doesn't concentrate solely on the important grounds, like the Stade de France, the venue for the 1998 World Cup Final. There is also room for village grounds like the one in Hertfordshire, England, 'where the grass is often too long, the white lines are never straight, nettles grow just inches from the pitch, the river is only a few yards away and dog dirt is a problem, as is climbing through barbed wire fencing to get stray balls back from the adjacent field where horses graze'.

Contact: *Groundtastic*, 75 Littlebury Green, Basildon, Essex, SS13 1RF, UK.

The (Air) Guitar World Championship

This is about what every adolescent boy does with his hands in the privacy of his bedroom.

Yes, playing an imaginary guitar, accompanying his favourite rock music tracks!

Under the rules of the Air Guitar World Championship, which is held in August in Oulu, Finland, every air guitarist takes to the stage for two minutes: the first minute is the compulsory round, which requires all the contestants to mime a solo to the same piece of music – Deep Purple's 'Smoke on the Water', or Nirvana's 'Smells Like Teen Spirit', say – while the second minute allows contestants to play to a backing track of their choice, or even without music at all. The judges then award marks from 4.0 to 6.0, taking into account such factors as the naturalness and the joy of playing.

Players may be marked down for a too 'choreographed' performance; but on the other hand – literally – a past winner particularly impressed the judges because he played left-handed.

Contact: Mika Ronkainen, Rommakkokatu 5-7 C 58, 90120 Oulu, Finland.

Tel: +358 (0) 40 5829143 or +358 (0) 8 3119941
Fax: +358 (0) 8 3128023 E-mail: matron@mimas.otol.fi

The Gurning World Championship

Contrary to what you might believe, it is *not* necessarily an advantage to be ugly to begin with: the winner of the world championship in gurning – the art of pulling an ugly face – often makes the biggest *transformation* in his features. Though it *does* help to have false teeth: many contestants take their dentures out – or put them in upside down.

Contact: Alan Clements, 14 Dent View, Egremont, Cumbria, CA22 2ET, UK.
Tel: 01946 821554

Gut Barging

Two bargers attempt to barge each other off the mat using only their stomachs. That's a one-sentence description of a sport in which the participants' beer-bellies *alone* cry out for paragraphs.

Contact: The World Gut Barging Association, Fons Albert, 33 Silver Street, Bradford-on-Avon, Wiltshire, BA15 1JX, UK.

H

H.A.I.R.

I asked my partner, Elaine, how she would react if I gave her a bracelet made of human hair. 'You'd get it back in a flash,' she said, adding that I'd probably want to give her a pair of furball earrings next.

Yet in the nineteenth century, not only bracelets, but also watch fobs, rings, necklaces, and brooches were made of braided human hair. There were hairy bookmarks, hairy riding whips, hairy artificial flowers – and in Paris, in 1855, an artist even displayed a full-length life-size human-hair portrait of Queen Victoria.

It seems that public tastes changed around the time of the invention of photography: why give a mere lock of hair as a keepsake, when you could give a photograph? To make matters worse, hair from deceased relatives *was* still kept as a keepsake – thus, hair-work came to be associated with death, and eventually disappeared altogether.

Until now. The group known as H.A.I.R., or Hair Art International Restorers, is trying to bring back this lost art. In fact, the members of H.A.I.R. also make some items from animal hair – so the idea of furball earrings isn't so far-fetched.

Contact: H.A.I.R., Ruth Gordon, 24629 Cherry Street, Dearborn, MI 48124, USA.
Tel: 313 277 2479

Hack'd

This is one of those touchstone items, which demonstrates the difference between usual and unusual leisure. It's the difference between a yawn and a contemplative 'Hmmmm . . .'

Thus, a magazine about bikes and bikers wouldn't get a second look, as far as I'm concerned. But a magazine about sidecars and sidecarists – 'Hmmmm . . .' *Hack'd* is just such a magazine, devoted to 'motorcycling's extraordinary third wheel'. According to an article in a recent issue, if you have been asked the following three questions and held your head high, you are a sidecarist:

Question 1: Does your wife get into it? (Answer 1: Rarely does anyone get into it.)
Question 2: Why did you put it on there? (Answer 2: It was the result of watching a World War II movie as a child – 'Ever since seeing a German general come riding in one, I've wanted one.')
Question 3: What happens when you go round a corner? (Answer 3: 'Sometimes, when I go around a curve enthralled by the beauty of the day, I forget to allow for some centrifugal force, and I scare the hell out of myself.')

Contact: *Hack'd*, PO Box 813, Buckhannon, West Virginia 26201, USA.
Tel: 304 472 6146 Fax: 304 472 7027

Haggis Hurling

Or, shot put with a sheep's gut.

(The current world record for throwing a haggis is 163ft 9½ins held by Alan Pettigrew of Saltcoats, Scotland. The Haggis Hurling championships are held every autumn in Edinburgh.)

Contact: World Haggis Hurling Association, 5 Castle Terrace, Edinburgh, EH1 2DP, UK.
Tel: 0131 228 6262 Fax: 0131 228 6889

The Handlebar Club

This is a club that's all about personal growth. Nothing new-agey or psychobabbly, however: to join, you simply need a moustache – an *enormous* moustache. Or as the rules state, 'a hirsute appendage with graspable extremities'.

One member has a 63-inch handlebar, said to be the longest on earth; though its length is somewhat concealed by being kept in waxed finger-coiled rolls at either end. Wax helps to strengthen a handlebar. 'Otherwise it droops and looks like a wet rag,' advises one member. 'Though one time I had to use wet soap because I ran out of wax. On the way home it started to rain – it looked like a fit of rabies.'

Contact: Mr Rod Littlewood, Membership Secretary, 560 Walton Road, West Molesey, Surrey, KT8 2EQ, UK.
Tel: 0181 941 6923

The Happy Pig Collectors' Club

When Gene Holt was ten, he bought his first model pig. 'There was a dime in my pocket and it was the first time I had ever gotten loose by myself in Galesburg [Illinois]. I ended up at the five and dime store, looked over everything and settled upon a ceramic piggy bank for 10 cents.' In due course, the piggy bank would be joined by *thousands* of pig collectables; and Gene grew up to found the Happy Pig Collectors' Club, which caters for what he calls 'the strange affliction to collect pigs'. There are 150 members and an official club greeting: 'When I see a pig, I think of you.'

Contact: Happy Pig Collectors' Club, c/o Gene Holt, PO Box 17, Oneida, IL 61467, USA.
Website: http://www.iquest./~drdan

Hearse Enthusiasts

At Stanford-le-Hope railway station, I telephoned to say I had arrived, then waited on the steps, looking out for the car that would pick me up. It would, of course, be a *black* car.

Before long, the hearse pulled into the kerb. Alan Smart was at the wheel, and in one of the pallbearer seats was Dave Salmon. Neither man, I should tell you, is employed by an undertaker and neither has a morbid interest in death. They are both members of the Classic Hearse Register – a club for people who love funeral vehicles.

'Not everyone in the club owns a hearse,' Alan told me as we drove away, 'and even those who do own one usually have another car. But this is my normal, everyday vehicle. It's very useful in my job.' He explained that he worked as a representative for a carpet company – and so could put all his samples, or even a complete roll, in the back. 'I can also get a four-metre roll on the flower-rail.'

'But don't you get people giving you peculiar looks?' I asked.

'All the time,' he said. 'You get kids pointing and saying "Look at that, Mum". But the funniest thing is when I'm out in the car and – as occasionally happens – I come across a funeral procession. Because then you get a hearse with a coffin, followed by a hearse full of carpet samples – and people really do wonder what on earth is happening.'

Death of a carpet salesman. He just wanted to be buried with his samples . . .

A few minutes later, we arrived at Dave's house. Dave owns two hearses, a 1947 Humber Pullman and a 1960 Austin Princess, both of which he is gradually restoring to a roadworthy condition. For him, hearses are majestic: he admits to being fascinated by their ornate special features, such as the chrome posts, linked by chains, that are to be found on certain coffin-decks.

'They're cars with character,' he said. 'Some hearses have even got etched, gold-leaf windows – how can you walk away from anything as beautiful as that?'

Aside from hundreds of photographs of hearses, Dave has collected various bits-and-pieces of hearse memorabilia. On a top shelf in his home there was a row of turned brass objects, each about six inches tall, many of which were shaped like mushrooms. 'They're coffin stops,' he said. 'All decks in the back of hearses have got holes in them – and you put the stops in different holes, depending on the size of the body, so that the coffin won't roll around.' Though in fact, at 'Hearse Rallies' and other car shows, when the club puts its cars on display to the public, members are forbidden to put coffins in their hearses. Two other 'good taste' rules apply: no flowers in the car and no dressing up as undertakers.

'I'm sure that there are members who would like to do those things,' said Dave, 'but they can't do it, not when they're representing the club. I have to be *very* careful about how the club is perceived.' How careful? He remarked that when he puts together the newsletter, he always makes certain he uses the word 'anyone' rather than 'anybody'.

Contact: Classic Hearse Register, c/o Paul Harris, 121 St Mary's Crescent, Basildon, Essex, SS13 2AS, UK.
Tel: 01268 472313
Or: Professional Car Society (Although this society covers the range of professional cars, hearses are a primary concern.) PO Box 9636, Columbus, Ohio 43209, USA
Website: http//www.professionalcar.org/main.shtml
E-mail: blruff@freenet.columbus.oh.us

Heavy Dart Throwing

It is the genius of the Belgians to invent variations on aiming sports. Elsewhere you can read about Vertical Archery, Bottleshooting, and

Struifvogel; but Belgians also play a heavier-than-normal version of darts – the dart weighs 400 grammes, big enough for its point to rest on the palm, with the flight on the forearm. The dart is released not from eye-level, but from the hip, so that it travels in an arched trajectory towards the target, eight metres away. As the players say themselves: '*Javelotwerpers gooien niet met een belachelijk klein pijltje.*'

Or, translating from the Flemish: 'Heavy-dart throwers don't toss a ridiculous little arrow.'

Contact: Volkssportconfederatie, Warandelaan 10B bus 2, 8340 Sijsele, Belgium.
Tel/Fax: 05 35 84 62
Website: http://www.snv.be/vosco/ E–mail: VOSCO@snv.be

The Hellfire Club

There is a reason why Tina Bate has seen the movie *Flash Gordon* 523 times; that reason is Peter Wyngarde.

'He wears a mask throughout the film, so you can't actually see his face,' said Tina, 'but you can still hear his voice.' Indeed, she has listened to Peter Wyngarde say the lines of the evil Klytus so often that she could be his understudy in a stage adaptation. 'Even when *Flash Gordon* was on TV about a year ago, I still had to rush home from work to watch it yet again,' she said. 'I've always liked the fact that the script begins with Ming the Merciless saying, "Klytus, I'm bored, what plaything can you offer me today?" It's nice that the very first word in the film is the name of Peter's character.'

Tina is the driving force behind the Hellfire Club, the official Peter Wyngarde Appreciation Society. In the early 1970s, this would not have seemed an unusual hobby. Then, Wyngarde was famed for being the crimebuster Jason King in the British TV series *Department S* and its spin-off *Jason King*: a role in which facial hair seemed to hide almost as much of his features as Klytus's mask. Urbane, vain and never without a woman, King's forte was lines like, '*I* am my most favourite subject,' and 'It is possible *somebody* hates me.' A measure of the character's success is that in 1971 more baby boys in Britain were christened Jason than any other name.

But nowadays, Wyngarde is rarely seen on TV, and seems to have gone out of fashion, along with the gold medallions and frilly shirts he once wore. Why, then, is Tina running an appreciation society which she only founded in the 1990s? How did her passion for Wyngarde begin?

'I think I probably started liking Peter because my mum couldn't stand *Jason King*,' said Tina. 'I'm a bit confused as to whether I can actually remember *Jason King* being on television during my schooldays, but I do know my mum hated it, back then. But in 1980 I went to see *Flash Gordon* for the first time because I liked Queen, who were doing the soundtrack. I happened to go with my mum – I remember when Peter's name came up on the credits I said to her, "It's that chap from that show you don't like." I think that's when I started admiring him. My mum's renowned for not having any taste, so that probably got me thinking that he's wonderful.'

A fascination developed: with Peter Wyngarde's voice, with the way he walks, with his mannerisms. His is the first face she sees when she wakes in the morning, as her bedroom is practically wallpapered with his photographs. 'But looking at him, he's not my type,' she said. 'I don't like men with curly hair and sideburns. He's got blue eyes – I always went for brown eyes. And I never liked men in suits. But I also think he's a very, very underrated actor. He's possibly the best British actor of his generation.'

After more than a decade of collecting all the moustachioed memorabilia she could find, Tina decided to launch the Hellfire Club, taking its name from a seditious organization led by Wyngarde in a 1966 episode of *The Avengers*. She now has 275 recruits. 'At the time, people were saying I'd be lucky to get 15,' she said, proudly.

She openly admits that she founded the club as a means of compensating for an unfulfilling working life as a sales assistant in a video store. 'I didn't feel appreciated there – sometimes I thought I was just a *rubbing-rag*,' she said. 'I felt I could get up in the morning and leave my brain on the pillow, because at work, I was paid to *do*, not to *think*. But I found another way of being appreciated, of being useful.' She spoke of how much it meant to her when, for instance, a crippled member from Leicester wrote, saying that the newsletter had brightened up his day. 'I came alive at 5.30, when I left work at the video store and started working for the club,' she remarked. 'Even today, though I'm now in a different job at the post office, I often work for the club till midnight, putting together the newsletter and answering the correspondence. I spend virtually every evening, weekend and holiday at the typewriter. I put all the best of me into this club.'

Most importantly, in March 1993, she met Peter Wyngarde for the first time. 'He was so nice. He put me at ease from the word go. After a little while, it was like I'd known him all my life.' She now regards Wyngarde as a personal friend, sometimes speaking to him on the telephone two or three times a week. 'He's not like the men I've known before. He's a real gentleman,' she said. 'There may be northerners who are gentlemen, but I've not met any – they all seem to be blackguards who spend their time down the pub. But he's so courteous. Like, not so long ago, I hurt my wrist and he ran to help me with my coat. Here, they'll let you struggle all day.'

But surely Jason King was the ultimate chauvinist pig? There was even one episode in which a woman said to him, 'Jason, as far as you're concerned, I'm only good for one thing.' To which King replied, 'That remains to be seen!'

'Yes, I know Jason King was a chauvinist,' said Tina, 'and I'm all for women's rights. But you forgive him. Besides, now I've come to know him as a person, I can't connect him with the role of Jason King. He's just Peter to me now.'

Contact: Tina Bate, 41 Four Acre Lane, Clock Face, St Helen's, Merseyside, WA9 4DZ, UK.
Tel: 01744 814414

The Higgs Appreciation Society

I speak as one who treats unusual societies seriously; but when I heard about *this* society, I thought it had to be a joke. In a letter I sent to the secretary, Mr Rupert Boulting, I even commented that their aims were 'presumably tongue-in-cheek'.

The tone of his response suggested otherwise. ('Dear Sir, It was just as well that your letter was sent to me rather than Nigel Barlow [the society's Press Liaison Officer]. Your suggestion that the Higgs Appreciation Society was "tongue-in-cheek" might have received a stony reception.') A subsequent telephone conversation with Mr Boulting reinforced the tone. I can only say that if the Higgs Appreciation Society *is* tongue-in-cheek, then the jape is played with such utter coldness as to be a new category of humourless humour – post-deadpan, as it were. So I suspect it *is* serious: we are dealing with an appreciation society for a character in a radio serial who has spoken all of *twice* in twenty years.

Higgs is part of the British radio serial *The Archers*. He plays a chauffeur. In the first of his . . . manifestations . . . there is a raid on the local post office. This results in a heart attack for his boss, Jack Woolley, who instructs Higgs to get the Bentley. Higgs says: 'All right.'

Then there is 'the chrysanthemum incident'. The flowers have been over-watered and Higgs is to blame. We hear Higgs being criticized by Woolley. Higgs says: 'Yes.'

That's it.

Depending on whether you spell 'All right' that way, or as the more common (but not quite acceptable) 'Alright', Higgs's contribution to the airwaves is 10 or 11 *letters*.

Yet the Higgs Appreciation Society holds discussions on such issues as 'Higgs and the Ballot Box' – how would Higgs have voted in the 1997 British general election? Then there was the time the society was addressed by a professor of quantum physics from Oxford University – the theme was 'Reality and non-existence'.

'Higgs is a bottomless well,' I was told by Mr Boulting. He remarked that the chauffeur was 'a great Englishman', to be compared to Walter Raleigh and Winston Churchill. 'Higgs is like a ghost. If he's mentioned, it's always in a big context. He's a strong person.'

'How can you judge anything from someone saying "All right"?' I asked.

'It's a very incisive "All right". You can tell his concern. You can tell he cares for Mr Woolley.'

'But don't you think you're reading things into the script?'

'It's all there,' said Mr Boulting.

Contact: Higgs Appreciation Society, c/o Rupert Boulting, 34 Newland Street, Eynsham, Oxfordshire, OX8 1LA, UK.

Holmes in Scale

'Sherlock Holmes' is an interest too mainstream for inclusion in this volume – but there are societies devoted to *aspects* of Holmes, which deserve their place. Later, you will meet the Irregular Special Railway Company, the Praed Street Irregulars/Solar Pons Society and the Watsonians; but as a curtain-raiser, consider the society Holmes in Scale, devoted to Sherlockian scale-modelling.

'We encourage modellers to consider that Holmes was a world traveller,' says the editorial in the society's journal. 'Model him in Japan, or the Wild West, or Revolutionary Mexico.' Though the Sherlockian modeller need not confine himself to figure painting. Model train enthusiasts should consider a layout based on a scene from one of the 56 short stories and four novels, and model-shipbuilders should consider the vessels of the canon, too. And why stop there? There are Sherlockian horses: 'I painted his distinctive blaze . . .' goes an article which describes the modelling of Silver Blaze – an article which ends 'I hope to do "Shoscombe Prince" next.'

Contact: Holmes in Scale, William C. Thomas, 9507 E. 65th Street, #407, Tulsa, OK 74133, USA.

The Hubcappers

'Why collect hubcaps? Why not?' says Dennis Kuhn, who produces the newsletter, *The Hubcapper.* 'They are cheaper and larger than radiator emblems. But you must tell anyone who asks that they are not the snap-on type of hubcaps, but the threaded bolt-on type from autos and trucks built before 1930.'

Contact: Dennis Kuhn, PO Box 54, Buckley, MI 49620, USA.
Tel: 616 269 3555

The Human Powered Vehicle Association

Trains and boats and planes ... and other vehicles propelled solely by human muscles!

The members of the International Human Powered Vehicle Association build fuelless, engineless modes of transport: bicycles – of course – but also pedal cars, and even helicopters and submarines. (Okay, I may have exaggerated about the trains – but not by much. There are certainly members who build and operate human powered rail vehicles.)

Contact: The International Human Powered Vehicle Association, 1308 Broad Street #72, San Luis Obispo, CA 93401, USA.
Tel: 805 466 8010 E-mail: IHPVA@IHPVA.ORG

I

The Inn Sign Society

It was like a psychiatrist's word-association test.

'Okay,' I said, 'what about really unusual animals?'

'There's the *Gnu Inn*,' he said.

'All right.' I paused. It would be too easy to suggest World War II. 'The Falklands War?'

'The Falklands hero Major-General Jeremy Moore is on a sign.'

Hmmm. 'Inventors?'

'Well, you've got the *Jet and Whittle*.'

'Pop stars?' With the possible exceptions of Elvis and The Beatles, I doubted that there would be any at all.

'Who's that chap who died of Aids?' he said.

'You mean Freddie Mercury?'

'Yes. He's on *The Queen's Head* in Sussex.'

'Um . . . okay, cartoon characters?'

'Well, there's *The Cartoonist* . . .'

To acquire this level of knowledge about pub signs you have to work at it – and that is exactly what Jimmy Young has done: Jimmy has visited 23,980 drinking establishments, about one-third of the United Kingdom's total. 'I've always been drinking, and I'd stop at some pub or other, and I'd wonder: why is that called that?' It was only to be expected, therefore, that in 1988 Jimmy founded the Inn Sign Society: a group of 350 enthusiasts who, like himself, 'collect' visits to pubs . . . not necessarily because of an unquenchable thirst, but so as to see the sign outside and to understand the reason for the pub's name.

'Pub signs are full of history,' he said, as we downed a pint in his local, a riverside hostelry called *The Double Locks*, in Exeter. 'You've probably got every king since Canute on a sign somewhere in the country.' He went on to explain how common names like *The Rising Sun* and *The Half Moon* go back to the Crusades, while the commonest of all, *The Red Lion*, dates from the time of James I, who wanted public buildings to display the rampant lion of Scotland. 'Children should learn about pub signs in school,' he said.

Contact: Inn Sign Society, c/o Alan Rose, 9 Denmead Drive, Wednesfield, Wolverhampton, West Midlands, WV I I 2QS, UK.
Tel: 0 I 902 72 I 808

Insect Cuisine

Do curries leave you cold? Do you say 'I'll pass', when it comes to pasta? Does the thought of Sunday roast give you that Monday morning feeling? It's time to try out new recipes, to experiment, to be bold. Ever thought of a nice big plate of ... *insects*?

I went for lunch at the home of David Manning, who runs the animal consulting agency, Animal Ark, which specialises in supplying live beasts for film, television and photographic work. Although the main insect-eater in the Manning household is an African lizard, David himself is not averse to the odd creepy-crawly snack. So, he cooked me the following meal, which I hope you will try out for yourselves:

Locust Surprise

Ingredients:
3 small spring onions (diced)
1 small clove of garlic (crushed)
3 small felafel cakes (chopped)
1 tablespoon of chopped mixed nuts
1½ cups of pre-cooked rice
salt and pepper
1 dozen locusts
3 or 4 black crickets (or more, to taste)

Directions:
1. If desired, chop heads and wings off locusts.
2. Heat a little oil in a frying pan.
3. Add onions, garlic and insects to pan. Stir fry.
4. After 2 minutes add rice.
5. After another 3 minutes add felafel cakes and continue stir-frying for another minute or two.
6. Add mixed nuts, salt and pepper and serve.

Actually, Locust Surprise is not as awful as it sounds. When locusts are cooked, they turn pink, like prawns, which helps to conquer the initial repulsion. The taste of Biblical plague isn't bad, either – rather nutty. (Having said that, the presence of nuts in the recipe means it's difficult to tell when you're munching on a thorax and when a nut.) The crickets are more distinctive, being somewhat sour – but again, not unpleasant.

Another insect gourmet is Dr R.I. Vane-Wright of the London Natural History Museum's Department of Entomology. 'Caterpillar fried with tabasco is very good,' he told me. 'Bees aren't bad – they taste of honey. And I would also recommend wax moth larvae – which is a parasite found in honeycombs.' In his opinion, by far the tastiest bug-bite is the Mopanie Worm, the larvae of a wild silk-moth found in central and southern Africa. 'It's absolutely delicious. Better than steak,' he said. 'Mind you, it does get a bit gritty, because of the spines on the outside.'

However, if you really fancy entertaining with insects, you should subscribe to *The Food Insects Newsletter*. Here are just three dinner-party suggestions taken from its pages:

Ant secretions as salad dressing. Simply place some lettuce leaves near a red ant nest: after the ants have swarmed over the salad, they are shaken off, leaving behind a vinegary taste. ('I'm eager to try it,' writes a reader in the letters column.)

Pupa puffs. Or, wasp pupae deep fried in peanut oil for about 15 seconds. Says one correspondent, 'It's only weird when their eyes look at you.' It is recommended that the puffs should be served with lemon and fine herbs, such as parsley, basil, oregano, etc.

Sago Beetle Grub. Strongly recommended, though the head is a bit crunchy. The grubs are fried until they are brown, though inside they remain the colour and consistency of custard. 'Unlike anything I've ever eaten before,' says another newsletter correspondent, 'the closest I can come to describing the taste is "creamy snail".'

You may be wondering whether there are any insects that should be avoided in one's diet. I put this question to David Manning, who has eaten everything from sun-dried caterpillars to mealworms. He thought for a moment. 'I probably wouldn't eat dung beetle,' he said.

Contact: *The Food Insects Newsletter*, Florence V. Dunkel, Ph.D., Editor, Associate Professor, Department of Entomology, Montana State University, 324 Leon Johnson Hall, Bozeman, MT 59717-0302, USA. Tel: 406 994 5065 Fax: 406 994 6029 E-mail: ueyfd@montana.edu

The Insulator Association

I wonder whether anyone is reading this sentence while sitting on a London underground train? If you are, look out of the window *now*.

What do you see? A blank, black wall? Look again. Did you not notice something *white* flash by? As soon as it's glimpsed, it's gone – but here it comes, there it goes, throughout the tunnel. What exactly is it?

When the train slows down, those milky blurs will curdle and solidify into objects, each consisting of two porcelain disks: nothing hi-tech – just a piece of china used as an electrical insulator. Another example of an insulator can be spotted when you're on the platform, waiting for the train: namely, the white bowls that are placed along the track, between the rail and the ground.

Now unless you're a professional electrician, you're probably thinking, 'Who cares?' But there are people who *do* care about insulators, people whose *hobby* is insulators – people so passionate about low-conductivity artefacts that they will hang pictures of them on their walls, just as if they were Pamela Anderson pin-ups. ('Reserve your insulator calendar now!' says an advertisement in an insulator enthusiasts' magazine. 'Included will be 12 professional quality photos of colourful rare insulators. Enjoy their beauty all year long.')

The driving force in this hobby is the Insulator Association, which has 6000 members worldwide; and one of its former presidents, Len Linscott, a retired American, recently visited London. During his stay at the Hilton Olympia Hotel in Kensington, I paid him a visit – and he proved that he had left none of his enthusiasm for insulators behind.

'I was pressing my face against the window trying to see those insulators in the train tunnels,' he said. 'I just wish I could take a couple home with me.'

Len is a man who admits that he 'lives and breathes' insulators. His interest began some thirty years ago when he and his wife Jacqueline used to go out on walks. In those days, near old railway lines and abandoned telegraph poles, it was possible to find discarded insulators on the ground. Various materials were used to make these insulators – porcelain, wood, adobe, rubber – but Len was particularly attracted to insulators made of glass, which he simply found 'pretty'. It was as if there was a supply of antique crystal just lying around, waiting to be picked up.

So, Len began a quest to find as many insulators as possible – he now has about 1400 in his collection – and this is not such a safe hobby as you might think. 'Once,' he said, 'I was hunting for insulators, and passing through a swampy region, where there was a big mound of earth. Well, I stood on the mound – and beside it, in a little pond, were a couple of dozen small alligators, each about six to eight inches long. Then I heard a noise ...' All of a sudden, coming through the bushes was Mama Alligator – and Len left the scene faster than an insulator passes before the eyes in a tunnel. 'And there was also the time, near an old railroad,' he said, 'when I stepped on a rattlesnake's tail ...'

If I needed further proof of the importance of insulators in people's lives, Len showed me a copy of the specialist insulator magazine *Crown Jewels of the Wire*. I noticed a letter in which a subscriber recounted his experiences of cataloguing a miscellaneous collection, which the owner had decided to sell: '...I got up at crack of dawn to begin the long process of cataloguing everything. It felt just like Christmas morning! I sat on the living room floor for over seven hours going through these treasures and often stopped to pause in amazement as to what I was holding in my hands.'

It is not ludicrous to call them treasures. The moral here is that something worthless can become extremely valuable simply because people start enthusing about it – certain insulators have been known to change hands for $10,000. 'There are some die-hard collectors out there,' said Len.

Contact: Len Linscott, Insulator Association, 3557 Nicklaus Drive, Titusville, FL 32780, USA.
Or: *Crown Jewels of the Wire*, PO Box 1003, St Charles, IL, 60174-7003, USA.
Tel: 630 513 1544 Fax: 630 513 8278 E-mail: crnjewels@aol.com

The International Association of People who Dine Over the Kitchen Sink

I opened the letter from the association: immediately I was confronted by a photograph of a kitchen sink – only, around the sink's edges there was a wine glass, a bottle of wine, ketchup, mayonnaise, Dijon mustard, and a salt and pepper set. Oh, and a candle.

The idea of forming the International Association of People who Dine Over the Kitchen Sink came to Norm Hankoff in 1991, when he was standing at his kitchen sink, wolfing down tuna salad, using extra-strength potato chips as utensils. As soon as he established the association, the letters started to arrive:

'At last we are out of the closet, into the open,' said one. 'No more sneaky looks out the window to see if neighbours are around. No more pretending that only mangoes have to be eaten that way. Everything tastes better over the sink.'

'My childhood memories are interspersed with my mother yelling to us to "eat it over the sink", especially during the watermelon season,' said another. 'I've never lost the practice and have directed my family to all its benefits. It saves washing dishes, sweeping the floor and wiping off the counters.'

'I have practised sinkie eating Monday through Friday for approximately thirty-four years (breakfast and lunch),' said a third. 'It is a very practical simple way to eat and it works for me. Saturday and Sunday, I sit down.'

Or as a fourth said: 'Plates are for wimps.'

Contact: The International Association of People who Dine over the Kitchen Sink, SINKIE World Headquarters, 1579 Farmers Lane, #252, Santa Rosa, California, 95405, USA
Website: http://www.sinkie.com E-mail: normh@sinkie.com

The International Society for a Complete Earth

I've just noticed something. Look at the name of that society. Now, what's another word for 'complete'? Whole. And what does 'whole' sound like? Hole. I don't know whether it's a coincidence, or a hidden pun that one is *supposed* to find, but if the organization were called 'The International Society for a *Hole* Earth' you would have a pretty accurate description of its objectives. The members do believe that the Earth has a hole in it; actually, a hole at *both* polar caps – with a non-existent core. They believe the Earth is hollow.

Danny Weiss, the American who founded the society, has made it his life's mission to explore the hollow Earth – and he explains the somewhat cryptic nomenclature thus: 'I feel the name is significant as it suggests an "incomplete" Earth. I want the outside world to unite with the inner world.'

The society maintains that the hollow Earth has been an article of faith for many cultures – the Hopi Indians, the Ancient Egyptians, Tibetan monks; the land inside the hollow Earth may be the Garden of Eden, Valhalla, Avalon. But a central *modern* document for hollow-Earth believers is *A Flight to the Land Beyond the North Pole: The Missing Diary of Admiral Richard E. Byrd*. This purports to be an account of how, in 1947, Byrd went inside the Earth, via an opening at the North Pole, and met a strange, alien race. During his flight to the Pole, he claimed to have encountered not icy wastes, but mountains, vegetation, rivers, lakes, forests and even a mammoth.

Hollow may be too much to swallow, for some people. But at least you cannot accuse the members of this society of being ivory-tower theorists: at the time of writing they are planning to recreate Admiral Byrd's flight to the Pole. 'We've got to prove this matter, one way or the other,' says Danny Weiss.

Contact: The International Society for a Complete Earth, PO Box 890, Felton, CA 95018, USA.
Tel: 408 335 9329 E-mail: hotline@ix.netcom.com

The Irregular Special Railway Company

'I did wonder whether there would be enough material to keep going – because it has to be said that there are only two occasions when Sherlock Holmes displayed an in-depth knowledge of the workings of railways,' commented Dr Antony Richards, when we met, early one Saturday morning, at King's Cross station in London. 'But about 60 per cent of the Sherlock Holmes cases *mention* railways.' He remarked that Holmes took a train from King's Cross to Cambridge in *The Adventure of the Missing Three-Quarter*.

Dr Richards, a product manager for a computer software firm, is the Chairman of the Irregular Special Railway Company: a society of sixty people who, as it were, link the smoke-rings from the sleuth's pipe to the clouds at the steam-train's funnel. Founded in 1992, this is the only society in the world devoted to the railway aspects of Sherlock Holmes. 'At least, it's the only society, *as far as I know*,' said Dr Richards. And he began telling me about the adventure *Silver Blaze*, when Holmes calculated the speed of a moving train from the time it took to pass between successive telegraph poles: one of those two occasions when the detective showed off his railway knowledge.

After a short walk to the café at St Pancras station – where we drank a cup of tea in honour of the wedding breakfast, held in the old St Pancras Hotel, in Holmes's adventure *A Case of Identity* – Dr Richards passed me a copy of the society's annual publication, *The Sherlock Holmes Railway Journal*. In its pages the deerstalker truly meets the station-master's cap.

For instance, I noticed an article which attempted to answer the question: why does Holmes use London's Underground Railway on only one occasion in the entire canon? To shed light on this, the journal has reprinted a contemporary account of travel in the 1890s, when the smoke in the tunnels could leave the travellers 'coughing and spluttering like a boy with his first cigar'.

'No wonder Holmes preferred to use a Hansom cab,' said Dr Richards.

A particular interest of the society is to recreate the rail journeys of Holmes and Watson. So, Dr Richards took me to the various Sherlockian stations of London and explained their significance. At Charing Cross, I learnt that in the old first-class waiting room (now the Rendezvous Lounge), Holmes had his left canine tooth knocked out, as recorded in *The Adventure of the Empty House*; while at Waterloo, in *The Crooked Man*, Holmes had his only meal on a station – which led Dr Richards to remark that one day the society would probably have a dinner in Waterloo's restaurant; and at Paddington, I became aware of the importance of the mighty *Bradshaw*.

'In *The Boscombe Valley Mystery*,' said Dr Richards, 'Holmes sends Watson a telegram saying, "Meet me at Paddington – we'll catch the 11.15 train". But I've checked *Bradshaw's* railway timetable for 1889 and there *wasn't* a train at 11.15.'

One can only hope, I thought, that Dr Watson wrote his patients' prescriptions with greater accuracy than his chronicles of Holmes's adventures.

'You also get some people,' continued Dr Richards, 'who think that this adventure took place on a Sunday, because Watson had a late breakfast that day and he probably wouldn't have done so if he'd had his normal weekday surgery. But Sunday is impossible.' He explained his reasoning: firstly, according to *Bradshaw*, there was no train on Sunday until 2.30pm; and secondly, the tale mentions two other rail journeys made by Holmes on the same day – and only one set of trains is a close match for the times. 'So it has to be a weekday or a Saturday,' he said.

Then we took to the Circle Line to re-enact *The Adventure of the Bruce-Partington Plans*. This story, which features the second demonstration of Holmes's railway knowledge, is home to another discrepancy:

'Now, you tell me,' said Dr Richards, as our train left the tunnel near Gloucester Road, went overground and passed a row of houses, 'would it really have been possible to lean out of one of those windows over there and place a dead body on the roof of this train? The distance is just too great.'

He moved on to the question of whether the train, in its role as hearse, might have gone clockwise or anti-clockwise on its journey round the Circle Line: clockwise, via King's Cross, there are sharp bends in the track which would surely have thrown the body off; that would imply anti-clockwise, via Victoria – yet why then was the body not seen?

'The fog?' I suggested. I suddenly realized that I was getting caught up in all this.

'There's a little bit of Holmes in all of us,' commented Dr Richards.

Contact: Dr Antony Richards, 163 Marine Parade, Leigh-on-Sea, Essex, SS9 2RB, UK.
Website: http://mesmsg1.me.ic.ac.uk/sherlock/

(The Society for) Italic Handwriting

This sentence is written in italic handwriting.

Well, obviously it isn't. To see a paradox resolved, you must re-write the words after contacting the group that promotes the style. But when a leading member of the Society for Italic Handwriting, Janet Pamment, told me that *anyone* could learn italic, I held up my notepad. 'Even someone who writes like *this*?' I sometimes find it difficult to read my own notes after an interview.

Janet screwed up her eyes. She had to think carefully about the answer, but then she said: 'Yes.' We started at 'a'.

Italic handwriting – if my notes do not deceive me – is a style which dates back to the 1500s, when it was developed by scribes who needed to write with speed and clarity in conducting the business of the Pope. It was also the hand of Elizabeth I. Sometimes, it is said that the key to italic is the elliptical 'o', which sets the tone for the whole alphabet.

To inspire me, Janet brought forth some before-and-after examples of her students' handwriting: from jerky and disjointed peaks and troughs, to the beautiful tide of italic. 'Italic changes people,' she said. 'There are people I teach who say they feel wishy-washy and ordinary, and then when they find they can do italic it gives them amazing self-confidence.' Which leads to a reappraisal of graphology: perhaps it is not personality that determines handwriting, but the other way around.

So can I now resolve the opening paradox myself? Have I done enough practice? Let me merely say 'My handwriting used to look like this', but now 'It looks like this'.

Contact: The Society for Italic Handwriting, c/o Nicholas Caulkin, 205 Dyas Avenue, Great Barr, Birmingham, B42 1HN, UK.

J

The Japanese Tea Ceremony

Imagine that the instructions for self-assembly furniture were written by a master of the Japanese tea ceremony. The plans for a chest of drawers would include footnotes, in the haiku verse form, on the sincere state of mind to adopt when slotting plywood panels into grooves. There would be advice, too, on the most aesthetically pleasing method of turning a nut. Even the act of removing unassembled bits and pieces from their boxes would have rules for torso movements, hand positions and posture.

It is this combination of the everyday and the artistic that is the essence of the Japanese tea ceremony; as I discovered at the London branch of the Urasenke Centre, an international organization concerned with the teaching of *Chado*, the Way of Tea.

There, as in Japan, tea takes place on a *tatami* mat, a floor-covering made from rice-stalks. Guests sit on stools raised just a few inches from the floor – stools so low that one effectively kneels. As a concession to novices, it is permissible to sit cross-legged on the mat; this is improper, but necessary, because it takes many months for the muscles in the legs to become accustomed to the pain of sitting on the stools.

I have to admit that I did not stay for enough lessons to reach that anaesthetic point. I found the complexity of the tea ceremony overwhelming. Every action is codified. There are rules for the placing of feet when carrying utensils into the room, just as there are rules for the conversation between host and guest. As a specific example of one tiny part of the ceremony, for my first lesson I had to memorize the twenty-one separate movements involved in wiping a piece of lacquerware with a *fukusa*, a silken cloth. Although 'memorized' is the wrong word: every action should be invested with a special quality of attention, the mindfulness which lies at the heart of Buddhist philosophy. It could take ten years of training, and one would still be far from an adept.

As for the tea itself: it is green, and cannot be sipped until the bowl has been turned two quarter-turns clockwise in the palm of the hand. Strangely enough, bowls need not be perfect: there is thought to be a deeper beauty in the blemished than in the unblemished, and the pottery is particularly admired if it has been repaired. One haiku expresses the beauty of imperfection thus: 'The moon is not pleasing unless partly obscured by cloud.'

To which I shall comment: 'The mind is not pleasing unless partly obscured by ignorance.' And use this to justify my imperfect training in the way of tea.

Contact: Urasenke Centre, 4 Langton Way, London, SE3 7TL, UK.
Tel: 0181 853 2595 Fax: 0181 293 4088
E-mail: urasenke.london@dial.pipex.com
Or: Urasenke Chanoyu Center, 153 East 69th Street, New York, New York 10021, USA.

Jew's Harp Enthusiasts

'There are only three things in my life that have meant a lot to me: my children, my wife and my Jew's harp,' said Duncan Williamson, when I visited him at his home in Fife, Scotland.

'I couldn't live without my Jew's harp,' he told me. 'Even when I ran away from home when I was 13, and I travelled on my own without a sleeping-bag, with not even a coat, nothing, not a penny in my pocket, I always had my little Jew's harp. Because it was good company and if you were weary, you could play yourself a tune.' To this day, he ensures that every jacket he owns has a harp in the pocket. 'I would feel naked without a Jew's harp,' he said. With that, he raised the doorkey-sized instrument to his lips . . . For an instant, it seemed that an orthodontist had been at work, filling his smile with metal; and then his finger plucked and the room was ringing with 'Oh Susanna'. I found it impossible not to tap my foot.

'You could play this without stopping.' he said. 'You could go on forever until you go hungry or dry.'

Contact: The Jew's Harp Guild, PO Box 92, Sumpter, OR 97877, USA.
Website: http://www.cyberhighway.net/~mpossl/jhghp.html

K

Keeping Abreast

In 1845 Dr Elijah Pratt of New York patented the first rubber nipple.

I might never have heard of Dr Pratt without the help of *Keeping Abreast*, a newsletter for collectors of infant feeders. Although the focus of the newsletter is on the various devices that have been used to feed babies – the likes of the double-ended nursing bottle and the wide-mouth nursing bottle – you will also find articles on the history of breast-feeding. For example, the practice of wet-nursing, in which women would hire themselves out to feed other women's children.

One learns that some wet-nurses would soak the baby's bedding with water to convince parents that the baby was so well-fed that it was constantly wetting itself . . . when in reality the woman's milk had dried up and the baby was starving to death.

Contact: JoAnn Gifford, American Collectors of Infant Feeders, 1849 Ebony Drive, York, PA 17402-4706, USA.
Tel: 717 741 3351

(The International Guild of) Knot-Tyers

There had been a death in the London theatre. It wasn't in the script. The corpse was found trussed up in ropes – the cause of death being a fall from the theatre's balcony. Everything pointed to murder. So, to see whether the ropes would hold any clues, Scotland Yard called in an expert from the International Guild of Knot-Tyers, which promotes the art, craft and science of knotting.

'But it turned out to be suicide,' I was told by one of the Guild's founders. 'The dead man was a scenery-shifter – and our member recognized that the ropes were tied with scenery-shifter's knots.'

Contact: The International Guild of Knot Tyers, c/o Nigel Harding, 16 Egles Grove, Uckfield, TN22 2BY, UK.
Tel: 01825 760425

Knur and Spell

The knell of knur and spell has not yet sounded, not yet.

It seems that the Spring Rock Inn in West Yorkshire is the last place on Earth where the game known as 'poor man's golf' survives, though even here the future is far from certain. At the time of writing (1997), it is planned that a knur and spell event will take place at the inn in 1998, and it is hoped that a revival will take place afterwards. And what is knur and spell? It is a measure of the game's decline that I should have to define it for you.

The basic idea is to place a small hard ball (the knur) in a spring-loaded trap (the spell): the trap throws the ball into the air, where it is struck with a specially-constructed stick (the bat). The aim is simply to drive the ball as far as possible – and shots of between two and three hundred yards have been recorded.

In the 19th century, and before the First World War, this game attracted an enormous following, with heavy betting on important matches. Top players were treated as superstars of the day: they would be wrapped in blankets whilst waiting to strike to keep them at maximum efficency – and at the moment of striking, their friends would huddle round the spell to keep the wind from deflecting the knur's flight by so much as a hair's breadth.

With the correct setting of the spell, it was said that experts could hit the knur in the dark: an appropriate image for a game on which the sun has gone down . . . almost.

Contact: The Spring Rock Inn, Norland Road, Greetland, W. Yorks, HX4 8P2, UK.
Tel: 01422 375669

L

Lavatory Seat Hurling

'Where does the event take place?'
  'No place.'
  'It takes place somewhere.'
  'I'm telling you, no place.'
  'Come on, you know where.'
  'No place.'
  '*Where?*'
  '*No place!*'

With such a routine, Abbott and Costello could have staged a comeback. Lavatory seat hurling *does* take place at no place – or strictly, Noplace – in County Durham, UK. The record throw now stands at 152 feet.

'In our first contest, we used an old seat from the pub,' said John Taylor, the landlord of the Mary Inn, which hosts the event, 'but that was in warm weather, in May. The second contest was in August when the ground was harder. We shattered four seats.'

They had to scour the town for replacements.

Contact: Beamish Mary Inn, Noplace, Beamish, Nr. Stanley, County Durham, DH9 0QH, UK.
Tel: 0191 370 0237

The Letter-box Study Group

There is a problem which might be called 'letter-box amnesia'. It's that experience of walking up the road to post a letter . . . and afterwards being unable to recall actually putting it in the box. 'You must have posted it,' you tell yourself. 'You *did*.' You hope.

The amnesia wouldn't happen if we took more notice of the boxes themselves. One group of people would *never* take a letter-box for granted: the 700 members of the Letter-box Study Group, whose aim is to accumulate and disseminate information on all aspects of letter-boxes. I went to meet founder-member Ron Hall, who has collected photographs of letter-boxes from all over the world – yellow boxes from France, blue 'trashcan' boxes from the USA, and hundreds of red boxes from the United Kingdom. Like many within the group, he has carried out a complete letter-box survey of his home town, photographing every box on the streets of Leamington Spa. 'It's just one of those things,' he told me. 'I'm a born collector. The idea of having something to look for is important. I carry my camera everywhere, in case I see an interesting box.'

A talking point among members when I met Ron was the introduction of the so-called 'Model K' British box, a modern box, which has a functional, twenty-first-century look. 'Lots of traditionalists hate the Model K,' said Ron, 'but I like it. It has a good-sized posting slot, which is well-protected from the weather, and instead of having to insert numbers to indicate the next collection, it has a dial.' He handed me a miniature of the box – but I found myself on the side of the traditionalists: the little Model K reminded me of a pepper-pot you would find in a cheap café. Yet it was odd to have such thoughts – never before had I held *opinions* about letter-boxes.

After a discussion on the history of the letter-box from 1852 to the present day – covering early hexagonal ones, as well as the fluted boxes of the Victorian era and one-off curiosities such as the box with a gas-lamp on top – it was time to go. As my taxi went through Leamington Spa, the letter-boxes I passed seemed somehow *fresh*: the red bolder, the boxes more prominent. I was noticing differences in shape . . .

I *used* to suffer from letter-box amnesia.

Contact: The Letter-box Study Group, c/o Mrs A Harms, 13 Amethyst Avenue, Davis Estate, Chatham, Kent ME5 9TX, UK

The Lewis Carroll Society

There is a special sort of fancy-dress party at which people dress exactly as they normally do, in their ordinary, everyday clothes. Nobody told me that I would be attending a party of this particular kind – and so it was that I turned up dressed from toe to head as the Mad Hatter, complete with a 10/6 label in my stovepipe hat, while everyone else was in suits and ties. Of course, the concept of an un-fancy-dress party would be of interest to the Hatter's creator, Lewis Carroll – for Carroll is the man who invented the un-birthday party, to be celebrated 364 times a year. And to celebrate all of this man's achievements, from his deductions in symbolic logic to his dabbles in surreal literature, a Lewis Carroll Society has been formed. The society's Christmas party was a kind of wonderland in its own right . . .

And right from the start, I thought there was something, well, a little *curious* about the way in which Ellis Hillman, the president, introduced me to some of the members: 'Here's a geologist. And here's a geologist. And here's a theologian. It's all the same thing . . .'

Eventually, I found myself chatting to Selwyn Goodacre, the society's chairman. 'I have about 1500 copies of *Alice*, mostly in English,' he said. 'And I also have some of Carroll's mathematical works, such as *An Elementary Treatise on Determinants*.'

'Can you read it?' I asked.

'No,' he replied, 'not a word.'

Someone who could probably read the entire *Treatise* was Toby, a member who was trained as a mathematician and philosopher. Toby has the most extraordinary habit of referring to obscure texts, which I had never heard of, and adding after the titles: 'Which presumably you're familiar with.' He was also at pains to assure me that Queen Victoria was *not* the author of the *Alice* books. 'Two computer programmers in California,' he told me, 'analyzed the style of Carroll and decided that it was exactly the same as Queen Victoria's. But that's nonsense – look at the dates.' He told me that *Alice* was published in 1865 and Prince Albert died in 1861. 'The idea that a woman who was embarking on a 40-year mope could have written *Alice in Wonderland* is quite preposterous.' I told Toby that I would do my best to allay the fears of all my readers who were worried that Lewis Carroll was the former Queen of England.

The next person I met was Charles Lovett, chairman of the North American branch of the society. In his remarkable collection of Carrolleana is a pornographic novel called *Blue Alice*, featuring a girl 'with breasts as white as whipped cream'. I flicked through the pages and noted the following variation of Carroll's children's classic: 'Her ear throbbed and pulsed around the great thrusting thing that Horatio H. Dumpty was shoving into it. . .'

Deciding it was time to move on, I turned to Edward Wakeling, who has translated *Alice in Wonderland* into code. Edward also admits to owning a box of costumes (one Hare, one Hatter and two Tweedles) and is particularly fascinated by Carroll's use of the number 42, which recurs throughout the collected works. 'Once you know about 42, I'm afraid it'll be with you for the rest of your life,' he said.

And passing amongst the members, I heard about the Dutch woman who had collected an album of *Alice* quotes from the *Financial Times*; about the use of *Alice* imagery to advertise toilet paper; about the work of experimental fiction whose every tenth word comes from *Alice*; and about the semaphore version of *Jabberwocky*. As all these facts came thick and fast, and faster and thicker, and thicker and faster, everything seemed to blur. . .

'Wake up,' someone said. 'Why, what a long sleep you've had.'

'Oh, I've had such a curious dream about a very strange party,' I replied. 'At least, I *think* it was a dream. . .'

Contact: Sarah Stanfield, Secretary, Lewis Carroll Society, Acorns, Dargate, Nr. Faversham, Kent, ME13 9HG, UK.
Or: Lewis Carroll Society of North America, 18 Fitzharding Place, Owings Mill, MD 21117, USA.
Website: http://www.lewiscarroll.org

The Limerick Special Interest Group

They can offer you timeless limericks, such as:

> There once was a Curate from Kew
> Who preached with his vestments askew
> A lady called Morgan
> Caught sight of his organ
> And promptly passed out in the pew. (Anon)

As well as limericks of *our* time, such as the following on cloned sheep:

> Said the shepherd, 'When we are alone,
> I caress her erogenous zone
> While I blow in her ear,
> But I harbour this fear:
> Is she my real true love or a clone?' (William N. Nesbitt)

Contact: The Limerick Special Interest Group, Box 365, Moffett, CA 94035, USA.
Website: http://www.netcom.com/~pentatet/reply.html
E-mail: pentatet@ix.netcom.com

The Lindbergh Kidnapping Network

'It must have been Hauptmann.'
'It couldn't have been Hauptmann.'
'But if it wasn't Hauptmann, who was it then?'
'I think it was Lindbergh.'
'Or Lindbergh AND Hauptmann.'

The kidnapping and murder of the baby son of the aviator Charles Lindbergh is one of the most notorious crimes of the twentieth century. Although Hauptmann was found guilty, and executed, doubts have persisted about the verdict. The theory has even been advanced that Lindbergh himself was responsible – perhaps as a prank which went horribly wrong. The lingering uncertainties about the case motivate the members of the Lindbergh Kidnapping Network: they publish a newsletter called *Sourland* – Lindbergh's house was located in the Sourland mountain region of New Jersey, and 'this seemed to have the right flavour for such a sad story', says the Network. They also go on guided tours of the sites associated with the crime. ('Here's a photo of the group who toured the Bronx in August 1997. We're looking at the spot where the $50,000 in ransom money was transferred.')

'The best part of the case,' I was told by Nancy Attardo, the editor of *Sourland*, 'is that no one can figure out who *was* responsible for the kidnapping. The more you read and study, the more you just throw up your hands.'

Contact: The Lindbergh Kidnapping Network, c/o Nancy Attardo, 211 Browncroft Blvd., Rochester, NY 14609-7836, USA.
Tel: 716 482 0216 Fax: 716 654 9648

The Lock Collectors' Association

One member of this association recently published a book called *Manacles of the World* – a collector's guide to international handcuffs, leg irons, shackles and restraints. As the editor of the association's newsletter comments: 'I believe it belongs in every handcuff collector's library.'

Contact: The American Lock Collectors' Association, 36076 Grennada, Livonia, Michigan 48154, USA.

Loggets

Words die, and are buried in footnotes. So should you be reading *Hamlet* Act V, Scene 1, your eyes will lower when you reach the lines:

'Did these bones cost no more the breeding but to play at loggats *sic* with 'em; mine ache to think on't.'

At the bottom of the page, you will encounter a note defining 'loggats' as 'a rustic game similar to bowls'. However, for a better definition, you could visit the Stag Inn, in Hastings, where this rustic game is played. There is even an annual championship, featuring the Yorick Trophy.

The game was revived by pub regular Mark Pennington, who stumbled upon a mention of loggets (spelt that way) in a book on the history of Hastings. 'It said that in 1626, a pub was granted a licence on the condition that it didn't play darts, quoits or *loggets* – which the book simply defined as a game involving lumps of wood being thrown at a stick,' he told me, when I dropped into the Stag. 'I couldn't find much else out about the game, so I put my own interpretation on the rules.'

This was at the time of John McEnroe's on-court tantrums – which exerted a decided influence on Mark's process of reinvention. 'McEnroe was a pain in the butt,' he said. 'Things were getting too competitive. I wanted a game in which people didn't take themselves too seriously. A game which would defeat the seriously competitive player.' He opened a bag containing the target in loggets: a six-inch wooden man, with a blue hat, pink waistcoat, and yellow shorts. 'I whittled him myself,' he remarked. 'He had a nose at one time, but contact with loggets knocked it off.'

So, we walked behind the pub, to the playing surface: a garden featuring a steep grass slope, with many bumps and ruts. 'Loggets could be played anywhere,' he commented as he stuck the little man into the middle of the turf, 'but certainly not on a mown and even lawn.' He opened the bag again and handed me my three wooden loggets: a small, a medium and a large. They bore as much resemblance to smooth round balls as the lawn bore to the Centre Court at Wimbledon.

'There's no uniformity to them,' I said, turning them over in my palm.
'There's *some* uniformity.'
'Well, they're not spheres.'
'They're oblate *spheroids*.'

The game started. The object is to throw loggets at the little man, alternating throws with your opponent. When all the loggets have been thrown, the logget nearest the little man is the winner and scores one point. If the winner's second logget is nearer than the best of his opponent, then a total of two points are scored. If a third, three. The first to six points wins. It sounds easy . . . but the irregularity of the loggets, interacting with the irregularity of the lawn, means that there is very little control over events: your first throw might well land close to the little man – but then the next could roll 12 feet away and finish in a rhubarb patch. The game of loggets is *so* chaotic, that the best strategy could even be to attempt to lose. 'Once, I did deliberately try to throw a game in the pub championships,' said Mark. 'And that was difficult. I found myself progressing into the next round.'

Overhead, the seagulls of Hastings cried, as though in mockery.

Well, I was the loser, by six points to four, but that hardly mattered. The old saying about 'it's the taking part that counts' was no longer a platitude to console losers – it was true. There was just one mystery to the game that had to be cleared up: a piece of equipment that Mark had taken out of the bag, but never explained.

'What's that dumbbell-shaped piece of wood?' I asked.

'Oh, that's a dog distractor,' said Mark. 'When dogs are trying to interfere with the game, you give them something to play with.'

Contact: The Stag Inn, 14 All Saints Street, Hastings, East Sussex, TN34 3BJ, UK.
Tel: 01424 425734

The Loglan Institute

'Now, let me make myself perfectly clear . . .' If I *really* do mean that, I'd better stop writing this book in English, and continue in Loglan.

Never heard of Loglan, short for 'Logical Language'? You might have, if you're a science fiction enthusiast: it's spoken by Mycroft Holmes, the hero computer in Robert Heinlein's book *The Moon is a Harsh Mistress*. But, unlike other artificially created languages (see the entries on Fictional Languages and Volapük), Loglan is utterly unambiguous: its grammar may be thought of as the linguistic equivalent of symbolic logic. Consider, for instance, the English sentence: 'It's a beautiful little girls' school.' What does this mean? A school for beautiful little girls? A beautiful example of a school for little girls? A beautiful and little school for girls? In Loglan, 'Da bilti ge cmalo nirli cue ckela' means a school for beautiful little girls, and only that – and every other sentence in the language is unambiguous as well.

Thus, when I said at the start 'I'd better stop writing this book . . .', you might consider that I could have said that in several, more precise ways in Loglan, meaning: '*I'd* better stop writing this book.' (You, dear reader, could surely do a better job.) 'I'd better stop writing *this book*.' (There's more money in pornography.) Or even 'I'd better stop *writing* this book.' (Get ready for *The Ultimate Guide to Unusual Leisure: The Musical.*)

Contact: The Loglan Institute, 3009 Peters Way, San Diego, CA 92117, USA.

The Lottery Collectors' Society

It takes determination to be a collector of anything; but would you have the sheer willpower to collect lottery scratch tickets *in mint condition*? (Admittedly, some members of the Lottery Collectors' Society *do* settle for used; while others have a penchant for the extremely rare examples of used winning tickets *which were never cashed in*.)

Contact: The Lottery Collectors' Society, c/o Mr Richard Bertrand, 4 E. Main St, Brookside, New Jersey 07926-0419, USA.

Lying 1: The Biggest Liar in the World Contest

Clause 7 of the rules states that 'Members of the legal profession and politicians are barred from entry.'

This contest, which is held every November in Wasdale, Cumbria, England, honours the achievements of a very British Baron von Munchausen, Will Ritson, a publican who lived in Wasdale in the 19th century. Famed for his many tall tales, Ritson claimed that the turnips in Wasdale were so big that after the local farmers had quarried into them for their Sunday dinner, they used them as sheds to house their sheep.

Here's a typical lie from the contest: a few years ago, a man told of eating a piece of mammoth which had been frozen in ice. Apparently, the mammoth had aphrodisiac and rejuvenating qualities, and it worked for him, but alas there was very little left . . . and he finished off by taking a slice of horrible-looking meat from his pocket and handing it to the judges.

Contact: Whitehaven Civic Hall, Lowther Street, Whitehaven, Cumbria, CA28 7SH, UK.
Tel: 01946 852821

Lying 2: The Burlington Liars' Club

'You can become a lifetime honorary member simply by sending in one lie and one dollar,' said the letter from the club. 'You will then receive a membership card. There is a contest each year, judged in December, with the winner announced on December 31st.'

The Burlington Liars' Club is a lie that became the truth. In 1929, a Burlington journalist, Otis Hulett, was faced with a slow news week – and so he invented a story about a contest between the Burlington police chief, and sundry policemen and firemen, to see who could tell the biggest lie. (The winner was the police chief who said that he had never told a lie in his life.) The story made the papers, but the next year, Associated Press called, wanting to know whether there was going to be another lying contest – which resulted in Hulett forming the Liars' Club, and starting its lying contest, for real. The following are examples of winning lies through the years:

1933: My grandfather had a clock that was so old that the shadow of the pendulum swinging back and forth had worn a hole in the back of the case.

1963: Fishing around here was so bad this summer that even the biggest liars didn't catch any.

1966: The food at this school is so bad that if it were not for the salt and pepper, we would starve to death.

1974: We were so poor in our youth that our parents couldn't afford window shopping.

And finally, a break from the 'It was so . . .' style of lie:

1977: It was so hot that you could take a frozen hamburger patty out of the freezer, toss it in the air and when it came down, you had one cooked well-done.

(I lied.)

Contact: The Burlington Liars' Club, c/o Mr John Soeth, PO Box 437, Burlington, WI 53105, USA.

Lying 3: The Pegleg Liars Contest

The word of Thomas Smith was as genuine as his leg – that is, not at all.

'Pegleg' Smith lived in the early 1800s in the American southwest, and is said to have lost his leg in an Indian fight. That might have been another of his lies, of course – along with his claim to have discovered a gold mine in the Anza-Borrego desert. Pegleg usually discussed the mine in exchange for a few beers, and often served as a guide for those seeking the gold. It was never found.

The tale grew, and over the years there was much interest in 'lost mines' all over the southwestern US. The legend was kept alive by a man named Harry Oliver, who for a time lived in the Anza-Borrego area. Mr Oliver even went so far as to 'salt' the desert with phony peglegs so that those finding them would believe that they were near the lost mine. He also started the Pegleg Liars Contest in 1946.

The event is held in April, beginning about dark, and lasting until all the liars have had their say. Unlike the previous two lying contests, this one has a specific subject: lies must relate to the desert in some fashion, and preferably to the Pegleg legend.

For instance: the reason the gold has not been found is that it is not *actual* gold, but the rare sand gold *fish*. These exotic fish live not in water, but in sand, and in fact they disappear when they get wet – and in the year that Pegleg found his 'gold', there was an unusual amount of rain in the desert. The contestant telling this lie then showed some examples of the sand gold fish that he claimed to have caught, and proved that they did dissolve in water. (They were in reality made of sand in a fish-shaped gelatine mould, stuck together with liquid starch, and painted gold. When he put water on them, they naturally dissolved.)

Contact: Mr Ted Schroeder, 9209 Fletcher Drive, La Mesa, California 91941-4404, USA.
E-mail: lschroed@sdcoe.k12.ca.us

M

The 'Magic of Bewitched' Fan Club

Bewitched, as you will probably know, was a sixties sitcom fantasy starring Elizabeth Montgomery as Samantha Stephens, a woman who juggled the demands of three roles: wife, mother ... and witch. As a sorceress of the suburbs, Samantha could simply twitch her nose – and the housework would be done.

It took a lot more effort for Gina Hill Meyers, the founder of the 'Magic of Bewitched' Fan Club, to compile her recipe book: out of sheer love for the show, she has been through every episode, extracting all the references to food, and then compiling their recipes into *The 'Magic of Bewitched' Recipe Book*.

For instance, in episode #163, Samantha's daughter Tabitha turns herself into a raisin cookie – and so the recipe for raisin cookies is listed. Likewise, in episode #246, Samantha becomes annoyed when her mother Endora over-seasons the stew that she (Samantha) is cooking – and it can be inferred that this is beef stew, since Samantha's husband Darrin remarked in episode #138 that beef stew was one of his favourite dishes; thus, the recipe for beef stew appears in the book. For completeness, Gina even includes the very simple recipes (such as for a corned beef sandwich, mentioned briefly in episode #102); and, most endearing of all, she hasn't forgotten the witch food. Fancy the witch menu in episode #202, with the appetizers Pâté of Elephant Tail and Hummingbird Tongues Parmesan? Or go straight for the main courses: Pickled Eye of Newt or Kidney of Impala Bourguignon in neat's-foot Oil.

Contact: The 'Magic of Bewitched' Fan Club, c/o Gina Hill Meyers, PO Box 25122, Fresno, CA 93729, USA.

The Maledicta Society

I feel like running my finger up and down the symbols keys and making statements like !#"£?$%'!&*@!! and *&'%$£!!"£$ or worse still, !??<##!!"&!@!£($*%!!. There is no such coyness in the journal of the

International Maledicta Society; if you're offended by swearing and X-rated vocabulary, then DO NOT join this organization. Taking its name from the Latin *male* (meaning bad) and *dicta* (meaning words), the society is concerned with the academic study of abusive language, curses, imprecations and general verbal nastiness. Here's an example of what you will see on the contents page of the society's journal:

Talking Dirty in Cuban Spanish; Swearing in Australian Football; Black Excremental Poetry; Greek Fist-Phallus Gestures; Glossary of Fart Euphemisms; Elementary Georgian Obscenity; Offensive Rock Band Names – a Linguistic Taxonomy; Obscenity and Vulgarity in African Oral Folklore; Pet Names for Breasts and Other Naughty Body Parts . . .

The Maledicta Society was established by Dr Reinhold Aman, an American linguistic scholar, who sees it as his life's mission to collect and analyze every obscenity ever uttered by man. The quest to put his ear in the gutter began in 1965 when Dr Aman was translating an obscure 19th-century Bavarian text. He came across a sentence which he says jumped out and struck him like a lightning bolt: 'I'm going to hit you over the head with a spoon, you monkey.' Dr Aman wondered why a person would call another person a monkey. That night, he made a list of other animal insults: dog, pig, rat, snake. Then he went on to food-related offensiveness: you meatball, you cabbage head, you silly sausage. Once he got going he couldn't stop, making lists of insults relating to professions, nationalities, body parts. 'I found it very intellectually stimulating,' he says. Here, after years of study, are some of his favourite curses:

Yiddish: 'May all your teeth fall out, except one – so that you can have a toothache.'

American South: 'Yo' breath is so foul it would knock a buzzard off a manure wagon.'

Ghanaian: 'You smell like a white man's armpit.'

African: 'He couldn't track a buffalo in four feet of snow!'

Swahili: 'God curse you, and the curse is that you be what you already are!'

Thai: 'Talking to you is like playing violin to a water buffalo . . .'

During a phone conversation I had with Dr Aman, he tried to summarize the results of his investigations. In general, he told me, Anglo-Saxon cultures prefer insults dealing with excrement and body parts, while Catholic countries are fond of blasphemy. Cultures of the Middle and Far East have a liking for ancestor insults. There are also curses which only make sense within the context of a particular culture; in parts of New Guinea, the worst thing you can call someone is a yam thief. But Dr Aman admits to a particular liking for Yiddish insults: 'A good Yiddish insult will begin in a way that gets you to drop your defences – and then poke you right in the eye,' he said. So, you might have an expression like:

'May you have three shiploads of gold – and it should not be enough to pay your doctor's bill.' Or: 'May you become famous – they should name a disease after you.'

Contact: Dr Reinhold Aman, Maledicta Press, PO Box 14123, Santa Rosa, CA 95402-6123, USA.
Website: http://www.sonic.net/maledicta/ E-mail: aman@sonic.net

The Man Will Never Fly Memorial Society

The Wrights were wrong.

That's the guiding principle of this society, which was born at Kitty Hawk, the scene of the Wright Brothers' conquest-of-the-air hoax. Yes, hoax. For, despite what the world may believe, it is a myth that machines move through the air, with men 'flying' them. Oh, so you've travelled on one of these so-called 'planes', have you? You were conned. You were on board a bus with wings – and while aboard you were given the illusion of flight, by cloud-like scenery moving past your windows, carried by stage-hands in a very expensive theatrical performance. As the society says: 'Let's have no more talk of planes flying – unless they are thrown by carpenters.'

The society was started in 1959, when its founders, who had been invited to attend a meeting on 17 December honouring the Wright Brothers, began drinking and thinking on the evening of 16 December. They drank and they thought until the myth of the Wright Brothers' flight in 1903 become as hard to swallow as the bootleg rye they imbibed. Thus was born the society's motto: 'Birds Fly, Men Drink.' Since then, it has fought 'the hallucination of airplane flight with every weapon at its command save sobriety'.

Because, when you stop to think about it, do you actually believe that a machine made of tons of metal will fly?

Contact: The Man Will Never Fly Memorial Society, PO Box 1903, Kill Devil Hills, NC 27948, USA.

Marbles

From Ash Wednesday to Good Friday it's marbles season in Sussex. There's the rolling of spheres and the downing of beers at the Black Dog, the Red Lion, the Half Moon and the Bush. But on the season's last day, go to the Greyhound. The biggest marble of all – no less than the blue-and-green one, the planet – may be said to be at stake in the game; for every Good Friday, the Greyhound public house at Tinsley Green hosts the marbles championship of the world. One Sunday, I went for beer and sandwiches there to meet Sam McCarthy-Fox, the secretary of the British Marbles Board of Control.

'At Tinsley Green, the game goes back centuries,' he said. There is a legend that in Elizabethan times, two young men were rivals for the hand of a local maiden: they tried to settle the matter by competing against each other in various sports – archery, falconry and the like – but had always come out equal. 'In marbles there has to be a winner,' said Sam, 'so it was the obvious solution to their problem.'

The object of the game is straightforward: to knock marbles off a raised 6-foot-diameter ring, using your tolley or shooting marble. The best players can put topspin, backspin and sidespin on to their tolleys and, just like snooker or pool professionals, can manoeuvre themselves into the best position for the next shot. But it came as a surprise to me that it's hard to master the simplest of marbles' skills – namely, the flicking of the thumb.

'There's an approved way of doing it,' said Sam, 'which gives you maximum control over shots.' So I did as instructed, and with the tip of my index finger I cradled the tolley on the joint of the thumb. I flicked. And the tolley dribbled out.

Sam wasn't surprised. 'Why *should* you have a strong thumb?' he asked. 'Unless you're a marbles player, you won't have any need of the strength.'

He recommended a series of exercises. I could start by flicking a marble against the skirting board at home. Then I could change the angle at which I flicked, and then I could flick from further back. If I kept up the training, there might come a day when I'd be as strong as one of the greats of the game, Jim 'Atomic Thumb' Longhurst, who could shatter a beer glass with a single tolley. Jim believed in constantly flicking his thumb – even when he didn't have a marble – to keep it in shape. But he did not take as much care of his equipment as the fabled Wee Willie Wright – a 5ft 2in Welshman who had a hot water bottle sewn into his overcoat to keep his thumb warm and to help the circulation.

Realizing I wasn't going to be good enough to compete for several years, I asked Sam whether he'd seen any moments of great drama in marbles. He mentioned the sand, the game's 'baize', which is sprinkled over the surface of the ring. 'I've seen a situation where a marble was on the edge of the ring, held on by just a grain,' he said. 'People were stamping on the ground, trying to make it fall off.'

But for Sam, the marbles themselves are of interest, as much as the game. 'I love marbles, I collect them,' he said. 'I have a demi-john full of them on my windowsill. It's the nearest I'll ever get to having a stained-glass window.' Though he mentioned that materials other than glass have been used for marbles: stone, clay, metal. And that isn't all. 'In the 1950s,' said Sam, 'a lot were made out of old toilet bowls. I've got about half-a-dozen of those.'

Contact: Sam McCarthy-Fox, Secretary, British Marbles Board of Control, 50 Ham Road, Worthing, W. Sussex, BN11 2QX, UK.
Also: An excellent contact for collecting and playing marbles is Cathy Runyan-Svacina, known as The Marble Lady, who is listed under the entry on the 'Sorry Charlie, No Fan Club For You' Club.

Maximaphily

This is the philately of coincidence.

Let's say you are on holiday and are about to send a postcard home. From a vendor's rack, you choose a view of a bridge you crossed earlier in the day, and then you buy a stamp: to your surprise, the stamp features a view of the very same bridge. You shrug your shoulders, write the card, and stick the stamp on . . . and then just as you drop the card into the mailbox, you realize that its postmark will bear the name of the town where the bridge is situated. *There will be a three-way concordance between the stamp, the postcard and the postmark.* You start to think that there could be other examples of this phenomenon: a stamp and a card featuring a movie star could be posted in Hollywood; a stamp and a card featuring a famous painting could be posted in the city where the painting is on display; a stamp and a card featuring a species of bird could be posted from the bird's natural habitat area.

Such triple agreements are called *maximum cards*. The hobby of collecting maximum cards is *maximaphily*. Those who collect are *maximaphilists*.

Though if you're going to build a substantial collection you need to rely on more than coincidence. You need to *create* the combinations – and here, the greatest problem is finding a postcard on the same theme as a stamp. It's easy enough if the post office has decided to honour Humphrey Bogart, or even Bugs Bunny, but what if it's someone like the composer John Philip Sousa?

Ah, but couldn't you simply *make* a postcard, by reproducing a picture from a book?

Except that one of the rules of maximaphily is that the card should be an 'off the rack' type, such as you might find in a souvenir shop, and *not* specially printed for the purpose of making a maximum card. A made-up card would be just too damn easy. And hey, you want the fun of a challenge, don't you?

Contact: Maximum Card Study Unit of America, PO Box 761, N. Bergen, NJ 07047-0761, USA.

Mazes and Labyrinths

There is a brick path on the village green at Saffron Walden, inlaid like marquetry into the grass. To walk it is to walk a very long and very winding road. I would call it a second-cousin to a spiral: you start at the edge and let the whirlpool suck you in. Yet it is not a spiral, nor a spiral's sibling, nor even a first-cousin – it has a completely different dizziness *en route*, as it leads you to its core. It is a *labyrinth*.

I did not say maze. A maze has dead-ends; the path at Saffron Walden is unnecessarily long – one mile crammed into an area 35 yards across – but it never once leads you astray.

The person who taught me the difference between a maze and a labyrinth walked one step behind me on those bricks: Jeff Saward, one of the world's foremost authorities on circuitous routes. Jeff runs a society of maze and labyrinth enthusiasts, *Caerdroia*. (A Welsh pun, meaning both City of Turnings and City of Troy – the latter being a continental name for a maze or labyrinth.) Jeff clips out magazine advertisements like those for financial services – 'Find your way through the money-maze'; he keeps records of psychological experiments on animal learning – the old rat-in-a-maze test; and even Christmas presents from his wife are related to Caerdroia – she gives him children's games, such as *Heroes of the Maze*. ('Enter at your peril . . ')

Behind all this lies a serious interest in history and archaeology: labyrinths and mazes are ancient symbols, which have appeared in virtually all human societies. Their patterns were etched on Syrian pottery in 1300BC and on rock-faces in pre-Columbian North America. Scandinavian fisherman used the symbols to give magical protection against trolls; the Romans used them as graffiti. Where there are humans, you will find mazes and labyrinths. Why, though?

'I think people are fascinated by the distortion of space and time,' commented Jeff. How long will you be trapped inside? You do not know. Which direction will your journey take? You do not know. Your only option is to take the path and follow it, wherever it may lead. The path, of course, can easily become a metaphor for life: there is a member

---

154

of Caerdroia who employs mazes and labyrinths as problem-solving tools – he sits and stares at the designs, asks spiritual questions and relates the twists and turns to the turmoils of his own existence. Jeff keeps an open mind on the effectiveness of mazes when used for such purposes. 'If you stare closely at them, I'm sure you'll see all sorts of funny things,' he said.

Contact: Jeff Saward, Caerdroia, 53 Thundersley Grove, Thundersley, Essex, SS7 3EB, UK.
Tel: 01268 751915
Website: http://ilc.tsms.soton.ac.uk/caerdroia
E-mail: Caerdroia@dial.pipex.com

The Meccanomen

There are people who have memorized the part number for every part produced in the entire Meccano* range since the toy's inception in 1901. Pick any one of the hundreds of gears, brackets, strips with holes and axle rods and they are able to comment without a moment's hesitation: this is part 20a, the 1916 version of the 2ins pulley with turned lugs; or that is part 30b, the bevel gear with 24 teeth. Sometimes they can give a historical perspective, pointing out that part 159 was only around from 1927 to 1935. Or that part numbers changed: 117 became 168d; 170 became 130a and most intriguing of all, 217a (1¼ins) became 24a (1⅜ins).

These are not men, but Meccanomen; and in 1989 they formed themselves into an international society to promote the building of working models of water-mills, traction engines, and numerous other mechanisms with axles and gears – all having that sprayed-with-machine-gun-bullets look that characterizes the matter in the Meccano universe.

Yet I have learnt that you need not build any models at all to be a Meccanoman; one leading member has written a booklet on pure Meccano collecting. The idea is to snap up job lots of Meccano at flea markets; you may also strike it lucky in the lofts and attics of elderly friends and relatives. 'Meccano parts have a distinctive aesthetic quality which makes them a pleasure to sort and examine,' the author writes in his booklet. Though he advises that this should always be done on a tray with sides about half an inch high; then, any grub screw or other small part which falls accidentally from your fingers will not roll onto the floor

---

and vanish in a dark corner. 'If this does happen,' he says, 'rummage with a magnet.'

In some parts of the world, including the United States, Meccano is known as Erector.

Contact: The International Society of Meccanomen, c/o Adrian Williams, Bell House, 72A Old High Street, Headington, Oxford, OX3 9HW, UK. Tel/Fax: 01865 741057 Website: http://www/dircon.co.uk/meccano/

The Merrills Association

Merrills, marells, marls, marl, marlin, marnull, marriage, marrel, marril, madell, maulty, medal, merls, meryall, merryholes, merrymen, merrypeg, meg merrylegs, peg meryll, miracle, miracles, miraele, mill, morals, moris, morell, morrit, multi, murrells, mutti and nine men's morris . . . the game of merrills has as many names as the devil.

It requires Mephistophelian cunning, too. The action takes place on a board marked with three concentric squares, connected by lines radiating from the mid-points of the sides of the innermost square: think of it as rudimentary cobweb, made by a spider still learning its trade. For a full statement of the rules, you should contact the World – Merrills Association, which holds an annual championship – but in essence, the idea is to place counters on the intersections of the board, with the object of achieving three in a line, which is known as a mill. If you do form a mill, you can remove one of your opponent's pieces.

The most intriguing aspect of this game is that it gives you a 'second wind': in the early stages, your counters can only move to an adjacent intersection – but as soon as you are down to your last three counters, you can move them to *any* empty intersection on the board. So when one is weak, one is strong.

Graffiti versions of the merrills board are found in locations all over the world: the oldest known is carved on a roof-tile of the Kurna temple in Thebes, built by Rameses I around 1370BC. While in England, merrills boards are often scratched on the choir stall seats of old churches, suggesting that the game may have been a popular way to while away a dull sermon.

So the devil doesn't just find *work* for idle hands, but *play*, too.

Contact: The World Merrills Association, Ryedale Folk Museum, Hutton le Hole, York, YO6 6UA, UK.
Tel: 01751 417367
Website: http://www.tromboni.demon.co.uk/merrills/merrills.html

Meteor Shower Signalling

If the fate of mankind were to be the same as the dinosaurs', with a meteor as the poison pill for our species, then there would still be a compensation, still be a silver lining to the dust-cloud rising from the crater. Because, in those moments before Armageddon, a tiny group of radio amateurs could be fulfilled as never before. Just like other radio hobbyists, these people send messages to each other – only they do it by a deliberately difficult route: by bouncing signals off the trails left by passing meteors. A leading enthusiast for 'signal propagation by meteor scatter' is David Butler.

'Some radio amateurs, like me, need more of a challenge,' I was told by David, who works as the manager of a group that installs satellite communications equipment. 'Anyone could buy a radio, plug in a bit of wire and make contacts all over the world. You could speak to Australia any time of day, no problem. But that's too easy. I am interested in making contacts of extreme difficulty. By that, I mean picking up fragmented, very weak signals.'

The opportunity for communication via meteors comes about 15 times a year, whenever a regular, annual meteor shower – that is, the remains of a comet, on a fixed orbit around the sun-crosses the orbit of the Earth. Two meteor scatter enthusiasts arrange a scheduled contact (or, 'sked') to take place during the shower, when they will alternately transmit and receive VHF signals to each other on a given frequency, for a given time. The fact that they are using VHF lies at the heart of the hobby: VHF signals are generally regarded as having a very short range – perhaps from the top of a mountain one may manage to send a message a distance of 200km, though normally the range would be even less. But if the signal is lucky enough to be reflected off the ionized trail of a meteor burning up in the Earth's atmosphere, it is possible to make contact with another enthusiast up to 2000km away.

So, on 3 January, at 8pm, during the Quadrantids meteor shower – the first shower of the year – I sat down with David at his transceiver in Herefordshire as he tried to make contact with Boris, based in Slovenia. The information that they hoped to exchange was the barest minimum: call-signs and perhaps a pair of numbers to represent the strength and duration of any signals received. But since meteors are typically the size of a grain of sand, even this level of communication is hard to accomplish. In the course of an hour-long sked, when the same message is repeated over and over again, it is quite possible that no more than half a call-sign will be received. When a message *does* break through, it can be heard as a garbled 'splodge' of speech lasting, perhaps, half a second, which then fades; or, if speeded-up Morse is used, which compresses the same information into a considerably shorter fraction of time, a distinctive 'ping' noise might be heard, like the echo-sounder of a submarine. Apart from that, the hobby just involves waiting and listening to the background crackles and hiss.

'To an outsider, it might seem a bit strange that I have spent the past 35 minutes on the radio and received no more than six letters during that time,' said David, commenting on the receipt of his call-sign, G4ASR, in two fragments, G4A and ASR. 'Especially as I could speak to the same person on shortwave with no problem at all. I don't know whether I could compare this hobby to anything. I suppose it's as pointless as fishing, really. Once you've caught a fish you throw it away. It's exactly the same with this – because there's really no need to do it. But it's a challenge because it's so difficult to achieve, and there's a kick from knowing that there's someone else doing a like-minded thing.'

Every year those like-minded people who practise meteor shower signalling gather for a meeting in Weinheim, in Southern Germany. 'The Czechs drink a lot, the Swedes drink a lot, but the worst drinkers are the Ukrainians,' said David. 'It's like a *beerfest*, but only for people who do meteor scatter. Socializing, and eating and drinking, are a large part of this hobby. *And*, of course, telling everyone how big your aerials are. . .'

Contact: David Butler, Yew Tree Cottage, Lower Maescod, Herefordshire, HR2 0HP, UK.
E-mail: davebu@mdlhrl.agw.bt.co.uk

M.I.C.E.

What would life be like if you saved every single piece of junk mail? Probably like John Townsend's life – who has boxfuls of the stuff all over the house. 'It's even on the staircase,' he says. 'Though there's a gap down the middle of the hall where I walk.'

When John receives junk mail, he divides it into two types: *paper mail*, which he keeps for posterity, for the future collectors of the paper ephemera of our era, and *card mail*, which either goes into his own collection, or is swapped with the other members of the organization known as M.I.C.E. That stands for the Modern Information Collectors' Exchange, and its 100 members are fascinated by the advertising cards which are distributed freely by commercial companies. (Being free is the important consideration: no commodity purchase must be involved – so an item such as a bubblegum card wouldn't count.)

Under the pseudonym Anonymouse, John sends out packages of these cards to M.I.C.E. members, who extract the cards they want for their own collections, replace them with an equal number of swaps, and post the package back to John; and so the process continues. I have received several mailings from M.I.C.E., with ads for the likes of *Quiet Life Tablets* ('For everyday stresses and strains') and for a disco called *IF?*, showing a picture of a woman in a zebra-skin outfit.

'Everyone is a collector,' says John. 'It's part of human nature. Even a housewife will collect furniture or things for her mantelpiece. It's just that some of us take it a bit further.'

Contact: M.I.C.E., 4 Stiles Avenue, Marple, Stockport, Cheshire, SK6 6LR, UK.

Milk Bottle Collectors

The song was inaccurate by a factor of 130: there were not ten green bottles hanging on the wall, but 1300. Actually, I must confess that they weren't green, either – but I was in a place where it was impossible to avoid thinking of that song, where if I stumbled, or if I talked too much with my hands, a bottle *would* accidentally fall. 'So what?' you might say, 'It's not as if you were in a wine cellar.' How true. These bottles did not, had never, contained *wine*.

'We started collecting milk bottles in 1975,' I was told by Mike Hull – the 'we' including his wife, Naomi, who took up the story of how their life became full of empties.

'We were living in Highgate at the time,' she said, 'and one morning we noticed that the Express Dairy had delivered a pint in a bottle that came from a different area.' She explained that the Express had taken over a dairy in Cricket Malherbie in Somerset, and was using up the latter's bottles. 'Being an English leacher,' she said, 'I was quite interested in the name – Norman, *mal herbe*, or bad grass.'

Mike tried to locate that inspirational item: it took a moment or two, because there was shelf after shelf of empty bottles. Some were displayed to give the impression of milk, by being filled with white polystyrene beads; but most were simply transparent, apart from the company logos, featuring dairymaids and cows. One or two old, rare bottles were in fact green. Then Mike said, 'Ah.'

The bottle that he handed me seemed very ordinary – one of the least distinguished of the collection. 'I'm surprised you even noticed there was anything different about it,' I said.

'But it made us wonder how many dairies there were,' said Naomi. 'Fifty maybe? We soon found out that there were *thousands*.' So the Hulls began collecting: finding old milk bottles in ditches, in woods, on rubbish tips, at picnic sites. In time, they launched a newsletter, *Milk Bottle News*, now taken by 130 subscribers. 'This hobby isn't like stamp collecting, where you can buy a catalogue and find out all the stamps there are,' said Naomi. 'We're perpetually surprised by what we find. It's one long adventure.'

Contact: *Milk Bottle News*, c/o Mike and Naomi Hull
Tel: 01453 884922. (UK)
Or: The National Association of Milk Bottle Collectors, c/o The Milk Route, 4 Ox Bow Road, Westport, CT 06880-2602, USA.

The Miniature Piano Enthusiast Club

What counts as a miniature piano? In this club's eyes, anything piano-shaped and 'small'. Some will have playable keyboards; others will be piano-shaped music boxes; still others will be silent ornaments. The enthusiasm extends to any object with a piano design: pin-cushions, pencil sharpeners, even *panties*.

'This year at our convention we had a concert of toy piano music that included "Alexander's Ragtime Band", "Dance of the Sugar Plum Fairy", and "Putting on the Ritz",' says Janice Kelsh, who founded the Miniature Piano Enthusiast Club in 1990. 'And next year, we're hoping to feature a toy piano played by a parakeet.'

Contact: Janice Kelsh, 633 Pennsylvania Avenue, Hagerstown, MD 21740, USA.
Tel: 301 797 7675

The Mitten Cat Association

Remember in *The Sound of Music* when Julie Andrews warbled that her favourite things included 'whiskers on kittens' and 'warm woollen mittens'? I am tempted to comment: had she been aware of the Mitten cat, Julie would have been able to combine these two enthusiasms.

Just as the Manx cat has no tail, so the Mitten is a breed with another peculiarity: an extra, fifth toe on each paw. The Mitten's front paws are so versatile that they can amuse themselves for periods of time when

160

their owners are busy by throwing their cat toys into the air and catching them. They can even be taught to hold small items in their paws, such as spoons.

Though Mittens are not as well-known as Manxes, they do have their supporters: the Mitten Cat Association, who are fond of saying 'You'll be smitten by a Mitten.'

Contact: International Mitten Cat Association, c/o Joan Hamel, PO Box 472, West Hill Station, Scarborough, Ontario, Canada M1E 4Y9.

Model Rocketeers

If you were now to stare at nothing but pointed objects for half an hour – packets of needles, sharp pencils, marital aids – you might acquire an after-image on the retina so that, wherever you looked, you would have a haunting impression of the inside of Trevor Sproston's garden shed. Or, perhaps I should say, his rocket factory. Trevor is one of the UK's leading model rocketeers – the vehicles he builds blast off and they leave the Earth. Yes, these rockets are small, but their principles are pure Cape Canaveral: some model rocketeers have achieved speeds of 300-400 mph and altitudes of 14,000 feet.

But instead of demonstrating a 'conventional' model rocket to me, such as a miniature Saturn Five, Trevor decided to demonstrate an atypical one: a flying saucer, about 10 inches in diameter.

So we stood in a field by his mission control, the launch box that sends an electrical current to the motors. There was a fizzing sound. The saucer went straight up . . . and then came straight down. It was in the air for less than ten seconds and went to a height of 50 feet. Well, I know I only wanted a taster, and I know that this was a short-range vehicle, but it seemed to me you could get more fun from shaking up a lemonade bottle. Trevor wasn't surprised by this reaction. A non-rocketeer, who hasn't had the pleasure of building a vehicle, will typically say, 'Does it just go up and down, then?' To which Trevor's standard answer remains: 'If it just went up and stayed there it would look very silly indeed.'

Contact: The National Association of Rocketry, PO Box 177, Altoona, WI 54720, USA.
Website: http://www.nar.org

Model Submariners

'No way would you get me down in a submarine,' said Bernie Wood. 'If you've got a key to get out of a room, that's okay. But with a submarine, there's this overwhelming fear of being locked in somewhere you can't get out of.'

Sitting in his lounge in Sidcup, Kent, he proceeded to describe the horrors of being depth-charged.

'Imagine being bombed underwater. That's the most terrifying thing,' he said. 'When you *know* you're going down.' There is the flooding, the lack of air, the increase in pressure as the ocean floor approaches. 'The rivets come out, the joints give, the plates buckle . . .'

With each of these details, he brought his hands closer together: the fingers bent round as though they were themselves the ribs of a submarine's hull. 'Until . . .' His hands met in a clap.

That is why he restricts himself to *model* submarines.

Other people across the world have come to the same conclusion – and today there are about 100 boating-lake Captain Nemos in the UK alone who form the Association of Model Submariners. The radio-controlled vessels they construct are able to dive to a depth of at least eight feet and some even fire live torpedoes. Primed with minute explosive charges, the torpedoes are used to launch attacks on 'dummy' surface ships floating in swimming pools.

So, we prepared to put a model U-boat into action. There was, however, one problem: Bernie had been to the local pond earlier and discovered the water level was too low. Undaunted, he lifted the U-boat from its cradle in his shed . . . and carried it to the goldfish pond in his back garden.

He showed me the principles of operating the controls – and, at my command, the submarine submerged. Then I worked the propeller and was able to send the submarine an inch or two forwards before it struck the side of the pond. I pressed another control and it surfaced.

'With ordinary model boats you can only go forwards, or left and right,' said Bernie. 'But I think what a lot of people get out of model submarines is the extra dimension of going up and down.'

'What about the fact,' I asked, 'that you can't actually *see* the submarine when it's underwater. Doesn't that make it all rather pointless?'

'I can see it,' said Bernie. 'I can see it in my mind's eye.'

Contact: The Association of Model Submariners, c/o David Austin, The Rise, Takeley Street, Nr. Bishop's Stortford, Herts, CM22 6QS, UK.
Tel: 01279 870917
Or: USA Sub Committee, c/o Mr E. Berger, 105 Long Bridge Road, Hampton, Virginia 32669-2020, USA.
E-mail: SubComGene@aol.com

Moist Towelette Collecting

'I really *do* collect moist towelettes,' I was told by Michael Lewis, a computer programmer from Orlando, Florida, in an e-mail. He added that he has well over a hundred lemon-scented facial wipes from all over the world; his favourites come from Israel, with their elegant spare-no-expense design. 'Each moist towelette is like a miniature work of art,' he said.

Michael will go down in history as the man who established the first ever website devoted to moist towelette collecting. 'It's just so darn hard to be the FIRST any more, and now I can proudly proclaim to have the first site dedicated to my hobby!' At the start, he did wonder whether *anyone* else shared his fascination for moist towelettes – but on the website he decided to include some tongue-in-cheek references to 'a large group of moist towelette collectors'.

Or rather, these references were *originally* tongue-in-cheek. As Michael told me: 'With the many responses I've received, I now believe it myself.' Yes, there *are* other collectors – and on the website, they at last have an opportunity to discuss the latest towelettes to come on the market, their aromatic ingredients, and whether or not the term 'handy wipe' is an acceptable substitute for 'moist towelette'.

Contact: Modern Moist Towelette Collecting, c/o Michael Lewis, 3000 Highway 19A – Suite 2, Mt. Dora, FL 32757-3419, USA.
Website: http://members.aol.com/moisttwl E-mail: MoistTwl@aol.com

The Mosquito Killing World Championships

I have no desire to feature blood sports – but should that prohibition extend to the Mosquito Killing World Championships? Its inclusion in this book will undoubtedly offend practitioners of the Indian religion Jainism, which holds all life as sacred. Jainists even wear face masks to prevent themselves accidentally breathing in an insect. But, hey, we're talking about pretty pesky things, here. And one of the rules is that death should come swiftly with a hand slap:

163

it is absolutely forbidden to torture the damn little bloodsuckers.

In the championships – which are held in July in the Finnish village of Pelkosenniemi, north of the Arctic Circle – competitors are given five minutes to kill as many mosquitoes as possible. As it says in the English translation of the rules provided by the organizers: 'Only totally dead, and creatures which are former mosquitoes, will be counted.'

Contact: Pelkosenniemen Kunta, 98500 Pelkosenniemi, Finland.
Tel: 016 826 111 Fax: 016 851 457

Musical Saw News

Rock stars may talk of playing their axes, but when the subscribers to the specialist publication *Musical Saw News* talk of playing their saws, they mean it. Their instruments, unlike Clapton's or Hendrix's, could cut a block of wood after cutting a track.

'If this was sharpened, it would be very good for sawing wood,' I was told by a London-based subscriber, John Moran, as he held up the tool. 'It's just that the teeth have had the edge taken off to protect the trousers.'

He sat down and wedged the saw handle between his knees. Bending the blade to one side, he stroked it with a violin bow . . . and the first few notes of the song 'Maggie' emerged, wailing like the wind across a moor. It is hardly surprising that the instrument appears in the soundtracks of old Laurel and Hardy films when Stan and Ollie are in fear of a ghost: the sound is ethereal, yet too exaggerated to be terrifying.

'When I perform, people are most curious about how it's played,' said John. 'Some even suggest it's me whining under my breath that's making the noise. They can't believe it's actually coming from a saw.'

Beginners, though, should be prepared for many ugly noises along the way. My first attempt at the tune 'Three Blind Mice' sounded like the rodents were squealing in agony as their tails were sawn off.

Contact: *Musical Saw News*, PO Box 84935, San Diego, CA 92138-4935, USA.
E-mail: SAWNEWS@prodigy.com

Mutant Plant Spotters

You may have seen a four-leaf clover – but what about a poppy that is white, not red? Or a thistle whose roots are flattened, like ribbons? Or a greater plantain that has divided and then reunited, leaving a hole in the stem? These are the sorts of aberrations discussed in *That Plant's Odd* – a newsletter for those who are intrigued by mutant plants.

'When you work in a garden for eight hours a day, you notice that there are certain things that plants do that they're not supposed to do,' said Martin Cragg-Barber, a professional gardener since 1982, and the man who edits *That Plant's Odd*. 'You notice things like flowers with no petals, or with too many petals, or even with petals growing out of other petals. Once you become aware of the possibility of aberrations, you can hardly go on a ramble without seeing them. It can add a whole new dimension to one's enjoyment of the countryside.'

Contact: Martin Cragg-Barber, *That Plant's Odd*, 1 Station Cottages, Hullavington, Chippenham, Wiltshire, SN14 6ET, UK.

The Muzzle Loaders' Association

The shot was muffled by the ear protection I wore, so smell was the sense, not sound. Clouds of smoke billowed around the barrel and I had the whiff of the powder in my nostrils. Remember, when you were a child, that odour of caps from a toy gun? Only I was firing no toy.

I had fired an 1853 Enfield, a rifle that saw service in the Crimean War. If you draw back the cock, it isn't difficult to imagine the weapon defending the honour of the Empire against flashing sabres and charging cavalry . . . and more than a hundred years later, the lock, stock and wrought-iron barrel are still in perfect working order.

I had come to the rifle-range as a guest of the Muzzle Loaders' Association, a group dedicated to firearms that have a loading-ritual: first you take your flask and pour the black grains down the barrel; then you drop in a bullet which has been lubricated with tallow and beeswax; then you use the ramrod. What's more, when fired, the bullets travel much more slowly than those of a modern rifle – through a lens, you can actually see the bullet approach the target, like a bumblebee of metal.

'Your line was perfect,' said the instructor, after my shot. 'It's just that you were a bit high.' The hole in the target was aligned in a vertical axis with the bullseye, but a couple of inches *above* the scoring circles.

It is appropriate to say: had I been at the Battle of Balaclava, I might, with a bit of luck, have dislodged a helmet.

Note: There are many muzzle-loading groups throughout the world – but the following are three very useful initial contacts.

***

Contact: The Muzzle Loaders' Association, The Exhibition Hut, Bisley Camp, Brookwood, Woking, Surrey, GU24 ONY, UK.
Or: National Muzzle Loading Rifle Association, PO Box 67, Friendship, IN 47021, USA
  Website: http://www.nmlra.org
Or: Mr Kim Atkinson, 27 Honeysuckle Drive, Hope Valley, South Australia, 5090.

N

Nail Enthusiasts

'Don't get into this hobby if you want to make a fast dollar. The money you spend on gas looking for that special nail will almost never be recovered in cash, but rather in that feeling of elation and satisfaction you will get from adding one more difficult nail to your collection.'

To be fair, we are not dealing with any old nails – only a special collectable sort, known as date nails, with numerals on the head. Hammered into timbers that are exposed to the elements, such as railway sleepers and fence posts, these nails are a record of the age of the timber, and therefore give a reliable indication of when it will rot, and will need replacing. This is a hobby that offers you the experience of a wide variety of head shapes (round, square, oval, pentagonal), lengths (¼in to 3ins), shafts (round, square, two-pronged, tapered), material (steel, malleable iron, aluminium, copper and even plastic), and typeface. Oh, and the numerals are either raised or indented.

Some enthusiasts have collected over 4,000 different nails: an astonishing achievement when you bear in mind they have to swear not to damage property in pursuit of their hobby. (They'll be drummed out of the Date Nail Collectors' Association if they do.)

Contact: Jerry Waits, Secretary/Treasurer, Texas Date Nail Collectors 'Association, 501 W. Horton, Brenham, TX 77833, USA.
Tel: 409 830 1495

Note: in spite of the 'Texas' in the name, this is a worldwide association.

The Narrow Bandwidth Television Association

It was a black-and-white photograph of a human face, but the features were dissected by vertical lines; like one of those automated billboards at the moment when the slats have started to turn.

If I told you the picture was taken from a television screen, you would guess that atmospheric conditions had affected the broadcast; but the truth is, the lines would be there come what may. It would be wrong, too, to talk about broadcasts: the picture was transmitted no farther than the width of a room, and faces are the only images the set ever receives. Images of members of the Narrow Bandwidth Television Association, a group which aims to promote the development, study and widespread use of *low-definition* TV. That is to say, the members build obsolete devices that cannot pick up signals from modern television stations; their passion is mechanical television, as pioneered by John Logie Baird – technology abandoned in 1935 when cathode-ray tubes replaced spinning discs.

The group was founded by Douglas Pitt, a physics teacher (now retired) who was nostalgic for the very early days of television. 'I built my own TV when I was 15,' he told me, as he put one of his creations on the table – a set capable of receiving a picture the size of a cigarette-card. Many years later, in 1972, Douglas put an advert in the magazine *Practical Wireless*, asking whether anyone else was still interested in Baird-style TV. 'A surprising number of people replied,' he said. 'They were reminiscing about the old days, saying they wished they'd bring mechanical television back again, in spite of the fact that the pictures weren't a patch on modern TV.'

Douglas sees building obsolete televisions as having a similar romanticism to driving steam locomotives. And even if technology is outmoded, it can still improve – for the members are constantly striving for better quality 32-line pictures. This leads to the paradox that digital enhancement techniques that are state of the art may be applied to technology that went out with the ark. That isn't all. At the group's annual convention, when members transmit and receive their own faces, an astounding array of home-made TVs are put to work, many of which don't even look like televisions – you might think they were hypnotism machines, or death-rays – combining, as they do, rotating drums, tilted mirrors and goodness knows what else. You cannot even exclude the possibility of the kitchen sink being a component. Douglas told me that one of the members built a mechanical TV as a teenager, but in his part of the country there was no electricity – so, to solve the problem, an electricity-generating turbine was hooked up to a tap, making a water-powered TV. 'When it was working,' said Douglas, 'you couldn't go to the lavatory – otherwise the picture went.'

Contact: Mr D.A. Gentle, Treasurer, NBTVA, I Sunny Hill, Milford, Belper, Derbyshire, DE56 0QR, UK.
Or: D.B. Pitt, I Burnwood Drive, Wollaton, Nottingham, NG8 2DG UK.

Narrow Bandwidth Television: The Sequel

'No matter what your age,' said Andrew Emmerson, 'there's some era of TV you've got a soft spot for.'

If you have just finished the previous entry, you'll know that the Narrow Bandwidth Television Association is devoted to obsolete television technology. The NBTVA is not the only organization with such an objective. There is also 405 Alive, a society concerned with the obsolete technology of the succeeding era – namely black-and-white 405-line TV, the age of valves. A member of 405 Alive, though, has broader interests than a narrow bandwidth fan, because apart from an attachment to the technology of their chosen period of obsolescence, a 405 Aliver also hankers after the old programmes, and the members avidly track down videos of black-and-white commercials and shows. 'For me,' said Andrew, who runs the society, 'black-and-white is a totally viable medium. Nobody criticizes Charlie Chaplin.'

Contact: 405 Alive, Larkhill, Newport Road, Woodseaves, Stafford, ST20 0NP, UK.

(The Society of) Natural VLF Radio Monitors

'The atmosphere was electric.' At last I can use that cliché and feel no shame.

It was an atmosphere evoked by playing a double CD, 'Electric Enigma'. As a first approximation to the truth, I can state that this album consists of over two hours of *crackles* – the sound of lightning bolts picked up on a radio receiver. The booklet accompanying the CD seems to acknowledge that this 'music' may not be to everyone's taste, and offers advice on listening: 'While to some, the popping and crackling might sound like "static", keep in mind that each click or pop is a lightning-stroke flashing somewhere.'

Of greater importance are the other noises, interspersed among the crackles – the most common being a 'whistler', that lasts a second or two, and has a downward-falling tone. This noise, too, is produced by lightning: by a complex process of interaction with the Earth's magnetic field, lightning bolts can create naturally occurring, very low-frequency *radio* signals – and listening to whistlers is the pastime of the natural radio enthusiast. So I'll sign off now and let Stephen McGreevy, who recorded the CD, and founded the Society of Natural VLF Radio Monitors, describe the experience:

'Serious and regular natural radio listening began in February 1991, when nearly every Sunday morning well before sunrise – the prime time for whistlers – I would pack my favourite whistler receiver, a small reel-to-reel tape recorder, and lunch, into a knapsack and bicycle to the nearby hills. Here I would dismount, and walk to my favourite listening spot, an elevation about 600 feet above sea level which I began calling "Whistler Hill". I was rewarded by many beautiful sunrises and many nice whistlers . . .'

> Contact: Society of Natural VLF Radio Monitors, Stephen McGreevy, PO Box 928, Lone Pine, CA 93534-0928, USA.
> Website: http://www.triax.com/vlfradio/index.htm
> E-mail: vlfradio@triax.com

The Nine-Volt Battery Collectors' Club

I asked Clifford Watts, the founder of the World Nine-Volt Battery Collectors' Club, whether he was solely interested in one sort of battery – the sort that is typically used in smoke detectors. 'Well, I do save some other batteries,' he said, 'just in case I can swap them for nine-volts with someone who's interested in another voltage.'

> Contact: World 9-Volt Battery Collectors' Club, c/o Clifford Watts, 51 Glendale Rd, Brantford, Ontario, Canada N3T 1PJ.
> Tel: 519 753 9049 E-mail: novtrans@worldchat.com

Ningle Jumping

It is a French word, *ningle*, but I do like to pronounce it in an English way. 'Ningle Jumping' (to rhyme with 'single bumping') is reminiscent of the language of *Jabberwocky*, of things that go whiffling through the tulgey wood, of vorpal swords that go snicker-snack.

The ningle is a long pole made out of chestnut, which historically was used to vault across watery ditches, in the Le Perrier region of France.

Originally, this was a method of travelling from farm to farm, but in the 1930s a competition was established to find the person who could jump the longest distance via ningle: a sort of watery pole vault, except that the aim was to achieve the greatest length, not greatest height. The competition died out, but it has been revived in recent times, with a record jump of nine metres being set in 1997.

Although there is intense rivalry amongst the serious ninglers, many participants appear to *enjoy* the failure of reaching the other bank – ending their attempt on the record with an almighty splash. (Whereupon, presumably, they gyre and gimble in the wabe.)

Contact: Mairie de Le Perrier, Comité des Fêtes, Département de la
Vendée, 85300 France.
Tel: 02 51 68 09 05 Fax: 02 51 68 14 30

The Nixon Collectors' Organization

Any potato bears a resemblance to Richard Nixon. In *Nixco News*, the magazine of the Nixon Collectors' Organization, you will find examples of Nixonia which are far more rare: such as the Nixon look-alike eggplant found in the produce section of Ralph's supermarket at the corner of Third and Vermont in Los Angeles. (I should stress that Nixon simulacra are just a minor side-issue in the magazine. The real meat, to go with the vegetables, is the memorabilia: anything from a Nixon cream pitcher to a pair of dancing Nixon and Agnew music boxes.)

Contact: NIXCO, 975 Maunawili Circle, Kailua, HI 96734-4620, USA.
Tel: 808 262 9837
Website: http://www.aloha.net/~eldon/nixcol.htm
E-mail: eldon@aloha.net

O

Oil-Wrestling

Boxers hang up their gloves; oil-wrestlers hang up their *zembils*.

A *zembil* is a sack woven from reeds, containing the leather trousers, or *kispet*, worn by the greased contestants in this Turkish form of wrestling: a sport in which it is as difficult to grip (or be gripped) as climbing (or being lassooed by) a rope made of knotted eels. Retired oil-wrestlers literally do hang their zembils on the wall, as a message that they will never don the kispet again.

Contact: Turkish Tourist Office, First Floor 170/173 Piccadilly, London, WIV 9DD, UK.
Tel: 0171 629 7771/0171 355 4207 Fax: 0171 491 0773

The Old Appliance Club

As I have noted in the preface, a few years ago I wrote a forerunner to this book, called *The Bizarre Leisure Book*. Soon after it was published, I received a letter from a reader asking for help: did I know of a club for people who were interested in old washing machines, vacuum cleaners and other bygone household appliances? Alas, I did not – *then*.

Now, in the magazine of the Old Appliance Club, I see the likes of beautiful reproductions of 1950s advertisements for refrigerators – 'The Space-Thrifty Coolerator is only 28 inches wide, yet it provides $9^{2/3}$ cu. ft. of safe cold refrigeration.' So if you're thinking of sending a letter asking whether some unusual club exists, I can tell you the answer already: 'It's only a matter of time.'

Note: The Old Appliance Club can offer assistance on a range of old appliance questions/problems, including the search for obsolete spare parts.

Contact: The Old Appliance Club, PO Box 65, Ventura, CA 93002, USA.
Tel: 805 643 3532 E-mail: jes@west.net

Old Familiar Strains

I have already described the Insulator Association. Deserving of separate treatment is the specialist magazine, *Old Familiar Strains*, which is for collectors of *just one particular type* of insulator: the 'radio strain insulator'.

'On my trip to southern California last spring, I stopped at a few antique shops along Interstate 5,' writes Dan Howard, the editor, in a recent issue. 'Always the optimist, I answered honestly when the proprietor of one shop asked, "What are you looking for?" After repeating myself slowly several times, I think that he finally began to understand that I was looking for "those funny glass jobbies that folks used to hold up radio antennas out on the farm". Then he related the often-told tale of the "bucket full" that he threw out because "nobody wants them".

Contact: *Old Familiar Strains*, c/o Dan Howard, 2940 SE 118th Ave, Portland, OR 97266-1602, USA.

The Old Lawnmower Club

The extraordinariness of the collector is directly proportional to the ordinariness of the collectable. In other words, the more mundane and commonplace the item, the more fascinating it is that anyone should collect it. This is why I have excluded the rich man's hobby of vintage-car collecting from this book – but *lawnmower* collecting definitely deserves a mention. Some members of the Old Lawnmower Club own over 500 grasscutting machines.

Contact: The Old Lawnmower Club, Milton Keynes Museum of Industry and Rural Life, Stacey Hill Farm, Southern Way, Wolverton, Milton Keynes, MK12 5EJ, UK.
Tel: 01908 316222 Website: http://www.artizan.demon.co.uk/olc/
E-mail: olc@artizan.demon.co.uk

One-Hit Wonder Enthusiasts

The theme of a thousand ballads is 'I finally found him/her, my perfect love, but then he/she went away – oh, please come back, boy/girl, and let us re-live that golden moment ...' But sometimes, the one who went away was the artist who made the record: one-hit wonders have a poignancy all of their own.

'When I was growing up in the sixties,' said Steven Rosen, 'I'd listen to the countdowns on the radio, and I'd even write down the names of the songs, and how they did, and I'd save those charts. And then six months later, I'd realize that an artist who had a hit record had dropped out of sight and was never heard of again.' What in the world had happened to the Ran-Dels (who recorded 'Martian Hop'), John Fred and the Playboy Band ('Judy in Disguise') and the Corsairs ('Smoky Places')? 'I wondered if I was missing out on something – if these people were having spectacular careers somewhere else, that I didn't know about because I was too young to be there. Later, I realized the opposite – they had vanished. I thought this unfair, especially if their one hit was a great song.'

For a while, Steven produced a magazine, *One Shot*, which explored the phenomenon of the one-hit wonder. (Although this has now folded, he has plans to replace it with a website.) And on his 40th birthday, 25 September 1990, he decided to establish One-Hit Wonder Day – when he would get in touch with fellow fans, and also do radio interviews to promote the art of the one-hit wonder. The tradition continues.

So, on 25 September *this* year, raise a glass to Frankie Ford who recorded 'Sea Cruise', the Teddy Bears, who recorded 'To Know Him is to Love Him', and of course the Tuneweavers, who recorded 'Happy, Happy Birthday, Baby'.

Contact: Steven Rosen, 1420 East Bates Avenue, Englewood, CO 80110, USA.

Ophthalmic Collectors

There are people, like Stephen James, who believe that beauty is just in front of the eye of the beholder – people who believe that spectacle lenses are aesthetically pleasing. 'I like the shape and the feel of them,' he told me, as he raised to his eye a quizzing glass, a hand-held monocle used by gentlemen about town in the early 19th century to scrutinize the charms of lackies. Other members of the Ophthalmic Antiques International Collectors' Club specialize in glass eyes, eye baths and opticians' test charts.

But should you start collecting antique spectacles, be prepared to remove your rose-tinted ones about the accuracy of television's historical dramas. 'I do wish that producers would get it right,' said Stephen. He cited the example of the British television series *Sharpe*, set during the

Napoleonic wars. 'They may have got the muskets right, but one of the characters was wearing spectacles of a kind that was developed 100 years later.'

Contact: Mrs V. Mellor, Membership Secretary, Ophthalmic Antiques International Collectors' Club, 3 Moor Park Road, Northwood, Middlesex, HA6 2DL, UK.

The Outhouse Preservation Society

Charles Collins has travelled all across North America for 15 years, conducting research on outside lavatories. His investigations have led him to discover that the average distance of an outhouse from a house is 33 yards, and the longest 98 yards. 'When you knock on a person's door and ask if you can measure the distance from their house to their privy, you get some pretty strange looks,' he remarks.

Contact: The Outhouse Preservation Society, PO Box 25067, Halifax, NS B3M 4H4, Canada.

Outhouse Racing

Held every year since 1977 on Canada's Labour Day Weekend, the Great Outhouse Race describes itself as 'The event that is more than just another bathroom fixture.'

A team of four push an outside lavatory on wheels along a three km course in Dawson City, in the Klondike. The course contains a great var-iety of terrain: level, rough, uphill, dry, muddy, open and narrow spaces. Meanwhile, a fifth team member is seated inside, on the . . . er, passenger seat. (Though he or she can swap places with any of the pushers, provided that the change is made on the run, or the outhouse is temporarily halted.)

Contact: The Great Klondike International Outhouse Race, c/o Klondike Visitors' Association, PO Box 389, Dawson City, Yukon, Canada, Y0B 1G0.

Tel: 403 993 5575 Fax: 403 993 6415
Website: http://www.dawsoncity.com E-mail: KVA@dawson.net

The Owl Collectors' Club

They call themselves *owl-coholics*. Cushions, tea-cloths, pyjamas, pots – they'll buy them all, provided the design features an owl.

'I don't know how many owly things I've got,' said Elise Mann, who founded the International Owl Collectors' Club, and who edits their magazine *Life's a Hoot*. 'I stopped counting when I reached a thousand.' She continued: 'My plates have got owls. My cups have got owls. I've got at least six owl-teapots . . .' Really, she didn't need to *tell* me this, for it is difficult to *move* in Elise's lounge, because of all the owl-abilia: money-boxes, clocks, shoe-horns, cake tins – and a huge pile of cuddly owl toys.

'Some people come in here and are appalled,' she said, as she showed off her owl cider-jug, and owl honey-pot. 'They often say to me, "How do you dust them all?" Well, I don't dust them. I admit you can't be that houseproud with a collection like this. But I'll sometimes run a vacuum-cleaner over them – with something over the end to stop the smaller owls getting sucked up.'

Contact: The International Owl Collectors' Club, 54 Tiverton Road, Edgware, Middlesex, HA8 6BE, UK.

P

The Palindromist

This book encourages you to spend your spare time in unusual ways. It can therefore be summarized as:

ODD:DO!

Well, it's not the greatest palindrome in the world; you'll find much better examples in *The Palindromist*, a magazine for people who like reading and writing sentences that are the same backwards as they are forwards. In a recent issue, there was an astonishing 175-word palindromic poem, *Ode to Evita*, written by the editor, Mark Saltveit, which begins 'God, deliver an ode to deviative Evita, cover star' and ends 'Rats, revocative Evita, I've doted on a reviled dog.'

'Palindromy is no more difficult than a tough crossword puzzle,' says Mark. 'But when you complete a gem like "Sex, even if fine, vexes" you have done more than solve a puzzle; you have created a work of art.'

Contact: *The Palindromist*, PO Box 471258, San Francisco, CA 94147, USA.
Website: http://www.realchange.org/pal
E-mail: palindromist@realchange.org

The Pantomime Horse Derby

On the same day in Bognor that men try to be birds (see section on the Birdman Rally) other men try to be horses.

Or cows, giraffes, even moose – you and a friend can dress up as *any* four-legged animal and gallop for the finishing tape. (You also need a third team member, as a 'trainer', who races to collect you from the starting position, and guides you along the course.)

Contact: Pantomime Horse Derby, Bognor Fun Bus Co. Ltd., 35 Lyon Street, Bognor Regis, West Sussex, PO21 1BW, UK.
Tel/Fax: 01243 869922
Website: http://www.arunet.co.uk/fairplay/demo.htm
E-mail: fairplay@arunet.co.uk

The Peashooting World Championships

'Choose a nice straight one. And remember to blow, not to suck.' This was the advice as I chose a pink plastic peashooter in the village hall at Witcham, near Ely – home of the Peashooting World Championships.

Soon, the air was full of the noise of phut … phut … phut. In the first round, competitors fire five peas at a circular target and the sixteen highest scores progress to a knockout phase. I wasn't good at judging the required amount of puff – too much and you'll overshoot the target, too little and you'll fall short – so after I was eliminated, all I could do was watch.

I observed differences in style: one-handed versus two-handed grips. Also, some favoured loading peas one at a time, while others went for five-in-the-mouth and, by deft tonguing, managed to fire all five in machine-gun succession. One prominent advocate of five-in-the-mouth is Mike Fordham, five times world champion. 'It allows you to establish a winning stance,' he said. 'Get one pea on target and you can fire the rest in the same way, without having to re-load.' In the knockout phase, a contestant fires *alternately* with his opponent – which is designed to stop these five-in-the-mouth tactics, thereby proving ability at re-establishing aim and posture.

As the contest reached the final, we knew it would be a shoot-out between Mike Fordham and the 1990 champion David Trent. Then, the village hall was hushed. You could have heard a pin … make that a pea … drop. Mike was hungry for success: with ten peas he scored eight perfect fives and two threes, compared to David's six fives and four threes. 'He deserved to win,' said David, very sportingly.

I thought I detected a tremor of emotion on David's face, the natural disappointment of the man who came second. Was that a lump in his throat? Or maybe he'd swallowed a pea.

Contact: Judy Phillips, 21 The Slade, Witcham, Nr Ely, Cambs, CB6 2LA, UK.
Tel: 01353 778363

Pedal Car Enthusiasts

There are firms that specialize in new and used car parts. *Pedal* car parts, that is.

Collecting and restoring pedal cars is a hobby that is growing in size –

even if its practitioners are too big to fit into the vehicles. So if you cannot afford a real Rolls Royce, why not opt for a junior version? The toy manufacturer Triang once made a Rolls Royce Corniche Convertible – complete with working lights, horn, keys for the ignition, tax disc and even a log book!

Contact: Pedal Car Collectors' Club, 4/4a Chapel Terrace Mews, Kemp Town, Brighton, East Sussex, BN2 1HU, UK.
Or: *The Wheel Goods Trader* (a specialist magazine for pedal car enthusiasts), PO Box 435, Fraser, MI 48026-0435, USA.
Tel/Fax: 810 949 6282

People Forever

I asked Charles Paul Brown whether he expected to be alive and well in a million years' time. 'Yes,' he said, calmly. A million years is a blink of an eye when you believe you will live forever.

Let me make it absolutely clear that Charles was not talking about the immortal soul, or eternal life through Jesus Christ, or anything of that sort. He, and everyone else associated with the People Forever movement, believes that the *physical* body can go on and on and on, with as many years to live as there are digits in the expansion of pi.

Utter nonsense, you're saying. Yet I will leave you with this thought: it's well-documented that the placebo effect exists – if you believe you are going to recover from an illness, that belief will itself improve your chances of recovery. So, if you can convince yourself, to the innermost core of your being, that you will never die, isn't it possible that you will at least get more years on this Earth than if you didn't have that belief? Given that, is the idea of physical immortality really so stupid?

Contact: People Forever International, PO Box 12305, Scottsdale, AZ 85267-2305, USA.
Website: http://www.people-forever.org/. E-mail: herbbowie@aol.com

Philatelic Paraphernalia

This is my only example of a *meta*-hobby – a hobby about a hobby.

The magazine *Philatelic Paraphernalia* is aimed at collectors of material *relating* to stamp collecting: albums, catalogues, perforation gauges, tweezers, or anything else used in the hobby of philately – apart from the stamps, that is.

The magazine was founded in 1984 by Victor Short, a British enthusiast who has an extensive collection of stamp hinges, the small gummed pieces of paper used by philatelists to hold stamps in albums. 'I like things that no-one else is interested in,' said Victor, who gives lectures at stamp clubs on the history of the stamp hinge, and who admits to buying albums of stamps solely for the hinges they contain. 'To display my collection, I turn the stamps around, so that you can't see the faces – just the hinges.'

Contact: Victor Short, *Philatelic Paraphernalia*, Hunters Lodge, Cottesmore Road, Ashwell, Oakham, Rutland, LE15 7LJ, UK.

The Pillbox Study Group

In the centre of the town are one hundred tons of defiance: a six-sided concrete pillbox – a bulldog of a building, with a slit for a machine-gun to protrude like a Churchillian cigar. Though the box stands by the bridge for strategic reasons, its placing there seems to defend the town's very name against the invader: Bridgwater.

'This bridge would have been a Home Guard position,' said my companion, John Hellis. He pointed to the concrete blocks on both sides of the road which would have impeded the German tanks, had they invaded Britain in World War II. 'There would also have been foxholes and barbed wire, and some of these houses would have been taken over to cover the position. And if the first pillbox down the road didn't hold the Germans, then this second one would have blown the bridge.'

John had taken me to Bridgwater in his capacity as organizer of a 50-strong club of pillbox enthusiasts, the Pillbox Study Group. But what is there to study? Are not all pillboxes just a concrete hulk?

'There are different shapes,' said John. 'Regular hexagons, irregular hexagons, squares, trapezia. . .'

John estimates that group members have seen about 9000 pillboxes, so far. 'On some occasions,' he said, 'I've found the remains of, shall we say, other people's *entertainment*.' He remarked that in one box, he had found a pair of women's panties and a pair of stockings. 'But of course the most common use of pillboxes nowadays is as a public toilet.'

'Is that obvious?' I asked.

'Very obvious. When you visit a lot of pillboxes, you become hardened to it.'

Contact: John Hellis, 3 Chelwood Drive, Taunton, Somerset, TA1 4JA, UK.
E-mail: j.hellis@dial.pipex.com

The Pillow Fighting World Championships

USA, 4 July: Pillow Fighting Day.

For over 30 years' pillow fighters have gathered from all over the world to sit astride a metal pole mounted high over a mud pit in Kenwood Plaza Park, California, and proceeded to whack each other with regulation feather pillows.

'Our long-time champions take the pillowfights seriously and have perfected their technique over the years,' say the organizers, the Kenwood Firemen's Association, who use the event as a fundraiser. Undoubtedly, having firemen on hand is a great help at the championships: there is always someone standing by ready to hose off the losers.

Contact: PO Box 249, Kenwood, CA 95452, USA.
Tel: 707 833 2440 Fax: 707 833 4412
Website: http://www.kenwood.ca.us

The Pipe Smoking Contest

It was not an ordinary briar pipe but a long clay churchwarden.

I struck a match. The bowl was so far from my mouth it was difficult to see what was happening. I sucked, had a taste of tobacco, and then there were a few hairs of smoke. I sucked again. Nothing. 'Fifteen seconds to light your pipes,' said the referee. I panicked. Another match. This time Satan smiled on me: there was a glow . . . for a few seconds.

I was eliminated even before the contest had begun.

Every Shrove Tuesday, the Bull Inn in Harpole holds a pipe-smoking contest. The rules are simple: pipes containing a thimbleful of tobacco are issued to competitors; two minutes is given for lighting-up; and after that, the aim is to keep the pipe going as long as possible – and if a competitor has to leave the room, the pipe has to be left behind.

That last rule can cause a problem or two, particularly as the contest takes place in a pub, where drink is a factor. There was drama when a man had to run to the toilet, and then dashed back, hoping he could save his pipe. 'I ain't washed my hands,' he said. 'But I've got a weak bladder. I couldn't stop.' A woman beside him suggested that he could have done something with a plastic bag and a rubber band.

After an hour, we were left with just two competitors. Suddenly, one said, 'I'm going,' and he was out. The other blew smoke and said, 'I'm gone.' It was the closest contest in living memory: won by a single puff.

Contact: The Bull Inn, Harpole, Northants, NN7 4BS, UK.
Tel: 01604 830666
Or: *The Pipe Smoker's Ephemeris*, c/o Tom Dunn, 20-37 120th Street,
College Point, NY 11356, USA. (This is an excellent magazine devoted
to all aspects of pipe smoking, including pipe collecting, pipe fiction, and
pipe history. It also lists details of other pipe smoking contests around
the world.)

The Play Money Society

When a country changes the design of its coinage, it's common for the
new – and often smaller – coins to possess an air of unreality. The new
coin isn't *proper* money, it reminds you of the *pretend* coins you had as a
child. I suspect the only people who *wouldn't* experience this feeling are
those who regularly handle pretend money; people who would know the
precise look of unreal cash, and would never confuse it with the real
thing. I refer to the 40 members of the Play Money Society: grown-up
collectors of Monopoly currency, toy pieces of eight, interplanetary space
patrol credits and other examples of phoney dough.

Contact: The Play Money Society, Jack Phillips, 2044 Pine Lake Trail NW,
Arab, Alabama 35016-4541, USA.

The Plumb Line

Why would anyone collect plumb bobs? The following is a written
answer given by Bruce Cynar, who runs an association of bob collectors,
The Plumb Line.
Why bobs? By Bruce Cynar
'I bought my first bob, a three-pounder that looks like an upside-down
spade from a deck of cards, because I'd never seen one that shape. My
first few bobs were "Gee I like the shape." The next 50 or so were "I
don't have one like that yet." The subsequent 200 were "Honey, it won't
be too many more and I'll have a complete set." HA! How many collectors have said that? I now have over 600, mostly brass, and continue to
hunt for more. Is there a single reason, or are there 600 reasons? Mostly,
I like the shapes, some the patina, some the size and some the internal
reel or mechanism. But if I had to pick just one single reason, it would be

man's ingenuity and inventiveness. To the challenge "Put a weight on a piece of string" we have come up with thousands of solutions. I hope, in this case, we continue to reinvent the wheel.'

Contact: The Plumb Line, Bruce Cynar, 10023 Saint Clair's Retreat, Fort Wayne, IN 46825, USA.
Tel: 219 489 5004

The Poison Bottle Collectors' Association

I find the hobby of collecting poison bottles entirely understandable. A bottleful of death: if you were but to uncork it, and put it to your lips . . . one's mind takes a sip of the idea even if the bottle is empty. There's no need for suicidal tendencies to feel the fascination.

Some of the bottles have a strange beauty, as well. I wouldn't mind a cobalt-blue glass skull on my mantelpiece.

Contact: Joan Cabaniss, 312 Summer Lane, Huddleston, VA 24104, USA.
Website: www.antiquebottles.com/apbca/

The Polesitting World Championship

And from the people who brought us the Little Mermaid. . .

Every year, from late June to early July, rising from the waters at Karrebæksminde, Denmark, you will see, not a human with a fish's tail, but a human with a pole under his or her bottom. Actually, you will find a *set* of such poles, placed approximately 20 metres from the shore, each pole 3½ metres tall and a couple of metres from its neighbour. Though some poles will be human-less, emptied by the forces of backache and boredom: for the Polesitting World Championship simply requires you to sit – for *days*. Every year, since the first championship in 1991, the maximum time spent on the poles has increased by a few hours: at the time of writing, it is 130 hours, and about half of the 25 men and women who enter will stay the distance.

It is true that each pole is equipped with a small seat (30 x 50 cm), but there is no backrest, nor an armrest. Food and water *are* brought to the competitors by the organizers, but nothing else: the poles have three hooks for a competitor's equipment (sleeping bag, books, cigarettes, etc) – but if you drop anything, tough! No additional supplies can be brought out to you.

And the answer is 'Yes' to the question that I know is on your mind: 'visits to the bathroom' *do* take place on the pole.

Contact: Flemming Enggaard Hansen, Mikkelhøj 52, 4736 Karrebæks-minde, Denmark.
Or: Amy Philipsen, Tel: +45 55 44 26 74

The Pork Pie Appreciation Society

Just as magicians never say how a rabbit finds its way into a hat, so butchers never say how a pig is prepared for the crust: a good pork pie is filled with trade secrets. But even if the seasoning for a pie is a mystery, known only to the individual butcher, it is still possible to ask whether one butcher's pie is better than another. This 'pie connoisseurship' is practised by the Pork Pie Appreciation Society. In the ten years since the society was founded, the members have sampled about a thousand different pies, from mass-produced supermarket brands, with greasy pastry and cellophane, through to peculiar one-offs, such as pies topped with cranberries or apple sauce. But what qualities are they looking for in a pie?

First of all, the society's president, Kevin Booth, insists upon 'pie husbandry'. 'A pork pie should be at room temperature, like English beer,' he told me. 'If a pie's cold, it dulls the taste, and if it's a hot day, then the pie sweats.' This means that, in summer, pies should be kept in a cellar, or in a pantry, and in winter they should be kept in the kitchen. 'And above all, a pie should be fresh,' he said. 'There is a practice which we call "boosting", which means sticking the pie in the oven before eating it, to give the *appearance* of being fresh. But that's no good – it melts the jelly, and makes the pastry soggy.'

Then, there are some obvious fundamentals. 'The appearance of the pie is most important,' said Peter Charnley, the society's secretary. 'The pie should look well-done, well-cooked – but certainly not burnt or black. Ideally, there shouldn't be any jelly stains on the outside of the pie. Sometimes the pie is glazed, but that's rare these days.'

'But if it is glazed,' commented another member, 'there shouldn't be any fingerprints.'

'Next, there's the shape,' continued Peter, holding up a pie that had bulbous, bellowed-out sides. 'This one has got a traditional shape, which some people like, though most of us go for a straight-sided pie. What we don't like at all is a pie that looks like a custard tart, that starts narrow at the bottom and broadens out at the top.'

Does the shape really matter? To the members of the society, the answer is unequivocally 'yes' – and is a question of gender roles. They see the pork pie as a masculine, manly food, to be washed down with a pint of beer – and the custard tart is simply too feminine a form. 'We did have a woman member once, but it didn't last,' said Peter. 'It seems that women prefer watching TV to drinking beer and eating pork pies on a Saturday evening.'

The next consideration is the pastry. 'It shouldn't be like a biscuit. And you don't want it soft and soggy. The pastry should be thin, crusty and crispy,' said Peter.

'Like my mum's,' remarked a voice in the background.

And then came the first bite. All the time he chewed, Peter examined the pie, then he swallowed and said: 'You should take a look at the inside of the pie. You want the meat to be pinky and well-ground. And definitely no gristle. And the pie should be completely filled, with jelly in all the spaces under the lid, and around the sides, without any gaps. If there are gaps, we call them "rat runs".'

After each of the members had eaten a pie identical to Peter's, they made comments and passed judgements.

'Initially, it was completely devoid of taste, and the pastry was stodgy – I thought it was a shocker,' said one. 'But then halfway through, it had bags of pepper and improved a lot. I can't work it out. It's a pie of two halves. I'll give it seven out of ten.'

'It's a man's pie,' said another. 'With a high meat to pastry ratio and just the right amount of jelly. I'll give it nine out of ten.'

'A mild pie, fresh, it smelt porky as it should do,' said a third. 'Though I thought that it lacked a bit of salt. Overall, a nice pie. Eight out of ten.'

I was invited to comment; unfortunately, I lacked the insights of the connoisseurs. 'Quite nice,' I said. 'I'll give it seven.'

When all the marks were averaged, the result was 8.2: the highest mark for the year so far. It was then that the pie's fetcher, Bob Letven, revealed that it cost 42 pence and was made by Mrs Knight from Marsden, near Huddersfield. 'I think she's improved her pies recently by reducing the amount of salt,' he remarked.

'One of the tests of a pie is whether you need to put sauce on it,' said Peter. 'If the sauce doesn't come out, as with this pie, you know you're onto a winner. If it's lacking a bit of taste, you'll see people put brown sauce on it. And when people reach for the more exotic sauces – like oyster sauce or hot chilli sauce – then it's likely to be pretty rotten.' Very occasionally, a pie is so bad that it cannot be salvaged by any sort of sauce at all – and then the members have a special way of expressing their feelings.

'It doesn't happen very often, but sometimes we have to throw the pies into the stream near the pub,' said Kevin. 'You see them in the throats of the swans.'

Contact: The Pork Pie Appreciation Society, c/o The Old Bridge Inn, Priest Lane, Ripponden, Sowerby Bridge, W. Yorks, HX6 4DF, UK.

The Postage Due Mail Study Group

I have sinned as I sent, and been sinned against by senders: I have on occasions mailed – or received – letters with insufficient stamps on the envelope. Sometimes there has been no stamp whatsoever. If there can be redemption for these crimes, then it lies in the knowledge that collectors' items are thereby created: there is a society whose members are fascinated by unpaid and underpaid mail, and the way it is dealt with by the postal administrations of the world. Below is their contact address. I have no idea whether you will offend or enamour if you leave the stamp off your letter to them, nor do I know the protocol for enclosing an SAE.

Contact: The Postage Due Mail Study Group, Peter Williams, 41 Manvers Road, Childwall, Liverpool, L16 3NP, UK.

The Postal Mechanization Study Circle

Sorted: you've used the word – but have you had the experience? If not, join the Postal Mechanization Study Circle, whose members go on excursions to see post office sorting equipment.

'Unlike philatelists, we find the stamp the *least* interesting part of the letter,' said Tom Mullins, the circle's secretary, when I accompanied him on a trip to the Reading mail sorting office. 'In fact, the only thing that interests us about the stamp is the phosphor line which helps the post office to distinguish between first and second class mail.'

Most of the circle's 160 members, including Tom, did start off as stamp-collectors, though. This typically led to an interest in postmarks, then to an interest in the marks on letters connected with sorting the mail, then to the sorting machines themselves . . . Such as the machine I saw, which took a stack of thousands of identical white envelopes – presumably a mailshot from a large company – and which turned them into one continuous white horizontal blur.

'Even if you were to put a different coloured envelope into that pile, it would still be too fast to see,' said Tom. 'I should know – I've tried it.'

Contact: Tom Mullins, Secretary, Postal Mechanization Study Circle, 27 Elizabeth Road, Hunters Ride, Henley-on-Thames, Oxfordshire, RG9 1RA, UK.

Pot the Pudding

Toad in the Hole, Ring the Bull, Down the Slot – these old pub games are all in this book; and here comes a modern game to join them: Pot the Pudding.

Now played in twenty or so pubs across the UK, Pot the Pudding is essentially the ancient Asian game of caroms crossed with the more modern game of pool. The object is to use your finger to flick coloured counters into the corner pockets of a 30ins square board, mounted on a turntable. But why call it Pot the Pudding?

'We liked the traditional feel to the name,' said Martin Wilson, who invented the game with his business partner, Dennis Bradley. 'One of the pieces in the game is called a black pudding – and black puddings, of course, make you think of the north of England.'

Contact: The George Inn, Hubberholme, Skipton, N.Yorks. BD23 5JE, UK.
Tel: 01756 760223
(The above was the first pub in which I encountered Pot the Pudding. For details of other pubs that play the game, or to purchase a Pot the Pudding board, contact Bradley & Wilson on 01430 441231).

The Praed Street
Irregulars/Solar Pons Society

The most famous address in all literature is 221B Baker Street, London. To this day, the Abbey National Building Society, which occupies the site, receives letters addressed to Mr Sherlock Holmes.

There is another London address which concerns me here, namely 7B Praed Street – home to a fictional detective you are less likely to know about: Solar Pons. Created in 1929 by the American author August Derleth, Solar Pons bears a striking resemblance to Sherlock Holmes: Pons employs the same deductive methods to solve crime, is sidekicked by a doctor who narrates his adventures (Dr Parker), and he even possesses a more intelligent elder brother, Bancroft, to parallel Holmes's Mycroft. Pons is, of course, a pastiche of Holmes, whose exploits take place a few years after those of the great Victorian detective.

Solar Pons deserves his place in this book because he has his own appreciation society, the Praed Street Irregulars (PSI). Just as Pons is a tribute to Holmes, so the PSI's name is a tribute to the most famous Sherlock Holmes appreciation society in the world, the American-based Baker Street Irregulars. Furthermore, the PSI has a British-based scion society, the Solar Pons Society of London – which derives its name from the leading British Sherlockian society, the Sherlock Holmes Society of London.

Thus, in the Fountains Abbey Inn on Praed Street, I met Roger Johnson, the man who runs the Solar Pons Society of London. Perhaps I should say Roger Johnson *is* the Solar Pons Society of London . . . he is the only officer, he keeps no membership records, and the society doesn't actually *do* anything – there are no meetings and no publications.

'This wasn't intentional,' said Roger. 'It's just the way things worked out.'

Over a pint, he explained that he became interested in the Solar Pons stories in 1970, while he was a student. 'The Pons canon is scandalously little-known in Britain,' he said, adding that part of the charm of the 70 stories is the presence of egregious Americanisms, because August Derleth never visited London. 'So characters refer to a "stoop", not a porch,' he said. 'And people live *on* a street, rather than *in* it.'

The young Roger decided to correspond with the Praed Street Irregulars – correspondence among the members is the main activity of the PSI – and was asked by the founder of the PSI, Luther Norris, if he would establish a British scion. Being an impoverished student at the time, Roger agreed only on the condition that it involved as little work and expense as possible. Luther Norris accepted these terms – and he had membership cards designed and printed, and enrolled a number of American members.

'I in turn have enrolled numerous others over the years,' said Roger. 'Unfortunately, Luther kept no records, so I began not knowing who most of my members were. It seemed an omen. The society has continued along the same lines. It just *is*. It will exist as long as I enjoy the exploits of Solar Pons. But as the sole officer, I am more than happy to answer enquiries.'

So, I enquired. I learnt that Pons shares Holmes's love of the word 'meretricious'; has an arch-enemy to parallel Moriarty called Baron Ennesfred von Kroll; and that his 'Further Adventures' are being written by the British author Basil Copper. Pons smokes a pipe and wears a deerstalker, though he eschews cocaine. If anything, Pons is more theatrical than Holmes, with a great passion for disguises, even when they are unnecessary.

After that, Roger opened his wallet and passed me a membership card: I was now enrolled in the Solar Pons Society of London. It struck me that, by virtue of our conversation in the Fountains Abbey Inn, the society had held its first-ever meeting.

There was one final act: a society excursion. So we walked along the street to see the residence of the great detective. 7B, we discovered, is now a college of languages and societies. I toyed with the idea of sending the occupants a letter, addressed to Mr Solar Pons – but sadly, I am sure that it would be returned to sender, marked 'Addressee unknown'.

Contact: Praed Street Irregulars, Dr George A Vanderburgh, PO Box 204, 420 Owen Sound Street, Shelburne, Ontario, Canada, LON ISO. Tel: 519 925 3022 Fax: 519 925 3482 E-mail: gav@gbd.com And: The Solar Pons Society of London, Roger Johnson, Mole End, 41 Sandford Road, Chelmsford, CM2 6DE, UK.

The Princess Kitty Fan Club

When a human being is outstandingly intelligent, he or she is *brilliant*; if that contains a hint of sparkling like a gemstone, then here is intelligence which is *chatoyant*. That is, a jewel with the lustre of cat's eyes. . .

Princess Kitty has been called the smartest cat in the world, the Einstein of felines. Once an abused stray kitten, shot at by a BB gun and half-starved, she wandered into the yard of Karen Payne of Miami when she was no more than six months old. 'I took her to a vet,' said Karen, 'and he gave her injections and said, "This is a very intelligent animal. You should teach her some tricks".' Karen took the vet's advice – and the results were extraordinary, proving that you *can* teach a young cat new tricks. Princess Kitty can now perform over a hundred: she sits, stays, jumps through a hoop, slam-dunks a little basketball, and even plays a toy piano. (Her favourite tune is 'Three Blind Mice'.) She is also the only cat in the world with her own fan club – members can learn about Princess Kitty's latest adventures, including her modelling assignments

189

and TV appearances, in the newsletter *Paw Prints* ('All the *mews* that's fit to print') and a video of her tricks is available for purchase.

'Princess Kitty knows her place,' said Karen, 'which is slightly above everyone else.'

Contact: The Princess Kitty Fan Club, PO Box 430784, Miami, FL 33243-0784, USA.
Tel/Fax: 305 661 0528 Website: http://www.princesskitty.com
E-mail: kittyprin@aol.com

The Procrastinators' Club

I have sent out many letters to this club or that, asking if they would kindly send me a back issue or two of their newsletter. When I sent a similar letter to Les Waas, the President of The Procrastinators' Club of America, he replied: 'You asked for a back issue of our newsletter. You should know that *all* of our issues are back issues.'

With 10,000 members worldwide – and probably half a million more who haven't got round to joining yet – the club is mostly concerned with jokes about procrastination. ('About 14 years ago, an attorney in Edwardsville, Ohio, wrote asking the first step in forming a chapter. We sent him information. Recently he wrote again, asking, "What's the *second* step?" ')

Nonetheless, there is a serious side to the club. Les, a lifelong procrastinator (he only recently replaced his black-and-white TV) seeks to praise procrastination as a habit of well-adjusted, effective, happy people. 'The alternative to the procrastinator is the anti-crastinator,' he says. 'And *they're* the ones who get the heart attacks and ulcers.' He also believes that procrastinators often do the best work. In his business, which is advertising, the best ideas are often those that come at the last minute, right up against the deadline.

'A good procrastinator,' commented Les, 'enjoys life more.'

Contact: Procrastinators' Club of America, Box 712, Bryn Athyn, PA 19009, USA.

Psychic Questing

There was a cinema-sized audience in the hall in Holborn, London, and on the screen at the front a slide projector cast an image: two brushstrokes of red on a white background, suggesting a sword. Everyone there would have known the significance: in 1979, Andrew Collins, the meeting's organizer, travelled to a secluded part of the Worcestershire countryside, where he unearthed a sword bearing Mary Queen of Scots' personal monogram. He used no metal detector, nor a map where X marks the spot; he was led to the sword by 'psychic clues'. Andrew, who has told the full story in his book *The Seventh Sword*, has in effect created a new form of psychic research: *psychic questing* – the retrieval of hidden artefacts located by psychic means.

Psychic questing can be carried out in many different ways. It could be that a quester will have a dream, or a hunch, about a hidden artefact; or maybe a group will start the quest by meditation. When Andrew Collins addressed the meeting he said: 'You could have a psychic vision in the bath, in the toilet, or down the pub.' However, the initial insight is unlikely to give the precise whereabouts of the object. Additional research will probably need to be done in libraries and local archives, so even if you're not terribly psychic you can still play a role in a questing group.

Since 1979, literally dozens of objects have been found by psychic questors. Or are *claimed* to have been found: the fruits of the questers' labours are so impressive that one is entitled to ask whether they come from a genuine fruit-tree, or whether they were purchased at a green-grocer's. But whatever the degree of one's scepticism, it's well worth attending the annual Psychic Questing Weekend. Here, questers give lectures about their latest discoveries: jewellery, silver boxes, crucifixes, daggers, and much more besides, are all exhibited in a display cabinet at the back of the hall.

Such a rich and varied jetsam has been found by these psychic beach-combers that Andrew Collins himself has now become rather jaded: 'I don't get a lot out of it any more,' he told me. 'I've seen it too often.'

Contact: Psychic Questing Conference, PO Box 189, Leigh-on-Sea, Essex, SS9 INF, UK.

Pumpkin Growing

If you know of the comic-book superheroes the Fantastic Four, then you will also know that one of the Four is the Thing. The Thing is a monster: orange, knobbly and huge. I mention this because the Thing is the only thing I know that is comparable to the orange, knobbly 1061lb *colossus* on the cover of the February 1997 issue of the World Pumpkin Confederation's magazine.

The confederation's members are dedicated to growing ever-larger pumpkins – and breaking the 1000lb barrier had been a club goal for over a decade. 'The accomplishment of this goal is a club victory and a victory for mankind as well,' says the editorial. The growers earned themselves a prize of $53,000.

So what now? Does the club disband? Not at all. 'The next big money will be on 1500lb,' continues the editorial. 'Now I've heard that "That's not possible!" Don't tell that to World Pumpkin Confederation members!'

Contact: World Pumpkin Confederation, 14050 Rt. 62, Collins, NY 14034 USA.
Tel: 716 532 5995 Fax: 716 532 5690 E-mail: lgourd@aol.com

Pumpkin Throwing

'There's a nominal prize of $250, but nobody plays for the money – the real prize is one year's bragging rights,' says John Ellsworth, a blacksmith from Lewes, Delaware, USA, a former world champion in the sport of pumpkin throwing. 'The title means a lot to me – you don't get many chances in life to crow that you're world champion of something.'

To become a pumpkin thrower, one needs to build a machine which might be compared to a Roman ballista – only instead of rocks, it hurls pumpkins; to become world champion, your machine needs to throw a greater distance than the other machines in the annual pumpkin-throwing contest in Lewes. And in fact, the machine doesn't have to be of the ballista-type: any pumpkin-throwing device will do, as is demonstrated by the classic contest of 1990.

In near perfect weather – a clear sky and temperatures in the high 70s – nine machines took part: three catapults, two slings, three centrifugal devices and . . . an aircraft. 'The guy just flew over the field and dropped the pumpkin from his plane,' says John Ellsworth. 'But his first two tosses landed short of the starting line because he was trying to keep the plane from crossing the line.' The pilot's third toss achieved 460ft – but this was not enough to win. It was overtaken by a giant crossbow catapult powered by the compression of 40 steel railroad-car springs, mounted on a dump-truck chassis – which threw 593ft; but even this was insufficient. The contest was won by the centrifugal Ultimate Warrior machine – a tall A-frame, with a throwing arm driven by a belt attached to the axle of a one-ton truck. This achieved a record-breaking throw of 774ft 7ins.

In recent years, compressed air cannons have smashed this record. In 1995, the record was 1617ft. In 1996, 2716ft. In 1997, 3718ft.

There are signs that the next generation of pumpkin thrower could smash even these distances. There are rumours that a man in Virginia is experimenting with a liquid nitrogen powered pumpkin thrower. Liquid nitrogen expands on contact with the air – and it is conceivable that such a machine could hurl a pumpkin *five or six miles*.

Contact: Amy Simpson, 1551 Savannah Road, Lewes, Delaware 19958, USA.
Tel: 302 645 0747

Pun Intended

There is the odd time in life when a pun is useful, such as when inscribing a card that bids farewell to a colleague. Someone called Ruth, say, moving onto a better job, might merit a comment like 'You have no pity, to leave us so Ruthlessly'. Once in a while, a pun is okay. It leaves the right taste in the mouth.

But once in a while is not good enough for some people. There are persistent punsters, whose favourite hobby is making cheap *jeux de mots*. They even have their own specialist newsletter – because *Pun Intended* is written in nothing but puns. Let's hear some examples, taken from its pages:

'I've heard that plants will grow better if you talk to them. I can't do that because I never studied any fern languages.'

'Bill Clinton says he smoked pot in the 1960s. Someone asked: "Did you smoke it in the rain?" "I may have smoked it in the rain," he said, "but I didn't in hail."'

'My friend had some trouble with the starter on his car. "Solenoid?" I asked. "Of course!" he replied. "Why should it bother anyone other than me?"'

'I might have been a psychic televangelist but I couldn't find anyone to fund a mentalist preacher. . .'

Et cetera, *ad nauseam*. The magazine is an offshoot of the American pun-making championships, the O. Henry Pun-Off (named after the American short-story writer who was himself a notorious punster) and every year in Austin, Texas, a crowd of up to 2000 gather to hear habitual punsters duel. A topic is chosen at random and then contestants are given up to five seconds to make a pun. Suppose for instance, the topic is Real Estate:

'I wanted to learn to fly a plane but there were more gauges than I could deal with.'

'Let's see. I've got a hat, shirt, pants and socks. That's four clothes.'

'I'm sick of these glasses. I'm getting contracts.'

'It's the lease you can do.'

'I've got some puns left in me, eight, nine, maybe tenement left.'

So it goes on, to the accompanying groans or even boos of the audience, until one competitor is gonged out for taking too much time, and the other goes through to the next round. The contestants are said to have developed a real sense of camaraderie – possibly because they would not be tolerated anywhere else.

Me? I have a problem. Or rather, had. I have been trying to come up with a pithy ending to this article – an ending which is itself a pun, hopefully of some sophistication, and one which summarizes everything in the previous paragraphs. My salvation came when I opened a dictionary of synonyms and discovered that an alternative word for pun is calembour. The solution was then obvious. Some people make lots of puns and others call 'em bores.

Contact: Pun Intended, c/o Gary Hallock, 1124-A Clayton Lane, Austin, Texas 78723, USA.
E-mail: c.hallock@mail.utexas.edu
O.Henry Museum Website: http://www.ci.austin.tx.us/parks/ohenry.htm

(The Worldwide Friends of) Punch & Judy

It was an elocution lesson, but banish all thoughts of the rain in Spain. For in this class, any approved vowels were made as if by comb-and-paper, while favoured diphthongs shared something with the cries of parrots and crows. 'Try: "Judy, Judy, Judy",' said the tutor, himself squawking. Then: 'Kissy, Kissy, Kissy.' And: 'Walky, walky, walky.' I did my best. But the words came out not so much as units of language but as a root-ti-toot-ti-tooey stream. It's not a simple art, this mastery of received pronunciation according to Mr Punch.

I was at the Worcestershire home of Glyn Edwards, a television producer who also happens to be one of Britain's leading Punch & Judy 'Professors', and founder of the Worldwide Friends of Punch & Judy. (For the violent puppet show is *not* just a British phenomenon – there is a Punch & Judy tradition in the USA, Canada, Australia and other countries.) Glyn is indeed the only one of the men of the booths to be in any way professorial; for he, unlike the rest, is prepared to teach students the traditional skills of Punch & Judy in regular 'That's the way to do it' courses. Even so, he is wary about too many people knowing the secret of Punch's squawk; and I can tell you only that a *device* is involved, and there is a knack to using it. 'Some people get the voice straight away,' said Glyn. 'With others, it takes six months. But when people do learn the trick, they walk around like bullfighters, full of pride.'

The voice is just one aspect of the professors' art. Glyn led me to a backroom where he had set up a blue-and-white striped booth. With a crocodile-puppet stuck on my left hand, Mr Punch on my right, and a string of sausages of my forearm, I stepped into the canopied anarchy of the Punch & Judy world. I proceeded to learn the basics of a 'behind you' sketch – the crocodile steals up on Mr Punch, but as soon as Punch turns around, the croc vanishes. It happens again and again, until, as you would expect, Punch gets to work with his club while the crocodile snaps at his nose. 'Kids do get a bit frightened of the crocodile,' said Glyn. 'They feel as if it could jump out and get them.'

Though there are variations in the show's plot, the one thing that never changes is Punch's contempt for society's conventions; a baby gets thrown about a lot, and for Punch there would be no problem in answering the question: 'Do you still beat your wife?' But Glyn is no sympathizer of bowdlerizing the script. 'Condemning the violence of Punch & Judy is about as sensible as condemning the violence of Tom and Jerry,' he said.

In any case, sensitivities about the show appear to be subject to fashion. In Victorian times, the wife beating and child abuse passed with few comments; but to the church-going audience of the day the appearance of the Devil-puppet was the cause of considerable disquiet. Similarly, twentieth-century campaigns against capital punishment have led to qualms about the scene in which Mr Punch tricks a hangman into executing himself. 'What next?' Glyn asked. 'Will animal rights activists protest about the mistreatment of the crocodile?'

I closed those jaws with a satisfying snap. I think the crocodile's safe. But what about the sausages? One day, there's sure to be a vegetarian who calls for their omission.

Contact: The Worldwide Friends of Punch and Judy, 'Professor' Glyn Edwards, Punch's Oak, Cleobury Road, Far Forest, Worcestershire, DY14 9EB, UK.
Tel: 01299 266634 Fax: 01299 266561
Website: http://www.primenet.com/-freshdlc/wwfPJ.html

Pyramidology

Ten miles south-west of Cairo, at the desert's very edge, stands the largest, the heaviest, and – so some would say – the most wonderful building on Earth. That the Great Pyramid at Giza is largest and heaviest has never been open to question. Containing the masonry for thirty Empire State Buildings; possessing four facets each with an area of five acres; being over two million individual blocks – who would deny this pyramid its wonder? Not I. Probably not you. And definitely not the 600 members of the Institute of Pyramidology – for whom the building at Giza has no-one but God as its architect; and for whom the pyramid's complex mathematical structure reveals the Almighty's plan for our world. Full of wonder about the institute itself, I went to meet its organizer, Fred Binns.

Fred had already posted me four volumes – handsomely bound, tooled in gold – containing the heart of the institute's message; so I felt well-prepared. Written by the institute's founder, Adam Rutherford, the pages of *Pyramidology, Books I to IV* greet you with an extraordinary mixture of square root signs and biblical prophecy. It is no exaggeration to say that an ardent pyramidologist will carry out trigonometric calculations to five decimal places in an attempt to prove the veracity of the book of *Daniel*. Pyramidologists believe that God's will is encoded in the building's dimensions, and that a careful study of the Giza geometry reveals such divinely-known data as the spheroidical shape of the Earth (that is, the amount by which the Earth deviates from a true sphere by 'flattening at the poles'); the mean distance of the Earth from the sun; and the volume of the Earth's crust above mean sea level.

'Do you ever wonder whether you're reading things into the pyramid that simply aren't there?' I asked Fred. 'Always possible,' he answered, 'and you can quote me on that.'

The reason for all this interest can be found in the book of *Isaiah*, Chapter 19, verses 19-20: 'In that age there shall be, in the centre of Egypt and yet at the border, a monument that shall be a sign and an altar to the Lord.' Could this be the pyramid at Giza? It stands at the centre of Egyptian life – to this day, Cairo buses run out to the pyramid – yet also it is on the country's border, for beyond there is nothing but the Sahara Desert. But a true pyramidologist will seek and find further confirmation of *Isaiah*. For instance, in the original Hebrew Bible, all the letters of the alphabet also represented numbers and so it is possible to add up the value of the words used in a biblical passage and arrive at a total. For the *Isaiah* quotation this turns out to be 5449 – which happens to be, in ancient inches, the exact height of our good old friend at Giza!

Most astonishing of all is the pyramidologists' claim that the building has an inbuilt calendar predicting major events in human history. By measuring the pyramid's passageways and adopting a scale of 1 inch = 1 year and by a careful interpretation of the building's geometry and architectural symbolism, pyramidologists claim they can find predictions of the Rise of Napoleon, the 1848 Revolutions, the Great War of 1914 and so on. It is worth noting, too, that in one interpretation of the pyramid's chronology, the year 1979 has special significance – for back in the 1950s, pyramidologists predicted that in that year would be the end of the world. I asked Fred how the institute's members felt when 1979 came and the cataclysm didn't happen. 'Very disappointed,' he said.

Contact: The Institute of Pyramidology, PO Box 136, Chesham, Bucks, HP5 3EB. UK.
Tel: 01494 771774

Q

Qigong

My feet were on the earth while my head was touching the heavens.

That was what my teacher, Simon Lau, told me to imagine as I stood motionless and breathed slowly. Also, I had to visualize that water was running down my body, as though I were under a waterfall. After a while of this, my leg muscles began to shake. I rocked on my feet, trying to make the spasms stop. My eyelids fluttered. Then my eyes opened and Simon's seemed to open at the same time. He smiled. We had been through the simplest of Qigong exercises.

Qigong (which means 'vital force') is a 4000-year-old Chinese system of physical, mental and breathing exercises. After about 100 days of Qigong training, a strange energy is said to circulate around the body. 'It felt as if my whole body was about to explode,' says a statement written by one of Simon's students. 'My head, which was whipping around in a frenzy, seemed set to rip off my shoulders and rocket into orbit. And all the while I moved around the room dribbling, panting and fighting an imaginary opponent. In short I must have resembled a drug-crazed evangelical epileptic.'

Well, I watched Simon do some advanced Qigong, including a rippling arm movement which I've seen breakdancers do, and a head movement which reminded me of a tortoise emerging from its shell. 'Do Qigong daily,' he said. 'Do it first thing in the morning, before you answer the phone, before you watch the news, before anything. Just do it, not for any specific reason.' And that's about it. I don't understand Qigong; except that the muscular spasms in my legs *may* have been the merest indication of what it's like when the energy flows. Yet I felt the most profound satisfaction for having met Simon: at last I had a 'Q' for the book.

Contact: *Qi Magazine*, PO Box 116, Manchester, M20 3YN, UK.
Tel: 0161 929 4485 E-mail: qimag@michaeltse.u-net.com

R

Radio Survey Collecting

When you're a teenager, the pop music charts dominate your life. By that I mean, the *music* featured in the charts – I don't mean the printed statement, the actual *list* of the top 40 or the top 100. That's a passion for adults.

Radio survey collectors collect charts such as the New York station's WABC77's weekly music survey, or the 93 FM WZAK Rhythm Roster – 'Here's your list of the hottest jams in Northeast Ohio!' At the heart of the hobby is the newsletter *RadioActive*. At one time, it was in fact called *Radio Survey Collector* – the new name reflecting a broadening of scope, to serve the interests of people who collect the likes of radio *jingles*.

Contact: *RadioActive*, Dennis Burns, 10248 Lola Court, Concord Township, OH 44077, USA.
Website: http://members.aol.com/DennisKQV/
E-mail: dburns@broadcast.net

The Railway Performance Society

There is a passage in G.K. Chesterton's *The Man Who Was Thursday* which describes the yearning for reality in general, and train journeys in particular, to be *otherwise*: 'Why do all clerks and navvies in the railway trains look so sad and tired? I will tell you. It is because they know the train is going right. It is because they know whatever place they have taken a ticket for, that place they will reach. It is because after they have passed Sloane Square they know the next station must be Victoria, and nothing but Victoria. Oh, their wild rapture! Oh, their eyes like stars and their souls again in Eden, if the next station were unaccountably Baker Street!'

Perhaps this is the key to the hobby of train timing, as practised by the Railway Performance Society, whose members sit with stop-watches, recording whether the train they have boarded is going fast or slow. Of course the journey itself can never change, never astound nor surprise, but the timing *can*. Further insights into the motivation of a train timer can be found in the society's booklet, *Train Timing: A Beginner's Guide*:

'Most participants enjoy a strong sense of sporting challenge. Even in these days of greater standardization, there is a thrill to be gained from studying the form and assessing whether the conditions are right for a fast run: the weather conditions, temporary speed restrictions in force, likely signal checks, the requirements of the schedule, and the motivation of the driver. Will the train be late enough to encourage the driver to regain time? Or is it so late as to dispirit him? Paradoxically, some of the best performances are obtained when the augury is unfavourable.'

Contact: Railway Performance Society, Bruce Nathan, 7 Salamanca, Crowthorne, Berks, RG45 6AP, UK.

Rat Fancying

It is probably the only magazine in the world with an obituary column devoted to rodents. For in *Pro-Rat-A*, the official journal of the Fancy Rat Society, mourners can find an opportunity to share their grief: 'I was heartbroken when Ricky and Percy died two years ago. I still get a lump in my throat every time I look at the holes in my curtains and the gnawed speaker leads.'

Needing to experience such rats myself, I arranged a meeting with Malcolm Cleroux, president of the Fancy Rat Society. 'The relationship of fancy rats to sewer rats is like the relationship of domesticated dogs to wild dogs,' he told me. 'Our rats are very affectionate. There's absolutely no truth in the myth that they jump for your throat.'

He proceeded to place a rat on my shoulder. 'They love cleaning your ears,' he said. 'They put their snouts in and they sort of wriggle around.'

I have to say that in a very short time, I too became a rat-fancier. They let you stroke them, they'll take chocolate drops from your fingers, they'll crawl up and down your arms. One of them scampered across my shoulders and tickled my neck with its claws. Yet for many people the mere thought of touching a rat would bring on a screaming fit. Why? Malcolm believes it has something to do with the tail, so naked, so worm-like. 'If rats had furry tails they wouldn't have such bad press,' he said. 'They'd be like squirrels. Though in reality, squirrels are very, very aggressive, not like rats at all.'

In Malcolm the rats have found their perfect PR man. I sat on his sofa, with a rat on my lap, as he sold me their virtues: 'Hamsters are a bit vicious, and ferrets – oh my goodness, do they smell; but rats are wonderful to hold and very clean. Some of our members have them running around the house.'

Contact: Angela Horn, Publicity Officer, National Fancy Rat Society, 26 King's Orchard, London, SE9 5TJ, UK
Or: American Fancy Rat and Mouse Association, 9230 64th Street, Riverside, CA 92509-5924, USA
Website: http://www.pacifnet.net/afrma/

Razor Collecting

'I've always had to collect, ever since I was a boy,' said Renzo Jardella. 'If I see more than two of anything, I'll collect them.' Twenty years ago, Renzo saw a couple of interesting razors in a market. 'That's how it began,' he told me. 'Now, if I don't get a couple of razors in a week, I get withdrawal symptoms. I'm a real junkie. I need a fix.'

A razor resembling an ice-cream scoop, for catching the lather; a Japanese razor that can be folded flat, like a credit card; a Shick Injector, in which new blades push out the old, like a bolt-action rifle; a semi-circular Roman blade from 500BC and a pennant-like Egyptian blade from 2000BC; a huge Bic, several feet long, used as a promotional device; hospital razors, sterilized and sealed for shaving body hair; women's underarm razors, children's toy razors, clockwork razors, electric razors . . . 150 words so far in this section. If every word were a different razor, I would still require twenty times the space to convey the experience of a visit to Renzo's home. Over 3,000 shaving devices in all.

'Do you use any of your collection to shave?' I asked.

'No,' he said. 'I use any old disposable.'

Contact: Safety Razor Collectors' Guild, PO Box 885, Crescent City, CA 95531-0885, USA.
Or: Renzo Jardella, 53 Selwyn Avenue, Richmond, Surrey, TW9 2HB, UK.

The Realm of Redonda

Skye is an island, Redonda is an island; and if I hum the song of the former, my soul sets sail for the latter:

> Speed, bonny boat, like a bird on the wing;
> 'Onward', the sailors cry;
> Carry the lad that's born to be king . . .

But if the helm in one's head is to steer a true course to Redonda, a little more is required. One needs to hear that tune – while imagining what that bird on the wing might be doing while he's up there . . .

'Redonda's only export was guano,' said William Leonard Gates, when I visited him at his home in Norfolk. 'And even that came to an end when a hurricane blew away the phosphate company's shacks.' He proceeded to describe this godforsaken island: one mile long, a third of a mile wide, and located thirty-five miles south-west of Antigua, Redonda is just a useless lump of rock. There is no beach, no landing place, no harbour – and not a single human inhabitant. Redonda, indeed, is but an aircraft-carrier for seagulls – and yet, Redonda is so much more.

I stood up in William Leonard Gates's lounge and read aloud: 'I, Stephen Jarvis, hereby solemnly swear full and faithful allegiance to His Majesty, Leo, Fifth King of Redonda, his heirs and successors, and do promise henceforth to be a loyal, true and trustworthy member of his Realm, to abjure imposters and to keep the laws of the realm always. GOD SAVE THE KING!'

Then Mr Gates – or King Leo, as he would now be known to me – bade me kneel on a footstool. 'If you would be good enough to bow your head,' he said, and with a sword – a small sword (well, all right, a letter-opener) – he touched my shoulders. 'I dub thee knight,' he proclaimed. 'You may stand – arise Sir Stephen!' Then he presented me with a book-let of stapled, photocopied papers, *The Realm of Redonda Members' Handbook*.

'Would you care to turn to page 17,' he said. 'You'll find there a copy of the national anthem.' Together we sang a noble hymn, 'O God Who Gave Our Island Soil', which describes Redonda as a 'hallowed place' and its beauty 'the treasure of our race'. After that, we sat down, and King Leo's wife, Queen Josephine, served us with tea and biscuits. The interview – or audience – began. Was it really true, I asked, that Redonda had a navy?

'Well, of course, it's symbolic,' said His Majesty. 'And just as we have dukes and barons, we naturally have to have the leaders of the armed forces – so, the navy, as well as the army, are represented. But we don't have anybody below the rank of officer because Redonda isn't like that.' Thus, there are no able seamen in the navy, just as there is no Redondan middle class, lower class, or peasantry. 'And we haven't actually got any ships at the moment – but we do have an admiral of the fleet.' He fetched a photograph of a man dressed in an admiral's uniform – this was Baron Sargasso. 'Of course, his uniform puts the army to shame,' said the King, 'because all they can manage is a couple of forage caps and a stick.'

Now, you are probably thinking that this is just a silly joke – a few men dressing up for a bit of play-acting and tomfoolery. And in truth, I could reinforce that impression by quoting selected passages from the *Members' Handbook*. Consider, for example, the crown jewels, whose chief glory is the great Ruby of Redonda. 'The full story of this magnificent jewel,' says the handbook, 'is one of the great romances of history; suffice to say that, having been lost for centuries, it was eventually found in use as a rear reflector on a lady's bicycle.' But what makes the Realm of Redonda a unique phenomenon is that it is both tongue-in-cheek *and* completely serious.

The story of Redonda goes back to 1493, when Columbus sighted the rock: he gave it a name – it is said that the outline of the rock reminded him of a church in Cadiz called Santa Maria de la Redonda – but being unable to land, Columbus never formally claimed the island. Redonda remained unclaimed – simply because it was physically useless – until 1865; then along came Matthew Dowdy Shiel, an Irish sea-trader from nearby Montserrat. Shiel, being overjoyed at the birth of his first son (his ninth child, after eight girls) decided to celebrate by taking a party of friends to Redonda – where he declared himself king of the island.

And so began a royal line which stretches to William Leonard Gates. Initially, the title was passed to Shiel's son, but since then the reigning monarch has chosen a friend as successor, and drawn up documents of abdication. It should be realized, though, that only the title is passed, not the ownership of the island. In 1872, the British Government annexed Redonda and handed it to Antigua. Indeed, the last time a king set foot on the island was in 1880.

'I first heard about Redonda thirty years ago when I attended an evening class in heraldry,' said King Leo, now 61, who when not engaged in royal duties, works as a teacher and academic historian. 'I happened to meet the man who designed the Redondan coat of arms.' He showed me a shield featuring three seagulls on a blue background with a white stripe across the centre – the stripe representing the guano. 'It struck me that here was a charming and unique quirk of history which should be preserved – I succumbed to the magic of Redonda and I've never been the same since.'

The odd thing is, I knew what he meant. Patriotism was building inside me: a love for the combination of bird-droppings and name-dropping which is implied by saying 'I had tea with the King of Redonda'. Like the twenty-five other currently registered members of the Realm, I had found my true nationality.

'Everybody I've told about Redonda ends up feeling that there is more to this than a funny club where you have a bit of a laugh,' commented His Majesty. 'There's this deeply psychological reaction that people get. Though in some cases it goes a bit too far. People get obsessed with Redonda.' How obsessed? 'Oh, obsessed to the point of thinking themselves king.' And he began telling me about the problems he has had with pretenders to the throne . . .

203

Postscript: The above piece was originally written in 1995; since then, there have been numerous developments in the Realm, whose membership is now about a hundred strong. For a start, Redonda's navy has at last acquired some ships – two, to be precise: a Caribbean sailing vessel, *The Mandalay*, which often passes near the island, and also, *The King of Redonda*, a model galleon on display in an Arts and Crafts Gallery in France. Furthermore, the Realm's armed forces have been augmented by a *space* fleet, able to offer the island symbolic defence against alien attack. And toe-wrestling – featured elsewhere in this book – has been adopted as Redonda's national sport!

Contact: The Secretary, The Redondan Foundation, World's End, Slip Road, Low Thurlton, near Norwich, Norfolk, NR14 6QB, UK.

Re-enactment Societies

Historical re-enactment is not just a hobby, but a vast subculture, with an estimated 1,500,000 participants worldwide, organized in thousands of societies, recreating the lives and warfare of every period in history. I have focused here upon one society, the Celtic Re-enactment Society, but at the end of this section you will find some general contacts for re-enactment groups.

It's difficult sitting down when you're wearing chain-mail. It's even harder standing up again.

The 26,000 washers that made up my singlet were not only heavy enough to make me overbalance and then totter like a wino, they did a fine job of chilling my skin. Imagine 26,000 doctors applying stethoscopes all over your front and all over your back and all at the same time – get the idea? As I sat in that lounge in Fareham, I was getting some ideas myself; like maybe those doctors would have to be summoned – and would my mail give me total protection against the swipe of a sword? 'No, not total protection,' said a man in a helmet. 'But it's better to have a couple of broken ribs than your lungs on the floor.'

All around, people were fingerpainting their bodies blue, adding snaky designs to faces and arms. Some had rinsed their hair with a dye and stiffener known as limewash, which gave a bleached, punkish look. As I prepared to go into battle alongside the members of the Celtic Re-enactment Society – a group devoted to recreating the lives of the ancient Britons – the talk was always of the invader. 'What did the Romans ever do for us, except build a few viaducts?' said a member called Karl (though he preferred to be known as Lucetius). 'In the

Rhineland, the Celts wiped out 12,000 of them,' said another of the lime-washed. He added: 'It was brilliant,' and told of how, sometimes, he dresses up as a legionnaire because 'everyone loves to beat up the Romans'. As for the fight on the menu, that was to be an inter-tribal skirmish, Celt against Celt. A lot of this went on twenty centuries ago, and if one tribe managed to kill the chief of another tribe his head would end up pickled in cider, kept for years and brought out at parties. 'Doesn't that strike you as a bit barbaric?' I asked. 'No,' said Paul, one of the youngest members, 'it's just like collecting football trophies.'

With the woad still wet upon our cheeks, we took a car, not a chariot, to the war zone, which happened to be the football pitch of the local school. Before long, the swords were windmilling through the air – but of course blows have to be pulled. 'Anyone can pick up a sword and hurt someone,' said Jane Smith, the group's organizer, as she gave me my first lesson in combat: our blades clashed in slow-motion. 'It takes real skill,' she said, 'to fight someone so that they leave with their arms on.'

Contact: Celtic Re-enactment Society, Jane Smith, 44 Iron Mill Close, Fareham, Hants, PO15 6LB, UK.
Tel: 01329 842055
Website: http://www.satellite.demon.co.uk/brigantia/index.html
E-mail: karl@lugodoc.demon.co.uk
Or: *Call to Arms* (A newsletter listing many re-enactment groups) 1 Lyng Lane, Diss, IP22 2HR, UK.
Website: http://www.calltoarms.com
Or: (For a website giving general information on re-enactment) http://www.compulink.co.uk/~novar/renact.htm
Or: Society for Creative Anachronism, PO Box 360789, Milpitas, California 95036-0789, USA.
Tel: 408 263 9305 or 800 789 7486 Fax: 408 263 0641

Reincarnation International

In seventeenth-century Germany, I was a quack doctor called Johannes Korman. With my pestle and mortar, I created medicines using ingredients such as ground bones, clay, flower extracts and wood. Sometimes I cured the sick, but on one occasion my potions led to the death of a patient. I was nearly lynched by a mob. They wanted to drown me – I can still recall my wife's screams as they dragged me to the river – but I pleaded with them, quoting my past successes as a man of medicine. Eventually, they let me go.

That was a 'previous life' that I recalled under hypnosis. Though I do not believe that it was a genuine case of reincarnation – I suspect that my subconscious conjured up all the images – I would certainly recommend hypnotic regression as an *experience*. If you'd like to find a hypnotist yourself, or simply want to read accounts of previous lives, then take out a subscription to *Reincarnation International*, the world's only magazine devoted to reincarnation.

By the way, I know how I died, as Johannes: I started experimenting on myself. When suffering from a head cold, I saw a rat swimming and this led me to think about the curative liquids which might be extracted from its organs. After all, rodents survive in the dankest and most inhospitable of environments – if only human beings had the resilience of rats. So, I picked up a branch, struck the creature, killed it, flayed it and chewed a piece of its skin. Soon afterwards I succumbed to a fatal fever.

Contact: *Reincarnation International Magazine*, PO Box 10839, London, SW13 OZG, UK.
Tel/Fax: 0181 241 2184 Website: http://www.dircon.co.uk/reincarn/
E-mail: reincarn@dircon.co.uk

The Remote Imaging Group

Central Europe looked like the surface of a brain; Alaska, like tree-bark; a mountain-range in Norway was a fern.

I was in a back room, surrounded by electronic equipment, and staring at images on a TV monitor. With me were two members of the Remote Imaging Group, whose hobby is watching the pictures of the Earth that are taken by weather satellites.

'That,' said one, pointing at a white blob on the screen that resembled a piece of cauliflower, 'is a thunderstorm over Africa.'

Contact: Remote Imaging Group, c/o Ray Godden, Wayfield Cottage, The Clump, Chorleywood, Herts, WD3 4BG, UK.
E-mail: 101602.376@compuserve.com

(The International Society of) Reply Coupon Collectors

I shall take this opportunity to remind readers that, if they're sending a letter to a society based abroad, they should enclose an International

Reply Coupon (IRC) to cover the cost of a reply. Although if you send IRCs to *this* society, they'll probably add them to their collections – as they did with the one I sent. 'The "4.95" in the lower left corner was new for Great Britain for me,' I was told by Dr Alan Hauck, the society's founder, in a letter whose postage he gladly paid.

The '4.95', in tiny print, meant that the coupon was printed in April 1995, two and a half years before I posted it. Concern with such minor variations is the very substance of IRC collecting. The basic designs of the coupons tend to remain unchanged across time (for *decades*) and across space (many countries use *identical* coupons). Thus collectors' eyes are focused upon the flexible elements, such as the price.

Contact: International Society of Reply Coupon Collectors, c/o Dr Alan Hauck, PO Box 165, Somers, WI 53171-0165, USA.

Ribbon Tin News

As surely as 'Video Killed the Radio Star', so the word processor killed the typewriter. Innocent bystanders caught in the crossfire included the typewriter ribbon, and the ribbon tin.

But ribbon tins still have their fans. Launched in 1993, *Ribbon Tin News* is a nostalgia-fest of office supplies. Only in this publication can you see a photo-feature about *Klean Type*, *Betterite*, *Plenty Copy* and other obsolete brands of spool. Or read about the sheer inkiness of *Bull-Frog Brand*, whose tin-lid once promised '75,000 impressions of the letter "E".' As one of the 90 subscribers remarks: 'As long as I have some, ribbon tins live on.'

Contact: *Ribbon Tin News*, Hobart D. Van Deusen, 28 The Green, Watertown, CT 06795, USA.
Tel: 860 945 3456

The Richard III Society

He was the wickedest wicked uncle of them all – a monster who killed his own nephews as they slumbered in their beds. A king? Yes, he was that; but one who schemed and murdered his way to the crown; a fiend, twisted in body as in soul – worthy only of stinking rags, never ermine. For this was Richard the Third, Richard Crookback: the foulest toad, the cruellest snake – in all of English history, the most rat-hearted, ravenous wolf.

Or maybe, you know, he wasn't so bad after all.

The idea that Richard III (1452–1485) has had a raw deal from history is what unites the members of the Richard III Society. In London, I met Elizabeth Nokes, the society's general secretary. 'He was almost certainly not a crookback,' she said. She told me that the famous portrait of Richard has been doctored, with a raised shoulder painted in afterwards. 'And there's no evidence he had a withered arm,' she added.

According to the society, Richard was quite an enlightened ruler. In his two-year reign, he helped the poor, fought injustice, reformed the machinery of the law and administration and was a patron of Caxton. He showed unshakeable loyalty to his brother, Edward IV, and had the good fortune to marry his childhood sweetheart. Could such a man *really* have killed the Princes in the Tower?

Richard, it seems, was the victim of a propaganda campaign mounted by his successors, the Tudors, who would do anything to blacken him and justify their hold on the throne. They were ably assisted by the man who wrote Richard's biopic, William Shakespeare. At one time, the society would put articles into theatre programmes, telling the audience that Shakespeare had written a pantomime version of history, with Richard as a boo-hiss villain.

Yet if Richard wasn't evil, then just how *good* was he? Elizabeth counselled a degree of caution: there are some people who go too far in the other direction. She mentioned in passing one book in which Richard was portrayed as so heroic he was almost St George.

'For his time,' she said, 'Richard III wasn't too bad a chap.'

Contact: Richard III Society, Membership Services Department, PO Box 247, Haywards Heath, West Sussex, RH17 5FF, UK.
Website: http://www.r3.org

Ring the Bull

If the Who had been *Ye Who*, a wandering troupe of medieval minstrels rather than a sixties rock band, then undoubtedly one of their greatest songs would have gone: 'He's a ring-bull wizard . . .'

Because in Ye Olde Trip to Jerusalem, reputed to be the oldest inn in England – it's been a brewhouse since 1070 – the regulars also play one of the oldest pub-games in England: ring the bull. Affixed to the wall is a genuine bull's horn, and several feet in front is a cord, suspended from the ceiling, to which is attached a bull's nose-ring. The object is to swing the nose-ring so that it lands on the horn. To be a real wizard, you should be able to do this by several different techniques: letting the cord swing three times back and forth before the ring lands; standing with your back to the horn as you launch the ring; and sitting beside the horn and launching outwards. I wondered whether any other pubs still played the game.

'Well, someone did tell me that there's a pub that plays it on the island of Fiji,' said Marilyn, the inn's manager. 'But we thought it was a bit too far away to start a league.'

Contact: Ye Olde Trip to Jerusalem, 1 Brewhouse Yard, Nottingham, NG1 6AD, UK.
Tel: 0115 9473171

The Road Roller Association

'Sometimes, I think that steamrollers are very nearly *alive*,' said Steve Arrowsmith. 'I mean, I'm an engineer and I know there's a logical reason for everything they do and the way they behave, but there are so many variables with steam, it appears as if the rollers have moods, as if they have a spirit and a will of their own. That's why I'm fascinated by them.'

Steve is the chairman of the Road Roller Association, a group of 450 enthusiasts dedicated to steamrollers and indeed to all equipment connected with road-making: water carts, tar boilers, stone crushers, grit spreaders, even road signs and hand tools. The members do not simply preserve this equipment – they *use* it, by holding weekend courses on roller driving and road-making. Can such labour be leisure? I had to find out.

The course began with Steve leading a group of novices, including myself, to the perimeter road of a grass verge. Here rested a ten-ton Aveling & Porter steamroller, built in the 1920s. Friendly as a kettle, practical as a tea-urn, splendid as a samovar – all these qualities could be seen in the roller. It was perfectly preserved in a livery you might describe as dragon-green.

'The first thing you do when you get on the footplate is to check the water level,' said Steve, climbing up. He indicated two glass cannisters and told us that if the water were too low, the firebox would explode. He pointed out the locations of the brake, the pressure gauge, the throttle and the gears. 'There are two speeds,' he said. 'Slow and even slower.'

So, I climbed up alongside Steve. For this initial run, he would be working most of the controls – I would simply have to steer. Anyway, off we chugged. I was feeling as proud as I imagine a rajah feels on an elephant's

---

209

howdah. Then Steve said, 'You're getting a bit close to the grass . . .'

'What's happened?' I said.

'We're stuck,' was the reply.

Steamrollers, I learnt, are not only slower to respond than a car, they behave very differently on grass. 'We'll have to dig the mud away from the back wheel,' said Steve, jumping down and assessing the situation. 'And then we'll need to get some ashes or grit down there. Grass is fatal for rollers.'

Twenty minutes later, we were still stuck and a tractor had to be summoned to pull us out with a chain. 'Has this ever happened on a course before?' I asked, hoping that it was a common occurrence. 'No,' said Steve, 'I have to say it hasn't.'

Contact: Road Roller Association, c/o Dave Crampton, 6 Norwood Close, Mackworth, Derby, DE22 4GA, UK.
Website: http://www.drayner.demon.co.uk/rra.html

The Road Transport Fleet Data Society

'I don't consider fleet data that unusual,' I was told by the secretary of the Road Transport Fleet Data Society, whose members are fascinated by garbage trucks, supermarket delivery vans, ambulances, and other vehicles organized in fleets. 'We're just filling a gap. There are plenty of societies for aircraft, buses and trains, but nothing else in the world, as far as I know, for the subjects we cover.'

Even the society's main activity could be seen as an exercise in gap-filling: for by various methods, including members' observations and contacts with fleet operators, the society attempts to record the licence plate number and locality of the vehicles in every fleet, with as few gaps in the data as possible. So here is a typical page of their newsletter, covering new service vans in the British Gas fleet in July 1996:

M835 XEV	Stretford	N306 CTW	Clifton	N784 DNO	Glasgow
M836 XEV	Cricklewood	N308 CTW	Cheadle	N819 DNO	Stockport
M855 XEV	Merseyside	N319 CTW	Harpenden	N849 DNO	Chesterfield

.　　　　.　　　　　.　　　　　.　　　　.
.　　　　.　　　　　.　　　　　.　　　　.

(64 lines of data omitted here)

.　　　　.　　　　　.　　　　　.　　　　.

| N848 DWC | Stockport | N869 FHJ | Oldham | N91 GVX | Caerphilly |

Contact: Road Transport Fleet Data Society, c/o Peter Jarman, 18 Poplar Close, Biggleswade, Beds, SG18 OEW, UK.

Rocket Mail Enthusiasts

Flick through the contact addresses in this book, and you'll understand that I have used a stack of blue stickers that say 'Par Avion/By Air Mail'. I have yet to use one that says 'Par Fusée/By Rocket Mail'. They do exist: created by enthusiasts who combine two hobbies in one – stamp collecting and model rocketry.

The idea is to design envelopes which proclaim their escape from the Earth's gravity; then, stuff as many as possible in the nose cone of your model rocket, blast off, and recover by parachute. I'm exaggerating – it is a *little* more complicated than that (the extra weight of the mail means that you have to use more powerful motors, for instance) – but if you successfully recover the envelopes, you'll have an instant collector's item. Some philatelists are prepared to pay good prices for pieces of rocket mail.

Now I wonder whether I can interest the model submariners in a similar idea . . .

Note: Although there is not a society or newsletter devoted exclusively to rocket mail, the hobby is promoted in the 'Rocket Mail Topics' section of the Journal of the American Airmail Society. *This section is edited by the gentleman below and his model rocketry club, the Paisley Rocketeers, is one of the most active groups of rocket mail producers.*

Contact John D. Stewart, 15 Bushes Avenue, Paisley, Scotland, PA2 6JR, UK. Tel: 0141 884 2008

The Roller Coaster Club

There was a time in Andrew Hine's life when he would see roller coasters everywhere. Going past a building site, he would notice a crane, and think: looks like a roller coaster. A glimpse of planks of wood on a truck would lead him to reflect: could be used in the construction of a support-lattice. No longer in a state of such obsession, Andrew is nonetheless still *interested* in roller coasters. How interested? Oh, he and his wife got married on one.

Contact: The Roller Coaster Club of Great Britain, PO Box 235, Uxbridge, Middlesex, UB10 OTF, UK.

Tel: 01895 259802 E-mail: rccgb@aol.com
Or:The American Coaster Enthusiasts, PO Box 8226, Chicago, IL 60680,
USA.

S

The Sacred Relics Research Group

If a comparison is obvious, it's unnecessary and shouldn't be made; but some comparisons are *so* obvious they are simply required. It would be peculiar – like a breach of etiquette – if I did not make a connection between Jonathan Boulter and Indiana Jones. Oh, there's no dust on Jonathan's hat – for the good reason that he doesn't wear one; and when we met, he didn't put the coils of a bullwhip down upon the table. What he shares with Indiana is a goal: Jonathan Boulter, a librarian from Willesden Green in London, intends to be the man who finds the Lost Ark.

At the time of our conversation in Ye Olde Swiss Cottage pub, Jonathan had just formed the Sacred Relics Research Group. As examples of the relics of interest to the membership, he mentioned King Solomon's Ring and King David's Golden Harp. But central to the group's endeavours is the search for the most famous filing cabinet in history: the Ark of the Covenant – the box of acacia wood and gold containing the tablets of the Ten Commandments.

'The Ark could be in Egypt. Or in Iraq,' he said. 'Some people claim it's hidden in the Vatican. Or on Mount Nebo. Or under the Temple Mount in the centre of Jerusalem. Or in Calvary – two American archaeologists claim to have seen it there. It could even be in Rennes-les-Chateaux in the south of France. A few years ago, it was reputed to be in Northern Ethiopia.'

It seems to get around a bit, then. 'Ah, but there could be more than one Ark,' he said. 'There could be replicas.'

I think it's time to return to obvious comparisons. I think we have to talk in terms of finding a slender metal thing, used in sewing, within a pile of dried grass. Jonathan isn't put off. 'I do believe,' he said, 'that I'll see the Ark one day.' He paused a moment. 'I'm open-minded as to when that might be.'

Contact: Jonathan Boulter, 4 Huntington House, St Paul's Avenue, Willesden Green, London, NW2 5SR, UK.
Tel: 0181 459 5520

The Saint Club

It's when he's doing nothing in particular that you know an adventure is about to begin.

He'll be sitting in a bar – and a man is shot with a blowpipe. He'll be walking along a bridge – and the wind carries top secret documents into his hand. He'll be making a phone call – and the man in the next booth drops down dead. (Heart attack? No. A small, broken glass phial is found on the booth's floor.) As Simon Templar puts it himself: 'Trouble is one of the things that sort of happen to me, like other people catch colds.'

But any man who had blown his nose *that* often, *that* much, would have worn out his sinuses long ago. Because Templar has encountered continual trouble ever since 1928, when Leslie Charteris, his creator, penned the first Saint novel, *Meet the Tiger*; and in television series, radio plays, films, comic strips, pulp magazines as well as in fifty-four books, Charteris fleshed out the career of an adventurer with no flesh at all: a stick-man with a halo.

Everyone has heard of the Saint. Most people of a certain age will be able to whistle the theme tune from the Roger Moore television series; but not so many will have heard of the Saint Club. One of the oldest surviving appreciation societies in the world, the Saint Club was founded in 1936, by Charteris himself. Its membership cards send up the fact that the Saint, unlike other crime-fighting heroes, has a downright disreputable side to his character:

'Notice to the Police: the bearer of this card is probably a person of hideous antecedents and low moral character and upon apprehension for any cause should be immediately released in order to save other prisoners from contamination.'

For the Saint is no goody-goody. He carries two ivory-handled knives – one called Anna, strapped to his arm, and one called Belle, on his leg. He will steal, he will murder. He *can* be considered a latter-day Robin Hood – taking from the unworthy rich and giving to the deserving poor – but he will keep ten per cent for himself as a fee. Above all, the Saint is no Sherlock Holmes. 'As a general rule,' Templar remarks, 'problems in detection bore me stiff – it's so much more entertaining to commit the crime yourself.'

Contact: The Saint Club, c/o Arbour Youth Centre, Shandy Street, Stepney, London, E1 4ST, UK.

St Michael of the Wing

'You could say that my attachment to the principles of monarchy is an interest like stamp-collecting,' said Malcolm Howe. 'And just like some stamp-collectors, I decided to specialize.'

As if to continue the analogy, he brought forth an album: it bulged with articles clipped from newspapers and magazines, all relating to the Duke of Braganza, the heir to the unoccupied throne of Portugal. '*Pretender* is not a word we use,' he commented. 'Portugal may have been a republic for 80 years, but it was a monarchy for 800 years before that, and I think it will become a monarchy again when the time is ripe. We say that the Duke is the *heir* to the Portuguese throne.'

Malcolm said 'we' not because he assumed a royal status himself, but because he was speaking on behalf of a group: the Association of St Michael of the Wing, a band of fifteen English men and women who seek nothing less than the restoration of the Portuguese monarchy. Affiliated to a parent association of about 100 Portuguese members, Malcolm and the other English Luso-monarchists meet three or four times a year, culminating in a church service on St Michaelmas Day, when they dress in white ceremonial robes and Portugal's old monarchist national anthem is played. 'Portugal is essentially Catholic, but here most of the members are High Anglican,' he said. More to the point, what is the origin of this group? And why should an *Englishman* like Malcolm be a member at all?

Malcolm told me that he experienced the first stirrings of monarchist sympathies in his schooldays. 'In 1952, I was at school in Bolton and we were all instructed to go to the hall. I thought some boy was going to get expelled, or that there was going to be a public flogging. But the head-master said that the King had died. I was very impressed – all the shops closed, there was mournful music on the radio. And remember, this was the aftermath of the War – and with the approach of the Coronation, Britain became a much more colourful place.'

Over the years, Malcolm came to believe that the alternatives to a monarchy were not worth having: a president, steeped in party politics, could never become a truly national symbol, nor hope to rival the tradition and charisma of royalty. 'A country that loses such trappings loses a great deal,' he told me. Nonetheless, why focus on *Portugal's* royal heritage?

'I like the Portuguese people,' he said. 'They have a lot in common with the English – their sense of humour is similar. And I like the ambience, the food, the wine and the history of Portugal. And through some friends over there, I met some monarchists. But I'm coming more and more round to the idea that there's something to kismet, to fate, to destiny,' he added. 'Because I happened to be on holiday in Portugal in 1983 soon after the ancient order of chivalry of St Michael of the Wing was revived.'

That order, in its original incarnation, dates back to 1171, when the Portuguese fought the Moors. On the battlefield, the King of the Portuguese, Afonso Enriques, invoked St Michael the Archangel – and, according to legend, a vision of St Michael's wing appeared across the sun. This vision inspired the Portuguese to victory; and, after the battle, the King rode to the Cistercian monastery in Alcobaça and founded an order of knights, St Michael of the Wing. 'The wing across the sun makes a beautiful story. And I believe in it,' said Malcolm. 'Though there are other people who say it was invented by a crafty monk.'

Although the original order was short-lived, its name was revived in modern times by Portuguese monarchists, who surfaced in the wake of the 1974 revolution, along with other organizations which had been suppressed by Salazar's regime. The revived order commemorates the legend in its white ceremonial robes, which represent the habits of the Cistercian monks and which bear the symbol of a wing against a sun, surmounted by a crown. Furthermore, at their church services, the members say a prayer to St Michael: 'St Michael, Archangel, defend us in the day of battle, be our guard against the snares and wickedness of the Devil.'

'When the Duke of Braganza visited England, he knighted all the members,' said Malcolm. 'Dubbing is a peculiarly English tradition, but the Duke tapped us on the shoulder – he said he had seen the film *Henry V* and so knew vaguely what to do.'

Contact: Malcolm S. Howe, 31 King's Court North, 189 King's Road, Chelsea, London, SW3 5EQ, UK.

The St Swithun's Society

On 15 July in the year 971, the body of St Swithun, Bishop of Winchester, England, was exhumed, and moved into the cathedral – in defiance of his wishes that he be buried in a simple grave, beyond the cathedral's wall. It is said that the occasion was marked by a very heavy rainstorm and that it rained for 40 days after. As the poem says:

> St Swithun's Day, if thou dost rain
> For forty days it will remain;
> St Swithun's Day, if thou be fair
> For forty days 'twill rain nae mair

One thousand years later, in a library in Ontario, Canada. . .

Three employees, Norman McMullen, Elizabeth Newberry and Kevin Dark had an in-joke: if they wanted to procrastinate, they would say 'I'll do it on St Swithun's Day.' But on 15 July 1974, they were getting together with friends after work at the library and realized it *was* St Swithun's Day. They simply had to celebrate. 'That marked the first official celebration of the day and the birth of the new St Swithun's Society,' remarks Norman McMullen.

The society now assembles three or four times a year, in the hope that it will rain. There was the time they went for a picnic on St Swithun's Day and there was 'an absolute downpour'. Then there was the time when they met at a bar and it was bucketing down. 'The other patrons wanted us to leave because they felt our presence had brought on the rain,' says Norman. Not to be dampened, they marched along the street in the rain, carrying their banner and singing appropriate tunes such as 'Stormy Weather', 'Raindrops Keep Falling on My Head', and 'Wait 'Til the Sun Shines, Nellie'.

Norman even keeps a jar of genuine St Swithun's Day rain in his freezer. 'Legend has it,' he comments, 'that any fruit or vegetable touched by St Swithun rain will be sweeter and juicier.'

Contact: Norman McMullen, President, St Swithun's Society, 427 Lynett Crescent, Richmond Hill, Ontario, Canada, L4C 2V6.
Tel: 905 883 0984

Sand Collecting

When Colin Fuller returned from his holiday in Cornwall, he brought home a souvenir: the beach. Three hundred polythene-bagfuls of sand – and even that was not enough.

'I haven't had time to look at these yet,' he told me, as he threw back a cupboard door in his hall, to reveal a pile of unopened parcels. From the postage stamps, I could see that he was in touch with Germans, Belgians, New Zealanders, Italians. These parcels could easily have been birthday gifts – only, if any were held to the ear, and shaken, there would have been an intriguing sound: something of a shuffle, something of a rattle. . .

'Unfortunately, a lot of packages of sand get opened by the Customs, looking for drugs,' commented Colin. 'I can't get anything at all from Bolivia.'

The parcels had been shipped to Colin by fellow members of the International Sand Collectors' Society. Members have different approaches to collecting – for instance, some are fascinated by 'historical' sand. Regarding a sample from Ulysses Beach in Italy, a collector writes in the society's newsletter *The Sand Paper*: 'For all one knows, this may have been the very sand on which, as Homer says, "the man who was never at a loss", slept after he was shipwrecked, following his adventures with the sorceress who turned his followers into swine.'

Then there is the collector who establishes a psychic link with the sand. Whenever she receives a new sample, she sticks her finger into it, and tries to receive extra-sensory impressions of the area from which it was taken. *The Sand Paper* remarks that 'Travel is not practical for her and this is her way of visiting new places.'

'Collecting means whatever you get from it,' commented Colin. His own approach to collecting seems – at first sight, anyway – to be more orthodox; a geological interest in sand, developed from a childhood curiosity about rocks and minerals. But then, he turned on his TV.

He took a phial of sand, magnified it with a microscope and, by means of a tiny TV camera, transmitted the image down a cable to his TV set: six or seven yellow grains filled the entire screen. I have to say that this had undertones of a religious experience – for surely no-one but God would study individual grains? Well, no-one but God and Colin Fuller.

'People say I'm mad, but I'm never happier than when I'm looking at sand,' he said. He explained that he did more than just observe. By means of a computer linked to the TV screen, he is able to analyze the smoothness of the surface of the grains – even to *measure* the grains; and if he sees one that is of particular interest, he takes action.

'I get a pair of tweezers and try to pick up the grain I like,' he said. 'But that's more difficult than you might think.' To demonstrate, he took a pencil and poked the sand under the microscope. When the pencil's tip was magnified, it was so large that it blanked out the TV screen. Exactly the same would happen with a pair of tweezers – so a search for a certain grain is effectively a blindfold fumble. 'It can sometimes take me a couple of hours to get the grain I want,' he said.

'Don't you ever feel,' I asked, 'that that's a waste of time?'

'No. Who's that poet who spoke about seeing the world in a grain of sand?' (It was William Blake.) 'Well,' he said, 'it's true.'

Contact: Colin Fuller, c/o Northamptonshire Natural History Society, The Humfrey Rooms, 10 Castilian Terrace, Northampton, NN1 1LD, UK.

Sand Marbles

Just as tennis is played on grass or clay, so marbles is played on ... no, to appreciate this game you have to begin by *scrapping* that analogy. Marbles and sand marbles have virtually nothing in common, except that marbles are used in both. Every year in Royan, France, 10 tonnes of sand is used in the construction of a sand marbles course, for the World Sand Marbles Championship. The sand is moulded into mountains, ravines, bridges, and tunnels; and threading up, down, on and through all these is a 60 metre circuit, featuring many twists and bends. The object of the game is to flick a marble around the circuit, in the minimum number of strikes. If sand marbles can be compared to any other activity it is perhaps . . . well, actually I can't think of anything to which it *can* be compared. But every year, representatives from 20 nations face each other in the championship.

Contact: Mondial Billes, Production 114, 114 Avenue Emile ZOLA, 17200 ROYAN, France.
Fax: 05 46 05 92 48

The Sausage Appreciation Society

'Some of the letters I receive do demonstrate *such* an obsession for sausages that sometimes it borders on the worrying,' said Robert Metcalfe, the man who runs the Sausage Appreciation Society.

Eating is just one aspect of the society's work. Even before the society was fully up and running, Robert was responsible for organizing a sausage song contest. 'There were 450 entries,' he said, 'in every musical genre.' With that, he turned on a cassette of sausage music. There was a reggae track, which had the lyrics:

> Don't want the stone age, the bronze age, the iron age
> I want the sausage
> I want to share my sausage with you.

Followed by a moody Irish ballad, of considerable beauty, which spoke of men who had:

> Strings of chipolatas
> For their inamoratas

Yet music is not the only food of love for people with this love of food. Robert spoke of organizing an exhibition of sausage *paintings*.

'Will you accept avant-garde?' I asked.

'Any style will do,' he said, 'as long as there's a sausage in it.'

Contact: Alison Cook, Sausage Appreciation Society, PO Box 44, Winterhill House, Snowdon Drive, Milton Keynes, MK6 1AX. UK.

Sedan Chair Racing

It is said that successful sportsmen win the 'inner game'; and mental attitude is more important in sedan chair racing than other sport. The three-person teams – two male carriers, one female passenger – must not only dress as Georgians, but *think* of themselves so, by not referring to events or people occurring after 1804. Judges are even empowered to add or subtract penalty or bonus time points, according to the dress, manner and general deportment of the teams.

Contact: Lancaster Tourist Information Centre, 29 Castle Hill, Lancaster, LA1 1YN, UK.
Tel: 01524 582394

SETI for Amateurs

In all likelihood you will have heard of SETI, the Search for Extra-Terrestrial Intelligence. You may not know that this activity can be carried out by *amateur* astronomers – there is no need for a huge radio telescope dish and a billion dollar budget.

One technique open to amateurs – and it's not the only one – is *optical SETI*. It works on the assumption that, if an alien civilization wishes to alert the universe to its presence, then it may well use laser beams to do so. Since all the power that a laser emits is concentrated into a very narrow band of wavelengths, its signal should show up against the huge quantities of natural radiation emanating from the aliens' planet and the star it orbits. So all you need to do is hook a telescope up to a filter that only transmits the band, and you could detect the laser . . . admittedly, you still need to *find* the band and this may take several lifetimes, but it's worth it if you make the greatest discovery in human history, isn't it?

Contact: *SETIQuest Magazine*, Helmers Publishing Inc., 174 Concord Street, PO Box 874, Peterborough, NH 03458-0874, USA.
Tel: 603 924 9631 Fax: 603 924 7408 Website: www.setiquest.com
Or: The SETI League, Inc., 433 Liberty Street, PO Box 555, Little Ferry, NJ 07643, USA.
Tel: 201 641 1770 Fax: 201 641 1771 Website: http://www.setileague.org
E-mail: info@setileague.org

Note: *SETIQuest Magazine* takes an eclectic approach to SETI, whereas the SETI League's primary concern is to build a worldwide network of amateur radio astronomers, who will use small dishes, a few metres in diameter, to scan radio frequencies in the hope of finding alien signals.

SHADO-USECC

Star Trek fandom is too mainstream for this book. I would rather mention the 100 enthusiasts who call themselves SHADO-USECC, which stands for Supreme Headquarters Alien Defence Organization – United States East Coast Control: fans of Gerry Anderson's lesser-known sci-fi series from 1970, *UFO*.

The basic premise of *UFO* was that aliens in spinning-top flying saucers would attempt to invade the Earth – and teams of SHADO operatives (led by Commander Straker, played by the American actor Ed Bishop) would attempt to shoot them down. Whilst some reviewers compared the acting to that of the performing puppets in another Anderson series, *Thunderbirds. UFO* does have a certain bizarre seventies chic. Who can forget the female operatives on Moonbase in their purple wigs?

The trouble is, those wigs, and *UFO* in general, *have* been forgotten. As an article in SHADO-USECC's newsletter states: 'In the past twenty years, how many articles about *UFO* have been published in the USA? There have been four – and two of those were linked to the *X-Files*, *Dark Skies* and *Independence Day*. And how many letters from *UFO* fans have been published? There have been seven, and I know this because I wrote five of them.'

Contact: Helen Weber, Commander, SHADO-USECC, 514 Delaware Ave, Lansdale, PA 19446-3417, USA.

The Shakespeare Oxford Society

My copy of the *Complete Works of Shakespeare* is leather-bound and in the centre of the cover is a gold-leaf portrait of Stratford-upon-Avon's most famous son. Or rather, there used to be a portrait, for three-quarters has worn away. To the members of the Shakespeare Oxford Society, that means a quarter too much is still left: for if they could, they would scratch with sharp fingernails until not a flake of Shakespeare's features survives. Then, they would have the book re-gilded with a new, aristocratic face: that of Edward de Vere, the 17th Earl of Oxford, whom they believe to be the true author of the greatest body of work in the English language.

To Oxfordians, the text is a hunting-ground – because events from de Vere's life, or his family history, may be alluded to within the plays. Take *Henry V*. There is a scene in a French camp when a nobleman asks a constable of France: 'The armour that I see in your tent tonight, are those stars or suns upon it?' This may be an allusion to a historical episode during the War of the Roses, when the de Veres, wearing the star of the Lancastrians, were shot by their own side's archers by mistake – a mist had descended upon the battlefield and made the star seem like the sun of York.

At its most extreme, the search for de Vere references leads the Oxfordians to re-examine Shakespeare's use of words like 'every', 'ever' or 'never', because he might be punning upon his own name. But why is this? What is the case for Oxford?

It begins with the mysterious life of William Shakespeare of Stratford. Scholars have scoured Elizabethan documents and have uncovered reams of information about major poets and many minor poets, but all they have about Shakespeare are three dozen references, not one of which describes him as a poet or playwright. Also, Shakespeare is supposed to have spent 29 years in London – yet there is not a single record of anyone seeing the great actor or playwright in the flesh. Strangest of all, in an era when the death of an English poet meant a lavish funeral and the composition of eulogies, Shakespeare's demise went completely unnoticed. Even Ben Jonson – who later claimed to have been a great admirer and friend of Shakespeare – expressed not the slightest regret when the Swan of Avon died. He didn't even mention the event.

In contrast, de Vere is *known* to have written poetry. It is also known that he wrote under a pseudonym (though that pseudonym is not recorded). Furthermore, being an aristocrat, he had personal experience of royal courts; he had exactly the right background to describe the events in the plays. And it is intriguing that the family crest shows a lion holding a spear.

Well, who knows, the Oxfordians may be right – and opinion may be swinging their way. Recently, I saw a copy of the book *The 100: A Ranking of the Most Influential Persons in History* by Michael H. Hart, and in this revised second edition, Hart has become so convinced by the Oxfordian arguments that he has handed Shakespeare's place to de Vere.

So a thought occurs to me: if the Shakespeare Oxford Society eventually comes to represent the received wisdom, will I one day find myself writing an article about a fringe group called the de Vere Stratford Society?

Contact: Shakespeare Oxford Society, PO Box 263, Somerville, MA 02143, USA.
Tel: 617 628 3411 Fax: 617 628 4258
Website: http://www.shakespeare-oxford.com
E-mail: everreader@aol.com

Shovel Racing

There are various ways of descending a snowy slope: skis, snowboard, skidoo, toboggan, luge, shovel . . . *Shovel*?

A quarter of a century ago, when snowmaking was in its infancy, ski resorts hired maintenance crews to repair bare patches on the slopes. Crew members were armed with a grain scoop (a large D-handled shovel) and eventually, they discovered that sledding down the hill while sitting on the shovels was the fastest way to get back to the bottom. This developed into the sport of shovel racing, which holds its championships every March at the Angel Fire Resort in New Mexico.

But to me, there seems to be a general principle of unusual leisure here: tools into toys. (Think of the musical saw, or blowlamp collecting, or axe racing.)

Contact: Angel Fire Resort, PO Drawer B, Angel Fire, NM 87710, USA.
Tel: 505 377 6401 Fax: 505 377 4200
Website: http://www.angelfireresort.com

Sick Bag Collecting

Some people ask friends and family to bring back a souvenir from a trip overseas; others will be delighted with an airsickness bag.

David Bradford holds the British record for sick bag accumulation – 1112 bags so far. Unfortunately, there is a disturbing modern trend in sick bags, which David hates: the generic bag, used by many airlines, which doesn't even have the airline's logo on the outside. Far more interesting are the likes of: the Finnaviation of Finland bag, which features a drawing of a reindeer spewing ice cubes; the Ansett New Zealand bag which says, 'If you need this, maybe you need *Sea Legs* – New Zealand's most popular travel sickness remedy'; and the Air Afrique bag, from the Ivory Coast, which has a drawing of a woman giving birth – presumably designed to suggest that no matter how bad you feel there are more painful experiences.

As you might expect, David's interest in sick bags began by using one.

'I was serving with the army in Cyprus, and I was offered a ride in a Phantom jet,' he told me. 'I was sick at the speed of sound.' The bag in question being *Bag, Air Sickness, Nato Stock No 8105-99-130-2180* – however, in his haste to eject into it, David completely forgot to switch off the microphone in the face mask. 'For a few moments the inside of the pilot's dome must have echoed like the sound-track of a monster movie,' he said.

Contact: Dr David Bradford, 40 Bolton Avenue, Richmond, North Yorkshire, DL10 4BA, UK.
Tel: 01748 824520
Or: The World Airline Historical Society, 13739 Picarsa Drive, Jacksonville, FL 32225-3265, USA.
Tel: 904 221 1446

Note: Sick bag collecting is not organized into its own individual society yet, but many collectors join the World Airline Historical Society, which deals with aviation memorabilia in general.

The Signalling Record Society

In the buffet bar at Coventry station, Peter Binnersley unfolded a yellowing diagram: a railway map, showing the area controlled by a single signal box in the Reading area during the 1960s. He indicated the four track main line, the double track goods line and then the numerals in the map's key. 'The number of levers in a signal box is a measure of its complexity,' he said. 'This box has 209 levers, which is near the maximum.'

Peter is a leading member of the Signalling Record Society, a group of 600 enthusiasts devoted to the study of railway signalling. 'As far as I'm concerned, the real magic of railways is the actual movement of trains,' he told me. 'I'm not specifically interested in engines. I did trainspotting for a while and got bored with it.' He estimates that he has seen about a thousand signal boxes throughout the UK, and his ultimate ambition is to explore the whole of Europe's railway signalling system.

'Have you ever read Charles Dickens's short story *The Signalman*?' I asked.

'Yes,' said Peter, 'and Dickens was pretty accurate about the signalling procedures of the time. You can't say the same for the film *The Great St Trinians Train Robbery*. The levers they pulled were all wrong. There's a scene where someone pulls a points lever and a signal moves.'

Contact: The Membership Secretary, Signalling Record Society, 44 Founcely Avenue, Dane End, Ware, Herts, SG12 0NQ, UK.

The Simplified Spelling Society

The word 'said' was spelt as 'sed'; while 'police' was 'polees'; and 'precious', 'preshus'. However, there were some mistakes in the booklet; these were duly pointed out on an errata slip. 'Replace "boy" with "boi",' said the slip, 'and "merger" with "merjer".' Anyway, let me offer you the first sentence of a story, *The Star* by H.G. Wells, which the booklet renders thus:

'It woz on the ferst dae ov the nue yeer that the anounsment woz maed, aulmoest simultaeneusli from three obzervatoris, that the moeshen ov the planet Neptune, the outermoest ov aul the planets that weel about the sun, had bekum veri eratik.'

The booklet was amongst literature sent to me by the Simplified Spelling Society. Yet although the passage above has a rule by which 'was' is spelt as 'woz', this is not accepted by everyone in the society. 'I feel the best spelling for "was" is "wz",' writes one member in the newsletter. In fact, new spelling schemes roll in at a rate of one a month.

To give some order to this situation, the society recently set up a Cut Spelling Working Group, to explore precisely which letters are redundant in English, and omit them. A resultant scheme has the advantage of saving about ten per cent of the time required to write, so 'Scoolchildren cud then devote th time saved in th act of riting to othr lernng activitis.'

Contact: Jean Hutchins, 13 Hurstleigh Drive, Redhill, RH1 2AA, UK.
Tel: 01737 765851 Website: http://www.les.aston.ac.uk/simplspel.html
E-mail: JeanHutchins@compuserve.com

The Skedders

There are die-hard sports fans; and there are die-hard sports *scheduling* fans. 'Sked' is short for 'sports schedule', a listing of all the games to be played by a team in a season. Somehow, a person acquires one or two, and then slips into the process of collecting 'sets', or a sked for all the teams in a given league. Such a person is then a 'skedder'.

Which sport? It doesn't really matter. Some skedders collect soccer; others, indoor lacrosse.

Contact: *The Sked Notebook*, [a specialist newsletter for skedders], c/o Marty Falk, 12 Foxchase Drive, Burlington, NJ 08016, USA.
Fax: 609 239 2045 E-mail: martylnd@bellatlantic.net

The Smurf Collectors' Club International

In France they are Schtroumpfs; in Italy, Puffi; in Spain, Pitufos; in Japan, Sumafu; in Denmark, Smolfs; and in Germany, Schlumpfs. Some avid Smurf hunters are willing to travel the world in search of elusive Smurf memorabilia unavailable in their homeland.

If you simply think of Smurfs as 'those funny little blue men in white hats', then consider that a collector looks at the *details* of the faces. All Smurf figurines are hand-painted, so sometimes there are defects and variations in the paintwork, making a figurine rare and even more desirable. A serious Smurf collector would give his eye-teeth for a misplaced eye or mouth.

Contact: Smurf Collectors' Club International, 24 Cabot Rd. W., Massapequa, NY 11758, USA.

The Snail Racing World Championships

The judge calls out: 'Ready, Steady, SLOW!' and off dash the snails. (The contest is held every July, over a 13-inch course.)

Contact: Hilary Scase, Little Congham House, Congham, King's Lynn, Norfolk, PE32 1DR, UK.
Tel: 01485 600650

Snuff-Taking (Competitive)

My eyes streamed. Again I spluttered. Meanwhile, Arthur Albin clicked the lid of his silver box and calmly tucked it back into his jacket. 'The first time I tried snuff,' he said, trying to sympathize with my distress, 'it blew my bloody head off. But I've been taking it for sixty years now.' By this time, I was busy blowing my nose ... and watching two mahogany-coloured streaks appear on the handkerchief. Despite having a novice of a schnozzle, I had travelled to the hall in Feniton, Devon, to take part in the United Kingdom Snuff-Taking Championships.

Championships? Granted, human nature has ever tried to parade vices as virtues, but is this the first example of a filthy habit becoming a competitive sport? Mr Albin, the Secretary of the British Society of Snuff-Blenders, was defensive. 'There's nothing filthy about snuff,' he said. 'I've sat watching people at dinner – and when you see the way that some people eat, *that's* what you call a filthy habit.'

Already, my thoughts were: I need some training. Ken Wilson, who called himself the Western Counties Snuff-taking Champion, helped by offering me samples of all manner of snuff-brands from a tiny chest of drawers. The names were seductive, like words from exotic reveries: Masulipatam; Morlaix; Old Paris; Orange Cardinal. And yet . . . 'Here, try some of this,' said Mr Wilson, smiling a little too much. He offered me a pinch of an Indian make. 'Don't you think it smells of –' I do not intend to quote the precise words of this description. Suffice it to say that a dog-owner could be fined for the substance that was put on the back of my hand.

Mr Wilson then said that if I wanted to do well in the championships, I would have to learn to take up the grains in short, sharp sniffs. He spread a gunpowder trail from my thumbnail to my wrist and invited me to go ahead. This time, the snuff was more pleasant – an odour of raspberries – and somehow I managed to ingest it all. I felt quite proud of myself, though I was beginning to feel decidedly woozy. Then Mr Wilson put my personal achievement in perspective. 'I wish I had my sword here,' he said. He told me that one of his party-pieces was to spread snuff all along the blade, from tip to hilt, and rapidly move his nose along, taking up every speck. However, he *had* brought along another training aid with him: his snuff-gun. This peculiar German-made device consists of a palette, with a spring-release mechanism, which literally *fires* a quantity of snuff up the nose. So, as a nasal bullet, I tried an Indonesian brand which smelt like fish-oil. I realized that if I wanted to be on my feet when the competition started, I'd better stop training. Besides, the Master of Ceremonies was calling everyone together for the start of the evening's contest.

Competitive snuff-taking involves edging along a lengthy table, snorting as you go. Behind this table sit twenty-five official servers, holding in their hands two spoons containing a pinch of snuff – so, in all, fifty different brands are represented. As a competitor moves along the line of servers, snuff is placed upon the back of his hand; the snuff is to be cleared as fast as possible – and every grain must go up the nose, and not drop on the table, or remain on the hand. Indeed, an eagle-eyed referee, who carries a stopwatch and follows each competitor, will allocate penalty-points for spillages and uncleared pinches. In a way, competitive snuff-taking resembles show-jumping, for both the total time taken for the course, and the faults incurred, will play a part in determining one's score. Though show-jumping does not have snuff-taking's rather unique disqualification rule: a sneeze, cough or splutter means you're out.

With the rules made clear to everyone, the referee blew a whistle and the first competitor was away: steaming down the table in a couple of minutes – nose down, elbow out, and accompanied by the crowd's traditional encouragement: 'Up! Up! Up!', whooped out like a war-cry. One by one, the contestants came forward. I asked Ken Wilson how he thought he'd done. 'I dropped a few,' he said. 'But I'm pretty pleased with my performance.'

Then my name was called. Still in a haze from my training, I was unsteady as I got to my feet. 'Think of England,' said Mr Wilson.

Off went the whistle. 'He'll never do it,' I heard someone say, and that was a goad. I knew I couldn't compete with the vacuum-cleaner nostrils of the serious contenders, but I was determined to complete the course. 'Up! Up! Up!' went the crowd, drowning out the sounds of my sniffs. All the perfumes of the snuff – strawberry, peppermint, lemon, eucalyptus – merged into one; my nose felt like it was being rubbed raw with a test-tube brush and bleach; and with that much tobacco being taken so rapidly into my system, I was virtually passing out. When at last I reached the fiftieth spoonful, and took it all up, I got the biggest cheer of the evening.

But later, as the winner, whoever he was, received his trophy and glory, I stood elsewhere: slumped over a poorly-lit backroom sink, bringing up a yellow-brown liquid that looked like a mixture of egg-yolk and naval shag. 'No,' I thought, as I emptied myself, as I came near the point of fainting, 'this is not a filthy habit, no, not at all. . .'

Note: at the time of writing, the future of the UK Snuff-Taking Championship is somewhat in doubt, following poor attendances in the 1997 championship. To find out whether the championship will continue, contact Mr Wilson below. However, the World Championship, which takes place in Bavaria, Germany, is very much alive. (See entry on Finger Tug of War for contact address.) It should be noted, though, that the World Championship uses different rules, with the object being to take as much snuff as possible (judged by weight) in a given period of time.

Contact: Mr Ken Wilson, Rosewell Cottage, Cross, Axbridge, Somerset, BS26 2EG, UK.
Tel: 01934 732811

The Society for the Eradication of Television

One person's God is another person's Satan. Later in this book, you will read about the Televisionists, who worship TV; the opposite point of – I was going to say 'view', but the Society for the Eradication of Television is so vehemently opposed to the medium I suspect that mere word would send a shudder through its ranks.

Blaming TV for a whole raft of social problems (everything from sleep disorders to falling educational standards), the 1500 members encourage people to smash their televisions, and any attempt to water down the message simply isn't tolerated. In one issue of their newsletter, *SET FREE*, a member dared to suggest that the title 'Society for the Eradication of Television' was a metaphorical one, and that it should really be interpreted as eradicating the *hold* that television has on certain addicted individuals, and that people should be able to join the society even if they do own a TV. The next issue was full of letters of outraged indignation, and mass threats to resign.

This is a society that summarizes its philosophy: the best things in life are TV free.

Contact: The Society for the Eradication of Television, 3406 Florida Street, San Diego, CA 92104-3208, USA.

The Society for the Preservation of Oversize Footwear

Imelda Marcos couldn't; nor Cinderella; though the Old Woman Who Lived in a Shoe could, and also Paul Bunyan; Elton John, in his role as the Pinball Wizard in *Tommy*, couldn't either, at least not completely. The rules as to who could, and who could not, qualify for membership of the Society for the Preservation of Oversize Footwear (SPOOF) are absolutely rigid: you need to find an old giant shoe, at least twenty inches long, made of leather. 'We have had many people desperately seeking membership,' said Danny Eskenazi, the president, 'but rules are rules.

Some people have attempted to join with *new* giant shoes, but alas they are only recognized as associate members until they find the genuine article.'

SPOOF was established when Danny made the astonishing discovery that three of his friends, who all live in the same area, and whom he had known for years through the antique trade, all owned a giant shoe, as he did. It was inevitable that they should form a society – and so they started to hold regular meetings at restaurants, each bringing along a giant shoe, which would sit on display as they laughed and feasted. In time, they were joined by other members, and recently Danny has started a Giant Shoe Museum in Seattle's Pike Place Market. This features more than 20 giant shoes arranged in a series of coin-operated display windows, including: a four-foot-long lace-up boot originally displayed at the 1893 Chicago Exposition; the world's largest military boot; the world's largest clown's shoe; and 'The Colossus', a 150-pound 60-inch handmade black leather wingtip which Danny believes to be the largest shoe in all the world. Even so, giant shoe collecting has to be one of the most specialized hobbies imaginable – what on earth could spark such an interest?

As a young boy, Danny was captivated by a pair of giant shoes displayed in the window of his grandfather's shoe repair shop. These weren't merely big shoes, but *huge* – size 37 AA – and had once belonged to the world's tallest man, the 8ft 11in Robert Wadlow. Danny has nurtured a fascination for big shoes ever since.

And here, as I am about to write the contact address for SPOOF, a page in this book will instantly turn into a 'WANTED' poster, with a $1,000 reward. You see, Robert Wadlow's shoes mysteriously disappeared from the store window when Danny's grandfather died in the 1960s, and haven't been seen since. Danny dreams of finding them one day – particularly as they are a matched pair, when everything else in his collection is a singleton, usually designed as window-dressing. As Danny says: 'The fact that there's a pair somewhere out there in the world is the impetus to keep collecting.'

Contact: Society for the Preservation of Oversize Footwear, Danny Eskenazi, President, 1909 First Ave., Seattle, WA 98101-1010, USA. E-mail: k7ss@wolfenet.com

Somewhere in Time Enthusiasts

For those of you who have never seen the movie *Somewhere in Time* – and that's most people, because it was a box-office disaster when it was released in 1980 – I'll try to sketch the plot.

Christopher Reeve takes the role of a playwright who, at a backstage party in 1972, is approached by an old woman, whom he has never seen before. She presses into his hand a pocket-watch and utters the words 'Come back to me'. She walks away. Eight years pass, and Reeve is staying at the Grand Hotel on Mackinac Island. Killing time before lunch, he visits the hotel's 'Hall of History' – where he spots a photograph of a beautiful young woman (Jane Seymour), whom he learns was a turn-of-the-century actress. For Reeve, obsession begins. After much detective work, he discovers that, sixty years after the picture was taken, she had aged into the very woman who handed him the watch! By sheer force of will, Reeve sends himself back in time to meet the young Jane Seymour – and the two fall in love. The spell is broken when the sight of a 1979 penny, that Reeve had been carrying in his pocket, sends him hurtling back to the future. He pines for his lost love, and wastes away. The two are reunited after death.

To the 700 members of INSITE, the International Network of *Somewhere in Time* Enthusiasts, this movie is a masterpiece. INSITE campaigns for a cinema re-release, produces its own quarterly magazine and, even as I type these words, is holding a weekend *Somewhere in Time* convention in turn-of-the-century dress at the Grand Hotel.

'I find myself fascinated by the notion of going back in time,' I was told by INSITE's founder, Bill Shepard, 'not as a sterile scientific experiment, but out of an obsession for a woman seen only in an antique portrait on a wall.' He remarked that when he first saw the film in 1980, it produced in him 'a feeling of being on the verge of tears, not from sadness, but from an indescribable sense of beauty'.

Is *Somewhere in Time* a cinema great? It's an unusual film, certainly worth a look, that seems to improve with every viewing. I have found myself calling it a nice film, a good film, then, 'It *is* a very good film.' I have even promised my partner Elaine that one day, we will stay in the Grand Hotel – assuming it's not fully booked by INSITE members.

'I've never really thought of INSITE as a fan club,' said Bill. 'To me it's more of a cause. We have a particular goal, that of influencing public and media perception of the film, to assure its recognition as the classic we know it to be.' Maybe Bill's dream will come true . . . somewhere in time.

Contact: INSITE, PO Box 1556, Covina, CA 91722, USA.
Website: http://homepage.interaccess.com/~addie/sit.html

The 'Sorry Charlie – No Fan Club For You' Club

He could have been an actor. He could have been a singer. But all he wanted to be was . . . a can of tuna.

Charlie the Tuna, a fish who wears a cap and spectacles, is known throughout North America as the mascot of the StarKist Tuna Company. In a series of animated TV advertisements which began in 1961, Charlie tried *desperately* hard to convince the company that he should be accepted by their fishermen on account of his erudition and good taste: he would quote Shakespeare, he would sing opera – but the boats would always throw him back into the ocean because 'StarKist want tuna that tastes good, not tuna with good taste'. Quite why he was so eager to be decapitated and stuffed into small cans was never explained; but still, he never gave up. That inspired Cathy Runyan-Svacina.

Ten years ago, Cathy, from Kansas City, was rejected by a former partner in a relationship that had gone bad – and she saw Charlie as the ultimate symbol of perseverance in the face of rejection. 'I admired his spunk,' she told me. 'And so I wrote to StarKist, asking for their permission to set up a fan club.' The response was as cold as a fish: 'Charlie does not have a fan club now, nor has there ever been one,' stated the StarKist high command. 'We do not see that it is appropriate at this time to start one.' Two subsequent letters from Cathy received a similar rejection.

'I can laugh about it now, but at the time it was shattering,' she said. 'It was like, how much lower can you get? Because this was a cartoon character that probably nobody else cared very much about. But then I just said, okay, they said no fan club, so we'll start the "Sorry Charlie, No Fan Club For You" Club, and we'll just come back.'

She has now recruited 5,000 members: each has a personalized lifetime membership card which entitles them to . . . not much . . . other than a positive reminder that they HAVE survived rejection before and they CAN do it again if it becomes necessary.

'I would love to be in your book,' she told me, 'but I realize your space will be limited. There won't be any offence if you don't include me. Because I CAN handle rejection.'

Contact: Cathy C. Runyan-Svacina, 7812 NW Hampton Road, Kansas City, MO 64152, USA.
Tel: 816 587 8687 E-mail: MarbleLdy@aol.com

The Souvenir Building Collectors' Society

Tucked among old furniture, vintage clothing and assorted cups and dishes, you encounter the Sydney Opera House.

Searching in junk shops and flea markets for models of famous buildings is a typical activity for members of the Souvenir Building Collectors' Society – though if you're thinking of taking up their hobby, I should warn you about *notabuildings*.

A notabuilding is one of those objects that you initially see and think is a souvenir building, but turns out not to be. Cheese graters can look like skyscrapers from afar. A fire hose nozzle can be mistaken for a steeple. In bad light, from a distance, a transistor radio can even seem to be an office building with rows of windows.

Contact: The Souvenir Building Collectors' Society, PO Box 70, Nellysford, VA 22958-0070, USA.
Tel: 804 325 9159

Space Autograph News

Buzz Aldrin, the second man on the moon, has two types of signatures: those signed Buzz, his legal name, and those signed Edwin E. Aldrin, the most scarce form of his signature. That's the sort of information to be found in *Space Autograph News*, a specialist publication for collectors of astronauts' handwriting.

But if you *are* considering taking up collecting for investment purposes, rather than purely for the fun of it, the cruel truth is that you had better think about which astronauts are likely to get to heaven first – because every time a famous space explorer dies, the value of his or her autograph increases dramatically. As the headline proclaims in a 1994 issue: *Deke Slayton's Autograph Value Increases Four-Fold After His Death.*

Contact: Michael E. Johnson, 862 Thomas Ave, San Diego, CA 92109-3940, USA.
Tel: 619 483 8632

The Spaghetti Bridge Building Contest

It so happens that a 'chord' is the name given to one of the principal members of a bridge truss. It so happens, too, that 'spaghetti' means in Italian 'little cords'. So there you have it: some sort of connection between spaghetti and bridge-building. A tenuous connection, yes;

but as 'tenuous' means thin, flimsy, and delicate there is surely no better way of introducing the idea of building a bridge out of spaghetti.

Every March in Kelowna, British Columbia, Canada, people construct bridges made entirely of pasta – lasagna and spaghetti – which span a distance of a metre. Ever-greater loads are applied, and the bridge which takes the greatest load without breaking is declared the champion. The current world record weight is 176kg (388lb) held by Bob Williams of Clyde, Alberta.

The competition is sponsored by the food manufacturer Catelli ... who provide pasta for both construction and the spaghetti dinner afterwards.

Contact: Spaghetti Bridge Contest, Okanagan University College, 1000 KLO Road, Kelowna, BC, Canada, V1Y 4XB.
Tel: Brad Rickards, 250 762 5445, local 7516 Fax: 250 470 6005
E-mail: BRICKARDS@Okanagan.BC.CA

The Spam Carving Contest

The world is divided into scientists and artists. If the previous section on the Spaghetti Bridge Building Contest sounds just too much like an engineering or physics project, and yet you still hanker after using edibles in a non-edible context, do not despair: there is always Spam carving.

Held every February in Seattle since 1990, contestants have 15 minutes to carve two cans of Spam into an entry. They can carve with whatever they want ... although, after an unfortunate experience the first year with a chain-saw, power tools have been prohibited. Previous winners include 'Spamhenge', 'Spam Descending a Staircase' and 'Spammy Wynette singing Stand by your Spam'. There has also been 'Spamsquatch' (= Spam sasquatch), 'Spamton of the Opera', 'Jean-Claude Van Spam', and the 'Venus de Spammo'. Some of the 100 contestants make good use of the jelly that comes in the Spam can – 'Spamcargot' featured a snail leaving a slime trail of Spam jelly.

'Spam is not just a meat,' said one competitor, 'it's a medium.'

Contact: Dana Cox, The Underground Tour, 610 First Avenue, Seattle, WA 98104, USA.
Tel: 206 682 5047 Website: www.Undergroundtour.com
E-mail: ugtour@aol.com

Spark Plug Collectors

Picture the scene at a flea market.

Browsing customer: 'Say, do you have any old spark plugs?'

Vendor: 'Yeah, I got eight of them.'

Browsing customer: 'Where are they?'

Vendor: 'They're under the hood of my car!'

Every spark plug collector has heard that one before. 'That's the answer I get nine times out of ten when inquiring about old spark plugs,' says leading collector Jeff Bartheld. 'But oh, that tenth one. . .'

That could lead to the purchase of a Devildog, a Lightning, a King Bee, an Inferno, a Hot Stone, a Never Miss, a Billy Hell, a Spitfire – or any one of 5,000 different types of spark plug. With such an array, I asked Jeff whether he had any advice for beginners. 'If history tells us anything,' he said, 'the rare plugs of today are many times the failures of yesterday. We may have to buy the plugs that are just plain no good, and save them for the future.'

Contact: Jeff Bartheld, Vice President Spark Plug Collectors of America, 14018 NE. 85th St., Elk River, Minnesota 55330-6818, USA.
Tel: 612 441 7059

(The International Society for) Spelæological Art

You may have heard of the *plein-air* school of French Impressionism: artists portraying the effects of brilliant sunlight. At the other extreme are those artists who paint in the utter absence of sunlight – or moonlight, starlight, or *any* celestial shining. Sketching by caver's headlamp-light is the method of the International Society for Spelæological Art. Packing their paper and pencils into waterproof boxes, the members venture underground, and become 'struggling artists'.

'I find the caving environment frightening and hostile. I am claustrophobic and I struggle every inch and moment, both mentally and physically,' says a leading member, Ceris Jones. Yet the cavers' world has a compelling fascination that outweighs the fear. 'The routine preparing and dressing in order to explore an alien and exciting world underneath us; the battle with all that rock and water; the human form, in these circumstances, must be paid a tribute and is well worthy of artistic expression.'

She adds that the human body of the caver is capable of an infinite range of movement and therefore lends itself to excellent poses.

Contact: Membership Secretary, International Society for Spelæological Art, Ceris Jones, 60 Sharoe Green Lane, Fulwood, Preston, Lancs, PR2 8EE, UK.
Tel: 01772 715947

Spoofing

Every Tuesday, at 9pm in the Alma public house, Wandsworth, London, Robin Gale's hand withdraws a certain number of coins from his pocket: it could be one, two or three that he selects – or, as a special case, none at all – but only he knows how many. He holds the coins in his fist, in front of him; and this action is copied by others. On a given evening, perhaps ten men will display their fists, all in a circle. For a few moments, these men will eye each other up.

Then, clockwise around the circle, everyone says a number: 'Seven' ... 'Eleven' ... 'Fourteen' ... and so on. Some use rhyming slang, or argot – so 'Harry Tate' is Eight, and 'German Virgin' is Nine. (Or, *Nein*.) The men are trying to estimate the total number of coins concealed by all the fists in the circle: that is, by powers of intuition, judgment, telepathy or plain guesswork they are attempting to solve an equation in which every parameter except one is unknown. This is the game of spoofing – and Robin Gale is the reigning English National Champion.

'I'd like to see more people take up the game,' says Robin. All the fingers have by now uncurled and a quick tally reveals that his call of seven was spot on – so the first round goes to the Champion.

Until closing time, Robin and the other members of his spoofing club, The Gentlemen Spoofers of Great Britain, will quaff half-pints of beer and yet try to avoid picking up the bill. They will hold successive rounds of spoofing, with the winner of each round being eliminated, until only two men are left – and the loser of that *mano e mano* spoof will buy drinks for everyone else. Then the process starts again. If you ask Robin how drunk he has been in the course of his spoofing career, he will merely reply: 'Drunk enough not to remember,' and argue that the greater the inebriation, the more accurate the calls.

Yet spoofing is not simply an excuse to drink. Experienced spoofers regard the game as addictive in its own right – there is even a World Championship, currently dominated by Australians and New Zealanders.

'I badly want to be World Champion,' remarks Robin. 'It would be the highlight of my sporting career.' Perhaps the question should be asked: is a spoofing title *worth* winning? Is it not just a game of pure guesswork?

'No, there's a definite skill in it,' says Robin. 'In a contest, you're weighing people up. Basically, if you're spoofing with a complete load of strangers, it's very difficult to work out a strategy. But if, as we do, you spoof with people on a regular basis, you can pick up a feeling of whether they're holding high or low – whether they're holding a lot of coins, or very few. And sometimes on an evening you just get it right.'

Contact: Gentlemen Spoofers of Great Britain, c/o Robin Gale, Tel: 0171 376 8836 (UK).
Fax: 0171 376 8856
(Other Gentlemen Spoofer groups are to be found in France, South Africa, Hong Kong, New Zealand, Australia and Guam. Contact Robin for details.)

Square Bowls

The counterpart to squaring the circle is cubing the sphere. When impossible geometry is applied to the French game of *pétanque*, the result is one of the most absurd games in the world: square bowls, played with wooden cubes, instead of steel spheres.

Every August since 1980, the town of Cagnes-sur-Mer in France has played host to the World Square Bowls Championship. Though the bowls cannot roll, they do tumble, much as dice would, helped on their way by the playing surface: the sharply-inclined streets of the town, featuring slopes of 10-18 degrees. The game originated when the town's pétanque enthusiasts were unable to play the normal game: the playing area in front of the chateau was ruined by being tarred over. So someone made the wild suggestion that. . .

I'm thinking that it *is* possible to reinvent the wheel.

Contact: Office de Tourisme, 6 bd Maréchal Juin, 06800 Cagnes-sur-Mer, France.
Tel: 04 93 20 61 64/04 93 73 66 66 Fax: 04 93 20 52 63

Stamps on Stamps Collecting

'The topic strikes me as a philatelist's dream – stamps depicting other stamps!' says Judy Hornaday. 'If you are attracted to stamps in the first place, how natural to find appeal in stamps that depict other stamps.'

Judy is a leading member of the Stamps on Stamps/Centenary Unit – 'centenary' because a principal motivation for a country to put a stamp on a stamp is to celebrate the hundredth anniversary of its first-ever issue of stamps. Overall, it is thought that some 4,000-4,500 stamps worldwide feature other stamps, although the ways in which stamps are featured can vary from detailed reproductions of previously-issued stamps, to mere 'blobs' in the corners of depicted envelopes.

'I've become a bit of a "niche" collector in recent years,' says Judy – and by that, she means a niche within a niche, concentrating on small sub-topics within the overall field of stamps on stamps. These include 'stamps under glass' (stamps that depict other stamps under magnifying glasses), 'turtles on stamps on stamps' (because she also collects turtles on stamps), and – I wondered whether this field could possibly exist, and amazingly it does – stamps featuring *other* stamps on stamps, or stamps on stamps on stamps. That's not the end, either. Judy also collects stamps on stamps on stamps on stamps. 'Truly fascinating in my opinion,' she comments.

One cannot fail to think of Swift's famous lines about fleas having 'smaller fleas to bite 'em/and so proceed *ad infinitum*' – especially as there *are* examples of the 'ad infinitum' stamp on stamp: a stamp which depicts itself, and thus has endlessly repeated stamps on stamps, the number visible depending upon the quality of the stamp, and available magnification.

Contact: William E. Critzer, SOSCU Secretary/Treasurer, 13385 Country Way, Los Altos Hills, CA 94022, USA.
Or: Judy Hornaday, 22446 Estallens, Mission Viejo, CA 92692, USA.

The 'Stand By Me' Club

'I was meeting a friend of mine in Bremen in Germany in 1980. We were in a pub called the Storyville – and "Stand By Me" came on the jukebox. I forget whose version it was now – probably John Lennon's. It was about a month before Lennon was sadly shot. And I said, "Oh, I've got two or three versions of that. I've got Ben E. King, Jimmy and David Ruffin, and John Lennon." And he said, "Oh, I've got another couple of versions." So it went from that and we thought we would collect different versions of the song.'

Mike Pentelow proceeded to play me Ben E. King's original 1961 recording of 'Stand By Me', and then cover after cover: performances by everyone from Demis Roussos to Muhammad Ali; in every musical style – punk, jazz, reggae; in foreign languages, such as Flemish and Chinese; even played by Hindu musicians on the Chitra Vina, a 21-stringed lute. In all, the members of the International 'Stand By Me' Club have located over 100 commercially-released versions of the song, and are still searching for more. To supplement this, the club actively encourages amateur musicians to record the song, and this has resulted in about 100 additional versions being added to the archive: 'Stand By Me' performed in spoken form as a cod-Shakespearean soliloquy; as an instrumental, on Northumbrian bagpipes; and in many more languages, from Arabic to Afrikaans.

Then there is the club newsletter. One member writes that she heard 'Stand By Me' performed by a drunk old tramp at Birmingham station, – though the tramp didn't get the words correct. Instead of singing 'When the night has come/And the land is dark/And the moon is the only light we see,' he bawled out: 'When the night has gone/And the room is bright/And the sun is the only light we see. . .'

The member gave him a pound coin for his trouble.

Contact: The International 'Stand By Me' Club, Flat 5, 21 Nassau Street, London, WIN 7RE, UK.

The Statue of Liberty Collectors' Club

'Once you establish that you will collect items related to the Statue of Liberty, it's amazing how your antenna activates,' comments Iris November, the founder of the Statue of Liberty Collectors' Club. 'You set off for a flea market, antique show, garage sale or whatever, and items "jump off" the tables and shelves to find you.'

With the assistance of her antenna and her husband, Mort, she has turned her home into a virtual Statue of Liberty museum: coffee tables, clocks, snow domes, china, ashtrays – over 800 items in all. Iris knows so much about the history of the Statue of Liberty that whenever the Statue of Liberty National Park receives a question they can't answer, they direct the question to her. Incidentally, a significant event in the statue's history was its refurbishment in 1986, when its nose was replaced.

The original nose is now in the apartment of one of the club's members.

Contact: The Statue of Liberty Collectors' Club, 26601 Bernwood Rd.,
Cleveland, OH 44122, USA.
Tel: 216 831 2646 Fax: 216 831 0497 E-mail: Lbrtyclub@aol.com

The Steven R. Addlesee Fan Club

You hear it said of certain celebrities that they are 'famous for being famous', but I hope to make the name of Steven R. Addlesee famous for being *not* famous.

Because Steven R. Addlesee, a 37-year-old American, is responsible for a conceptual breakthrough in the field of celebrity worship. He has had the imagination to set up a fan club that honours . . . himself. Yes, Friends Of A Legend, or FOAL, is a society dedicated to the achievements of a man who is not famous at all. Unbelievably, FOAL has recruited 36 members so far – there are badges, a fanzine, and recently there was even a convention, SteveCon, at which two of the attendees presented their hero with a brass key chain engraved with the message: 'Steve Addlesee, Living Legend.'

Sensing that there could be a lesson here for us all, I wrote to Steven R. Addlesee and received several back issues of FOAL's fanzine, *COLT*. Sure enough, it was just like a standard publication about a rock star or actor. Fans write in to ask questions – anything from 'What are your views on defence spending?' (Steven R. believes in a strong national defence) to 'Do you sleep naked?' (he wears undershorts). But whereas rock stars and actors tend to be amazingly successful, with money to burn, this fanzine is about the sheer struggle to make ends meet.

For example, when a member inquires about Steven R.'s plans for Christmas, the answer could almost come from Dickens's Bob Cratchit: 'Hopefully we'll be alive and well, with a roof to keep out the snow, and the utilities paid so that we can have lights on the tree and make the inside a few degrees warmer than the outside. We'll be doing good just to get cards out to friends.' And when asked where his career is going, he responds: 'Hopefully some place better than it is now.'

That career is the key to Steven R. Addlesee. His ultimate goal is to establish himself as a professional inker in the American superhero comics industry: an inker is responsible for applying his nib to an artist's pencil drawings of costumed crimefighters, so that every bulge of every muscle, and every hem of every cape, has a solid black outline, ready for reproduction. But unlike Superman, Steven R. Addlesee is not a highflyer – and the fanzine records the many rejections and setbacks in his career.

In 1983, for instance, he showed his work to Marvel and DC (the two major US comics publishers) and was told 'to keep dreaming'. Years later, he is still meeting with disappointment and dashed hopes. 'I met the representatives of a new publishing group called Graphik Publications. They signed me up as an inker,' he writes in *COLT*. 'Too bad they folded before I received any assignments.'

So it goes on – he always keeps his fans up to date with the latest career non-developments: 'Phil Francis has moved without leaving a forwarding address, so I assume Serendipity Publications is history . . . I haven't heard from Dan Vest in a while, so I assume I won't be inking *The Lords of Stone* series for Hot Comics.'

There does seem to be a ray of hope, though, when his wife, Cathy, takes an active role in promoting his name and talents. 'This resulted in numerous commissions and some decent money,' he writes. But . . . 'I later learned from Cathy that she paid for a lot of those commissions herself because the patrons didn't pay her.'

Reading about Steven R. Addlesee's frustrations in issue after issue of *COLT* is really quite absorbing – and I can understand why people would join FOAL. Undoubtedly, part of the appeal is rooting for the underdog: FOAL is not a fan club for the man as such, but for the quality of his perseverance. (And the fact that he has recently had a few published pieces of work, commissioned by smaller companies, makes you feel that there is just a chance that he might make a breakthrough and get the job he wants.)

On the other hand, it has to be admitted that there is something downright funny, a cruel humour, about seeing a person thwarted again and again – this is the comedy of the *Road Runner* cartoons, where fate always conspires against the schemes of poor old Wile E. Coyote. Surely, the Coyote will get the Road Runner *this* time . . . Surely Steven R. Addlesee will get a commission *this* time. Fate says otherwise.

I decided to find out more about Steven R. Addlesee's motives for setting up FOAL.

'When I was a kid,' he said, speaking on the telephone from his home in Sandy, Utah, 'I was a comics fan and had a number of favourite artists – but I didn't know how to contact them and tell them how much I liked their work. But if they had had a fan club, I would have joined. So now that I'm a comics talent, I'm making myself available to fans.'

But what about the fact that he is not famous? 'When I started FOAL in 1993, I thought: I'm not well-known. But there were people encouraging me and they said: "You will be".'

His method of recruitment to FOAL is to hand out flyers at comics conventions. He read one of these to me: 'Have you ever wondered what goes on in the life of someone working in the comics industry? Do they work in a basement? Do they rake in the money or do they deliver pizzas on the side?' (Actually, he *does* work in a basement. And he *does* deliver pizzas to earn some money.)

As a result of attending these comics conventions, Steven R. Addlesee has edged just a little closer to achieving fame. He has persuaded certain established artists he has met at the conventions to portray his face in crowd scenes, as a comic-book equivalent of a film extra. 'I was featured in an issue of *Wonder Woman*,' he said.

Contact: Steven R. Addlesee, 7919 Thornton Circle, Sandy, Utah 84093, USA.
Tel: 801 942 9266 E-mail: carcajou@fia.net

The Stone Sawing World Championship

I have covered lumberjack sports elsewhere. (See the entry on Axe Racing.) In Oamaru, New Zealand, there is a variation which could be thought of as lumberjacking in a *petrified* forest.

Many of Oamaru's buildings are made of the local limestone and this has inspired the town's annual Stone Sawing World Championship: two-man saw teams endeavour to cut through a rectangular block of stone (1 metre x 1 metre x 1.5 metres) in the fastest possible time. How fast is fast? About twenty seconds. 'It's like slicing bread,' I was told by the local tourist office. Presumably made from *stoneground* flour. . .

Contact: Visitor Information, Waitaki Private Bag 50058, Oamaru, Waitaki District, New Zealand.
Tel: 03 434 0372/03 434 1656 Fax: 03 434 1657

Storm Chasing

There is an eye of the storm, and an eye *on* the storm – the latter being the hobby of storm chasing. For the awe of it all, people will travel hundreds of miles in search of the elusive tornado: they will actually *hope* for bad weather when they are on holiday.

Contact: *Stormtrack*, c/o Tim Marshall, 4041 Bordeaux Circle, Flower Mound, TX 75028, USA.

The Street Lamp Interference Data Exchange

There was the case of the man who would drive to a meeting every Thursday evening. On the way home, a street lamp would go off when his car passed underneath. *And it was always the same lamp.*

I heard about this case when I met Mr Hilary Evans, a paranormal researcher and founder of the Street Lamp Interference Data Exchange, or SLIDE, a forum for those who are interested in the alleged ability of some people to switch off (or in a few cases, switch on) the lamps on our streets by psychic power alone. I should say that you don't have to possess this power to join. Hilary doesn't. He hasn't even witnessed it. But since establishing SLIDE, he has received well over a hundred letters from human switches. 'In 99 per cent of these letters,' he told me, 'there's a sentence which says something like "I'm so glad that somebody is taking this seriously at last".' One correspondent claims to put out street lamps whenever he makes love to his girlfriend.

Yet is not wiring failure the most obvious explanation? Or perhaps a light source, such as a car's headlamps, triggers the photo-electric cells inside the street lamps?

Hilary believes that some examples of street lamp interference do have a normal cause, but the vast majority do not. 'If the car headlamps theory is right,' he said, 'how could that explain the fact that the lamps stay on when someone else drives the same car? Or what about when someone is just out walking?'

Coincidence? I suggested. Surely with millions of people walking the streets every day, under hundreds of thousands of street lamps, there will be lamp failures? Hilary agrees that coincidence has to be taken into account, but he thinks there's much more to street lamp interference than a statistical fluke. He told me about two paranormal researchers who were walking back at night, discussing SLIDE, when suddenly a lamp went off. 'That has to be a coincidence,' said the more sceptical of the two. They walked further down the road and the next lamp they passed went off as well.

Contact: Hilary Evans, 59 Tranquil Vale, Blackheath, London, SE3 0BS, UK. Fax: 0181 852 7211

The String Figure Association

Why is it called a 'cat's cradle'? Show me the cat that would like to sleep in one.

More correctly, such constructions are known as *string figures*. You can suggest a wolverine in twine and a caribou in cord; also, the alligator's mouth, the howler monkey's jaw, and the Itoi bird's bill; a seasnake, or a fish lying under a piece of wood. Or, should you prefer inanimate objects: the Eiffel Tower, the Confederate flag, and the Chair of the High Chief of Tuvalu.

If some of these sound exotic, it is because string figures are known across the world. Some designs are believed to go back to the stone age – and for centuries, they have been used by storytellers to illustrate their tales, or as good luck charms to help ensure a bountiful harvest or successful hunt. On the island of Nauru, string-figure construction was at one time a competitive sport: a hundred years ago, there were all-island contests in which a competitor would turn his back, so that the others couldn't see his method of construction, then suddenly turn round, exhibiting a hideously complex figure. The others would thereupon endeavour to copy it as quickly as possible.

Some of the designs of Nauru were so fiendish that, in spite of being illustrated in a book of 1906, their methods of construction have only recently been deciphered ... by a member of the International String Figure Association, of course.

Contact: International String Figure Association, PO Box 5134, Pasadena, California 91117, USA.
Voice Mail: 213 214 7333 Fax: 818 305 9055
Website: http://www.isfa.org/~webweavers/isfa.htm
E-mail: marksherman@isfa.org

Struifvogel

They say a bird in the hand is worth two in the bush. But it could be worth twenty-five points in the middle of the target.

In the Belgian pub game of *Struifvogel*, or bird-dart, an artistically carved wooden bird is suspended from the ceiling by means of a cord. In the bird's beak is an iron pin, and under its tail a leather thong: competitors draw the bird back by means of the thong ... and then release it, so that the bird glides to the other side of the room, to stick in the target. Although it sounds easy, in reality it takes a great deal of practice to make the bird – which can weigh more than 5kg – go in a stable flight towards the bullseye.

Alas, the rewards of achieving mastery must rank as the lowest of any sport in the world: there is an annual event in which whomsoever achieves six bullseyes out of six wins . . . four sausage rolls.

Contact: Struifvogelmaatschappij 'De Kroon', Coördinator Achiel Van Parys, Sterrenstraat 6, 2500 Lier, Belgium.
Tel: 03 480 86 32

Stuntology

Stuntology: the science of stunts, tricks, practical jokes, and the like. Some examples.

In every bag of pistachios there are some that haven't cracked open in the roasting process. So why not save them for a year and then serve them in a bowl at a party? Watch people starved for pistachios riffling through the bowl for a single edible nut.

You pretend to sneeze. Prior to this, you dipped your hand in water – and as you sneeze, you flick the water at someone.

You say: 'I can get this pebble out from under this cup without touching the cup.' Then you put the pebble on the table, cover it with the cup, wait ten seconds with a look of concentration on your face and say, 'Okay, it's gone.' They say, 'No way.' But as soon as they pick up the cup, you remove the pebble.

You can find your soap opera name by the formula: middle name + name of the street you grew up on. (Try it – it works!) You can find your burlesque name by the similar formula: name of your childhood pet + your mother's maiden name.

You're in a fast food restaurant and someone at your table is drinking a milkshake. They go to the toilet. While they're away, you take a ketchup sachet, open it up, stick the end of their straw into it, and put the straw back in the milkshake. Then when they return and sip . . .

Those stunts were taken from *The Journal of Stuntology and Tuneology* (a magazine of stunts, with a few bonus pieces of sheet music) published by Sam Bartlett, a 35-year-old professional banjo player. I did wonder whether there were any *banjo*-related stunts in his archive – and there *was* one. 'If you plink a banjo near the bridge you get a very metallic sound,' he said, 'and if you conceal the banjo as you do this, and at the same time you pull out a nasal hair, then it will sound like you've got metallic nasal hairs.'

Contact: *The Journal of Stuntology and Tuneology*, c/o Sam Bartlett, 333 S.Jackson, Bloomington, Indiana 47403, USA.

The Sugar Packet Collector Club

When coffee arrives in the restaurant, faces fall – the sugar is in the form of unwrapped lumps.

As one Belgian enthusiast remarks: 'To make a super collection of sugar packets is not a hobby alone. It is a special life, a way of life, and for me that is a NEED.' While an American collector states: 'Collecting sugar packets, when one thinks about it, is akin to coming to terms with an ever-expanding universe, or the notion of eternity. Both concepts make minds become temporarily unstable! So when I look at my collection – to which I add almost every day – I quickly realize that hundreds (if not thousands) of new designs are being issued daily somewhere in the world. Never ending, always expanding, and of course impossible to catalogue.'

Contact: Sugar Packet Collector Club International, Mitzi Geiser, 15601 Burkhart Rd, Orrville, Ohio, 44667 USA-9618.
Tel: 330 682 7486 Website: http://members.iquest.net/~phillip/
Or: The UK Sucrologists' Club, Beryl Laishley, 30 Cavendish Drive, Waterlooville, Hampshire, PO7 7PJ, UK.
Website: http://web.ukonline.co.uk/email.ukscsugar

The Suitcase Championship

There are various ways of descending a snowy slope: skis, snowboard, skidoo, toboggan, luge, suitcase . . . *Suitcase*?

Okay, I used the same intro for the entry on Shovel Racing. The two sports are remarkably similar: instead of sitting on a shovel, competitors in this New Zealand-based activity descend a ski-slope while sitting in a suitcase. The first one to the bottom wins.

There is one problem with this sport: it is not clear whether it has a long-term future. To withstand the rigours of the 200 metre run, the suitcases have to be very sturdy; and even those that *do* survive are normally battered by the end. Each year, it's getting harder and harder to find people willing to turn their luggage into luges.

Contact: Destination Queenstown, PO Box 353, Queenstown 9197,
New Zealand.
Tel: 3 442 7440 Website: http://nz.com/Queenstown/
E-mail: queenstown@xtra.co.nz

The Sundial Society

In the age of quartz crystals and Stephen Hawking, it may seem strange
for anyone to be attracted to telling the time by shadows.

'We have quite a few mathematicians as members,' said David
Young, the Secretary of the British Sundial Society. He showed me a
copy of the society's bulletin, with pages of trigonometrical alphas,
betas and thetas, all to determine the position of the *gnomon*, the dial's
pointer. 'And some of the members are attracted to the mottoes on
dials,' he added, and quoted a few examples, most of which were to do
with human transience, like *Man fleeth as a shadow* and the punning
We must die-all. 'But sundials can be studied in so many ways. Art,
science, geography, astronomy, craftsmanship – sundials are a combination of all these things.'

David remains impressed by the accuracy of shadow and pointer.
'One of our members came across a dial that was reputedly made by Sir
Isaac Newton,' he said. 'It was made in 1620 – and it was accurate to
within ten seconds. Yet the nearby station clock was ten minutes slow.'

Contact: British Sundial Society, c/o David Young, Brook Cottage, 112
Whitehall Rd, North Chingford, London, E4 6DW, UK.
Tel: 0181 529 4880
Or: North American Sundial Society: Frederick W. Sawyer III, 8 Sachem
Drive, Glastonbury, CT 06033-2726.
Tel: 860 633 8655 Fax: 860 403 5295
E-mail: /frederick.sawyer.es.72@aya.yale.edu

Superman – The Adventures Continue

Jim Nolt is a retired teacher from Pennsylvania. This is what he said to
me in a letter:

'There is no way I can describe to you the influence he has had
upon my life. He was there when a young boy needed a hero and has

continued to guide me and help me through my entire life. I feel he is with me constantly. It was his sense of fair play, honesty, quiet strength, courage and stick-to-itiveness that continues to challenge me every day.' And: 'I feel he is partly responsible for my becoming a teacher. There were many days in the classroom when I'd think of him and wonder if he'd appreciate my efforts. He has inspired me to help children, to devote a portion of my time, money and energy to helping others.'

The person who has inspired Jim is not, as you might be tempted to think, Jesus Christ, but another figure with extraordinary powers – Superman. Or, to be strictly accurate, *one interpretation* of Superman: the 1950s low-budget television series featuring the less-than-musclebound George Reeves.

Ever since he was a kid, when he would put on a T-shirt with a towel pinned to the back, when he would pretend to fly and bend steel bars (aluminium foil rods), Jim has been influenced by George Reeves's – and *only* George Reeves's – version of Superman. When I asked him what he thought of near-namesake Christopher Reeve's interpretation of the Man of Steel, the answer was a curt, 'George Reeves *was* Superman, Christopher Reeve was a man *portraying* Superman.' Jim even starts using inverted commas when referring to Christopher Reeve's work, such is the contempt he feels. 'His "Superman" lacked spark, his "Clark Kent" lacked absolutely everything.' It's hardly surprising that, to keep the memory of the late George Reeves alive, Jim publishes a magazine, *The Adventures Continue*, devoted exclusively to the 1950s Superman.

Well, I managed to track down a video of a George Reeves performance, *Superman and the Mole Men*, a cinema film shot in less than a month on a budget that wouldn't even stretch to shoestrings. The special effects? You *won't* believe a man can fly. It also struck me that George Reeves's interpretation of Clark Kent is far too strong: there are times he seems more powerful than Superman. The effect is empha-sized by the clothes worn by the two-men-in-one: sharp suits for Clark, while for Superman's costume, the seams are as prominent as the S symbol. Surely something is flawed here? Jim doesn't see it that way. 'George's Clark was indeed a strong character,' he told me, 'in fact, so strong that I often thought I'd like to see a series solely based upon Clark Kent.'

Contact: Jim Nolt Enterprises, 1935 Fruitville Pike #105, Lancaster, PA 17601, USA.
E-mail: jimnolt@redrose.net

The Swizzle Stick Collectors' Association

Spoons for sipping . . . rods for stirring . . . forks and spears for retrieving olives and cherries . . . if you're looking for a hobby in which it is possible to acquire a *huge* collection, then swizzle stick collecting is probably the one for you. Some members of the International Swizzle Stick Collectors' Association have 20, 30, 40 *thousand* swizzle sticks – and the association's founder, Ray Hoare, has *50,000*. Ray, a barman for the Royal Canadian Legion, regards the art of conversation as an important technique for acquiring new swizzle sticks: 'I never cease to talk of the hobby, and it continues to pay off,' he says. 'Day after day, no matter who'll listen, swizzle sticks always come into the conversation.'

Contact: International Swizzle Stick Collectors' Association, c/o Ray Hoare PO Box 1117, Bellingham, Washington 98227-1117, USA.
Or: c/o Ray Hoare, PO Box 48793, Bentall Centre, Vancouver, B.C., Canada, V7X 1A6.
Tel: 604 936 7636

T

Talking to the Trees

The last time mankind mucked around with a Tree of Knowledge we all got into quite a bit of trouble. Like greatly increased pains in childbearing; having to eat our food by the sweat of our brow; and being hurled out of Paradise. With Chapter Three of *Genesis* serving as a warning-sign, I went to visit Martin Blount, founder of the group Tree Spirit – a society with the laudable aims of protecting and conserving woodland . . . though many of its members go further and ascribe a certain wisdom to wooden friends. In their magazine, you will find passages like the following:

'When we travel we talk to the trees where we camp. We tell them of the beautiful trees where we live, of how the Dorset hills look, or the Welsh mountains. We tell them of the weather in places other than their own.' Another passage advised readers to share their 'deepest feelings and secrets, treating the tree like a close friend. You can trust the tree, it will never tell anyone else.'

Martin took me along to a sycamore. He and I sat beneath a bough and began a conversation. Perhaps we were overheard by ears that rustled. . .

SJ: In your magazine, there are people saying they communicate with trees. Tell me about that.

MB: You show the tree respect. You open up, show affection. You try to get onto the same wavelength as the tree. It helps if you imagine you've got a root.

SJ: What do you say to a tree?

MB: Occasionally, if I've got a problem, I ask the trees for advice. We hug trees as well.

SJ: You hug them?

MB: There's nothing wrong with showing affection. One of our members has so much respect for trees that she changed her name to Hazel Birch.

SJ: What's the special appeal of trees?

MB: You can learn a lot from them. I always feel good when I'm with trees. Mind you, they're not always peaceful. Sometimes they're aggressive.

SJ: And what are your favourite trees?

MB: Silver birches are very feminine and happy and joyous. But they don't live very long – seventy or eighty years. Nothing for a tree. Yews can live for a thousand years. They grow so slowly, they've seen a lot of things. They're very wise trees.

SJ: I see. What do you think of wood as a raw material?

MB: I think it's excellent.

SJ: But doesn't chopping down a tree pose some ethical problems for you? Doesn't it make you feel guilty?

MB: What you have to do is to go out and explain the situation to the tree. You have to tell the tree why you're doing it. You show the tree respect and then you thank it for its timber. Some time ago, I went and talked to a walnut before I cut it down.

SJ: What message do you have for my readers?

MB: Go out and hug a tree. The more you do it, the more natural it becomes. Millions of people hug and talk to cats and dogs – it's the same thing.

Contact: Tree Spirit, Hawkbatch Farm, Arley, Nr. Bewdley, Worcs., DY12 3AH, UK.

Tarantula Breeding

Fraction by fraction, I moved my finger forward, closer to the bristles. On the table in front of me lay the skin of a very large spider. It lay like a broken-up wheel – no rim, but an axle and spokes. Or perhaps it lay like hand-me-downs; being just a skin, it was really a garment. Whatever, I was afraid. I touched one of the legs and moved my fingernail up and down the bristles. They were gingery. My heart went faster, my lips tightened. I was acting as if the ghost of the spider were about to return, as if one of those dead limbs were about to twitch. Arachnids may cast off their hides but I don't think I'll ever cast off my arachnophobia.

I was in a plain room, but one that smelt of rotting fruit. 'That's to feed the flies,' I was told. There were also boxes of chirping crickets and boxes of locusts and boxes of maggots . . . all the choicest food. For I was in the home of Paul Carpenter, whose hobby is breeding tarantulas.

Paul's fondness is for a particularly aggressive strain, African Baboon Spiders, which have legs as thick as pencils. As he opened a container –

and as I stood as far back as possible – I saw a prize specimen. 'Look at those fangs,' Paul said with glee, 'you could catch a trout with one of those.' I kid you not, the spider's eight eyes were staring at my two; and until that moment, I hadn't known that spiders made a noise – this one was hissing like a steam kettle.

As soon as the lid was on and not before, Paul and I began talking about the joys of spider sex. As you may be aware, for the male there is always the possibility of ending up as a post-coital meal: Paul pointed to a top shelf, where there was a container holding a female who had eaten four of her husbands. Given the cost of buying replacements, it's not surprising that Paul often resorts to prising the couples apart with a knitting needle.

Contact: Ann Webb [Honestly, that's her name!], Secretary, British Tarantula Society, 81 Phillimore Place, Radlett, Herts, WD7 8NJ, UK.
Tel: 01923 856071
Or: American Tarantula Society, PO Box 1617, Artesia, NM 88211-1617, USA.

Target Ball Enthusiasts

There is a period in the history of target shooting which might be defined as after claws, before clays: when shooting *live* pigeons had lost its appeal, but shooting *clay* pigeons had yet to start. This period, roughly the decade 1877–1887, was the heyday of the target ball: a glass globe, sometimes filled with feathers, which was hurled into the air by a trap, and shattered by its meeting with either a cartridge or the ground. To the readers of *On Target*, the world's only newsletter devoted to target balls, the unused ones are highly collectable.

Mind you, target balls did have a drawback: what do you do with all those shards of glass? One ingenious solution, as you can learn from *On Target*, led to another minor episode in shooting history: the target ball made of *manure*.

Contact: Ralph Finch, *On Target*, 20135 Evergreen Meadows, Southfield, Mich. 48076-4222, USA.

The Televisionists

'The time has come to lay down your false idols and turn to Your real God, the one you and I have worshipped for years. The Television.'

252

Such is the gospel according to the Televisionists, the 200 members of the group known as the TV Ministry. They openly admit that the TV is never off in their homes, and they sermonize further: 'TV is the centre of our lives and our living rooms. We adorn our TV altar with cable TV, VCRs, video games and now even Net TV. We take special care of our televisions and we're always saving up for a bigger and better TV. These days, God comes in many different models!' They continue: 'Without TV, we wouldn't know how to live, or think, or feel. Talk shows are the modern confessional. The holy book is the TV guide. All we know for sure is that TV is the single biggest thing in the lives of most every American today, and we are no exception. Our salvation lies beyond that screen. Rid yourself of the guilt you carry for your TV viewing. You know you want to.'

Gives a whole new meaning to the expression 'cult TV', doesn't it?

Contact: The TV Ministry, PO Box 136, Calumet City, IL 60409, USA.

The Test Card Circle

In some countries, a test card is called a test pattern. Rarely seen in these days of 24-hour-television, test cards were at one time broadcast in the gaps in schedules, to help television installers check on reception. The typical card consisted merely of an unchanging pattern of circles and lines, accompanied by a musical soundtrack.

'It first hit me when I was about four years old, about 1963. I tuned into the schools programme and on came this strange black-and-white pattern of circles and lines. I was transfixed.'

So said Paul Sawtell, the chairman and founder of the Test Card Circle, a group of 85 enthusiasts devoted to the study and appreciation of test cards and test card music. No, the horizontal hold of your brain has no need of fine tuning and yes, your eyesight is indeed giving you a perfect picture of these words. For I tell you, there are people who swap videos and tapes of the card and its soundtrack; people who admit that in their youth they would hurry home from school to get in some serious viewing before the programmes started; even people who are nostalgic for the British television strikes of the 1960s when the test card was shown all day. 'The only thing missing from a perfect day's viewing,' said one member, reminiscing about those long-ago strike-ridden times, 'was the lack of the national anthem at closedown.'

At the chairman's home, I watched a wealth of videos, featuring many test cards – including British regional variations, foreign cards, Christmas specials (with holly in the corners) and reduced power versions. Paul also explained to me the rudiments of the card's engineering functions: the 'letter-box' shape on some cards, for example, was actually used to test for high-frequency streaking, caused by a misaligned aerial. The centre circle, on the other hand, was a check on the curvature of the picture's geometry. Such a treasure-chest of fascination is embedded in the card and its soundtrack that at the circle's annual convention there is even a test card quiz. Contestants are asked about television installation and about obscure pieces of music, for example: 'Which types of aerials are most likely to cause ghosting?' and 'Who played the music in the middle section of the 1985 BBC tape featuring Markhu Johansen?' The competing quiz teams have buzzers set to operate at the tone-frequencies associated with the BBC1 and BBC2 transmitters – 1khz for BBC1, 440 hz for BBC2.

Paul admits that if test card enthusiasts have anything in common, it's probably an unhappy childhood. 'Most of us were the ones in the classroom who were picked on,' he told me. He admits to having few friends at school, and against a background of being bullied, he found a certain comfort in the screening of the card. What particularly attracted him was the music, which he maintains was more varied and of a higher standard than most of the sounds of the era; and by turning on the TV he had access to an extraordinary musical diversity: jazz, big band, classical – 'Even a man imitating a dog bark,' he told me. Nowadays, Paul works as a professional musician and composer and as he played me a tape of his tunes it struck me that they bore something of a resemblance to test card music, an influence which Paul does not deny. It seems that in his work, just as much as in his leisure, Paul Sawtell's whole life has been affected by a means of checking that televisions are correctly installed.

What is clear is that the Test Card Circle fulfils a need. Paul knows that prior to the circle's foundation there was 'a bubble of frustration about to burst' – and then there was enormous relief, as people suddenly realized that they were not alone, that it was possible to meet others who shared a belief that the rest of television's output was a 'mindless deluge'.

Contact: The Test Card Circle, Curtons House, School Lane, Walpole St Peter, Wisbech, PE14 7PA, UK.
Website: http://www.meldrum.co.uk/tcc/index.html

This Strange Earth

If you enjoyed the movie *Field of Dreams*, then you'll enjoy *This Strange Earth*, the Journal of Unexplained Rural Phenomena.

Devoted to what might be called 'Fortean Farming', mostly in the midwestern United States, the publication records the likes of the ghostly agricultural labourers who helped a farmer from Illinois to harvest his corn when his cornpicker had broken down and the mysterious 'hot spot' in the middle of a Wisconsin field – even on the harshest days of January, there's no ice or snow on the surface of the ground in just that one spot. In other words: while crop circles represent the 'normal' rural paranormal, this magazine concentrates on the 'abnormal' rural paranormal.

Contact: D. Brinkmeier, *This Strange Earth*, 1174 South Home, Oak Park, Illinois 60304, USA.
E-mail: brinkmeier@AOL.COM

The Thomas Crapper Society

There is a sort of urban myth which circulates about Thomas Crapper – and that is, that the man himself is a myth. Could anyone *really* be born with that name, and then go on to invent the flush toilet? So, when I contacted the International Thomas Crapper Society, my first task was to clarify whether or not Mr Crapper existed.

Andy Gibbons, the founder of the society, assured me that Thomas Crapper *did* exist; though Andy himself only became interested in Crapper because he, too, had heard the man dismissed as a myth, and wanted to know the truth.

Having said all this, Thomas Crapper did *not* invent the flush toilet: that invention belongs to no one person. 'But Crapper was an amazing builder and plumber, and a royal sanitary engineer,' said Andy.

'So what does the International Thomas Crapper Society *do*?' I asked. 'Talk about crappers, *et cetera*,' he said.

Contact: Andy Gibbons, International Thomas Crapper Society, 1153 N. 230 W. Logan, UT 84341, USA.
E-mail: gibbonscrapper@tcs.tcsourceone.com

Tiddlywinks

Tiddlywinks n. A game in which the players attempt to snap little disks of bone, ivory, or the like, from a plane surface into a cup. [Prob. from *tiddly*, a child's word for *little*.]

The etymology implies, that tiddlywinks can be dismissed as a kindergarten pastime; yet when I went to meet Charles Relle, one of the UK's foremost players, I met a middle-aged man – and within minutes of reading the rules and struggling to follow Charles's advice on tactics, it became clear to me that here was a game of considerable depth, a game which should be taken seriously.

Although the pot is the focal point, I found that the object is not simply to sink one's disks (winks) as fast as possible. Tiddlywinks has elements of attack and defence as a result of the so-called 'squop' rule: if at any stage a wink is covered by another wink, it is said to be squopped and cannot be played. Basic strategy then involves immobilizing or out-manoeuvring one's opponent, with the successful player establishing a military-style domination of the playing surface. Modern tiddlywinks thus combines skills both of the hand and of the mind. Try potting a crucial wink using a backspin shot – it's not easy.

What's more, a winks subculture has emerged. At its heart is the English Tiddlywinks Association, which publishes the specialist journal *Winking World*. Its American counterpart publishes a rival, the delightfully-titled *Newswink*. The pages of these magazines are awash with terminology: squidgers, gromp-shots, nurdled winks and cruds – words which themselves seemed designed to provoke public ridicule. In fact, it is the game's embarrassing image which seems, perversely, to attract many players. 'Most people start it as a joke,' Charles admitted, 'but eventually they see there is much more to it than they had thought.'

Tiddlywinks has spawned a world championship – currently dominated by the Americans – and at the highest level it is extremely competitive, whilst remaining good-humoured: tiddlywinks is simply not important enough for tantrums. As Charles put it: 'You might cry if you lost the Varsity Boat Race, but not the Varsity Tiddlywinks. After being soundly thrashed by your opponent you would probably go down to the pub together.'

Contact: English Tiddlywinks Association, c/o Patrick Barrie, 19 Benians Court, Cambridge, CB3 0DN, UK.
Website: http://www.cheng.cam.ac.uk/~pjb10/winks
E-mail: pjb10@cheng.cam.ac.uk
Or: North American Tiddlywinks Association, c/o Rick Tucker, 4651 Kinsey Lane, Alexandria VA 22311-4916, USA.
Tel: 703 671 7098 Website: http://www.tiddlywinks.org
E-mail: RickTucker@cpcug.org

The Tin Bath World Championships

I am afraid I can think of no pun or wordplay that can be used to form a link between 'bathtubs' and 'canoeing'; so, the Tin Bath World Championships – in which 65 competitors use paddlepower to propel their seaworthy baths to victory – will simply have to *be* that link, without any further verbal ado.

Mind you, there is more hope for me in the rule that says: the winner will be the first to finish, or the one covering the greatest distance *if they all sink*; for in that latter eventuality, they would not be bathtubs, but *bathy*tubs, from the Greek *bathys*, as in bathysphere, meaning of the ocean depths.

Contact: Wendi Kitching, 2 Arbory Street, Castletown, Isle of Man, IM9 1LJ, UK.
Tel: 01624 823850

The *Titanic* Society

There was no hour-hand on the pocket-watch. If you looked closely, there was a tiny arrow of rust, the hand's silhouette, marking the last time ever told.

'That's my father's watch,' said the old man. He pressed his finger against the glass of the showcase. 'I often come into the museum to see the time when it stopped – when the water got into the works.' He meant the time when his father died, along with 1500 others, because in 1912 the pocket-watch belonged to a steward on the *Titanic*.

There have been worse sea disasters – the Philippine ferry tragedy, for example, where double the numbers died. Unlike the *Titanic*, that disaster is largely forgotten. There is certainly no Philippine Ferry Society, whose members swap memorabilia and build models of the death-ship in every material from matchsticks to margarine; no Philippine Ferry Convention, along the lines of the one organized in Southampton by the British *Titanic* Society. As I stood in the maritime museum – one of the visits on the convention's schedule – I couldn't help wondering why people were still intrigued by the *Titanic* disaster, all these years after it happened. Why *do* people bother learning every fact they can about a sunken ship? And I mean *every* fact, from the colour of the carpet in the first mate's cabin, to the contents of the cargo hold.

Maybe superstition is a reason. Travelling on the train to Southampton, I had been engaged in conversation by a man who noticed that I was reading a copy of the *Titanic* Society's journal, *The Atlantic Daily Bulletin*. Although not a member of the society, he had read a great deal about the subject. He told me about a novel, *Futility*, published in 1898, which predicted the disaster with uncanny accuracy. In the novel, a ship called *The Titan*, of virtually identical tonnage to the *Titanic*, strikes an iceberg, with great loss of life. 'I believe the sinking of the *Titanic* was God's will,' he said, 'the book was a prophecy.' I wondered why God would want to kill so many people. My companion had a ready answer: 'Pride goes before a fall.'

In 1912, there was good reason to be proud of the *Titanic*. The ship was seen as mankind's finest engineering achievement – the largest vessel ever built, a symbol of industrial power. 'Man had come to the conclusion that he was better than nature, that he could do anything,' I was told by George Connor, one of the *Titanic* Society's leading members. 'Man was proved wrong.'

We were now travelling around Southampton on a bus, looking at *Titanic*-related sites, like the hotels where the passengers stayed on the eve of departure and the pub frequented by the *Titanic*'s captain. George told me that his *Titanic* obsession had led him to travel to the Arctic and Antarctic, just to get a better understanding of icebergs. 'People know everything about the *Titanic*,' he said, 'but not many people bother about the iceberg.'

At Southampton Docks we boarded a boat. If the *Titanic* disaster was God's will, then we would be following the first part of the Via Dolorosa, from the very bollards where the ship was tied up to the edge of the open sea. 'We're doing exactly the same line as the *Titanic*,' said a voice on the speaker. If anyone thought this a trifle morbid, they didn't let it show.

Later that day, on dry land, I was introduced to the society's guest of honour – a *Titanic* survivor, Edith Haisman, who was 16 at the time of the disaster. (She is, unfortunately, no longer alive.) 'I remember when my father walked up the gangway to board the ship,' she told me. 'He turned very pale. My mother said "Are you ill?" "No," he said, "I'm all right".'

The arrow on the pocket-watch pointed towards ten to two.

Contact: British *Titanic* Society, PO Box 401, Hope Carr Way, Leigh, Lancs, WN7 3WW, UK.
Or: *Titanic* Historical Society, PO Box 50153, Indian Orchard, Mass, 01151-0053, USA.
Or: *Titanic* International, PO Box 7007, Freehold, New Jersey 07728-7007, USA.
Website: www.titanicinternational.org

Toad in the Hole

This entry begins where another finishes. When my game of Loggets (*q.v.*) was over, I asked Mark Pennington whether he knew of any *other* unusual leisure activities I could include in the book. This is a primary method of research: many activities spread only by word of mouth. Still, I was hardly prepared for his reply, 'There's a pub just down the street where they play a game called Toad in the Hole.'

I was soon in the Lord Nelson. Amongst the normal pub furniture was a leaden-topped cabinet. It was scarred all over from people tossing 'toads' or small brass disks at it. A game was in progress – I heard a cry of, 'Come on Jim, get it in the hole!' The toad hit the hole's rim. There was a collective sigh of 'Ooooohhhh!' for the near miss.

Incidentally, I noticed a line on the floor of the pub, about eight feet from the cabinet, which players stood behind to throw their toads. In darts, this line is known as the oche. No-one knew whether there was a similar technical term for Toad in the Hole – though one player did suggest it be called 'the lilypad'.

Contact: The Lord Nelson, Eastbourne St, Hastings, TN34 3DP, UK.
Tel: 01424 423280 or 01424 430381

Toaster Collectors

A *poetaster* is the name given to a rhymer. The following makes me think I could slot an extra 'o' into that word:

It's a friendly little toaster, though it seldom ever works
It's a Toast-O-Lator toaster, it's got its little quirks.

That rhyme is in honour of a 1936 toaster, the Toast-O-Lator: a strange device, in which the bread is inserted at one end, traverses the inside, and comes out the other end. This is actually a very poor method of making toast; the Toast-O-Lator doesn't toast enough, and if you reinsert the slice, it comes out a golden shade of black. But odes to defunct toasters are just one aspect of the specialist newsletter for toaster collectors, *A Toast to You*. In one issue there was even an April Fool's gag that would only appeal to toaster collectors: a photo of the Sunbeam *Single*-Slice T-9. (Sunbeam only made a double-slice version. The single-slice machine was made by cutting a normal double-slice T-9 in half and soldering it back together.)

And you can order rubber toast from the newsletter, to make a terrific display for your collection.

259

Contact: *A Toast to You*, PO Box 529, Temecula, CA 92593, USA.
Tel: 909 699 5139 Fax: 909 699 8119

The Tobacco-Spitting World Championships

In 1978, a man stood against a hitching post in Calico Ghost Town, California. He spat on the ground and said, 'Why don't we hold a tobacco-spitting contest?'

There are now *three* separate contests in the town's annual tobacco-spitting world championships: Accuracy, Juice-spitting and Wad-spitting. In the Accuracy event, contestants spit tobacco juice at a metal stake: a hit on the top – which is about as big as a dime – counts as a bullseye. Top spitters (a description of their accuracy and their status) have been known to score five in succession. In the Juice-spitting event, the object is to achieve the greatest distance with your nicotine-flavoured saliva. The world record currently stands at 28ft 5½in. Crowds of thousands gather to watch . . . and probably wish they hadn't when the wind changes direction.

But those two contests are mere curtain-raisers for the great Wad-spitting event, in which the world record is currently 53ft 3in. Many of the competitors take great pains to prepare their wads; so they pick them up and re-use them, even though they have fallen in Calico's saliva-spattered dirt.

Contact: Calico Ghost Town, 36600 Ghost Town Road, Yermo, CA 92398, USA.
Tel: 760 254 2122

Toe-wrestling

Ye Olde Royal Oak Inn at Wetton in Derbyshire is approached by a sheep drovers' ancient trail – mile after mile of drystone wall, leading to this 300-year-old alehouse set in the heart of the Peak District. The Royal Oak is the type of watering-hole that wayfarers encounter when St Christopher is in one of his better moods: friendly staff, 17 brands of fine malt whiskey, and comfortable accommodation. Oh yes, and it is also the only pub in England with an active tradition of toe-wrestling.

Just how, and when, toe-wrestling began at Wetton is a mystery. The Royal Oak's current landlord, George Burgess, knows only that two years ago, when he bought the pub, the estate agent's particulars said that the Royal Oak was famous for the sport. Sure enough, behind the bar, George found a board setting out the rules, as well as a pewter cup engraved with the words 'Toe-Wrestling Champion'.

At the Royal Oak, George led me to a side-room and his son Kevin brought in the board of rules. It was obvious that this piece of painted wood was no antique – I would guess it was less than ten years old, including, as it did, a 'No steroids' rule. It also gave an approved cry of surrender – of 'Toe Much' – so you could begin to wonder whether toe-wrestling is just a spoof, an imaginary event along the lines of indoor hang-gliding or underwater choral singing.

But you must put such suspicions aside. For when George took over the pub, the locals confirmed that they had actually witnessed toe-wrestling contests and told of how sheer force of ankle power could throw a grown man off his chair. Anyway, I challenged George to foot-to-foot combat, he picked up the gauntlet (or sock) and he and I were soon sitting facing each other, ready for the barefoot showdown.

Now, human beings can fit their bodily parts together in a number of different ways. It is a remarkable fact that two big toes slot together rather well, like clips. Perhaps evolution designed them for this purpose. If you have not tried toe-linking before, I would recommend that you experiment at home with your partner.

As soon as we were interlocked, George and I started to wrestle. Toe-wrestling resembles arm-wrestling, in that the idea is to pin down your opponent, but there are differences. Under the rules, the non-participating foot has to be lifted off the floor, which makes it difficult to gain any sort of purchase – and it also looks exceedingly silly. Howls of pain are soothed by the balm of belly laughs.

George had victories over me in both left- and right-foot contests. Encouraged by his success, he is now considering hosting the first-ever toe-wrestling world championships. . .

Postscript: The above piece was written in 1993, for the earlier version of this book, *The Bizarre Leisure Book*. In June 1994, George did indeed hold the first-ever toe-wrestling world championship, which was won by Alan 'Nasty' Nash. The championship is now firmly established as an annual event at the pub – Nasty winning three out of the first four championships, thereby emerging as toe-wrestling's first superstar – and pictures of the sport have been shown on television programmes all over the world. I myself have entered every championship – though I have yet to win a single bout – appearing in particular as the world's only *masked* toe-wrestler, Kentoe Nagasocki (taking my name from a masked wrestler of the seventies, Kendo Nagasaki) and also as the world's only *three-legged* toe-wrestler, Jake the Peg (copying the false-leg routine of the Australian comedian Rolf Harris).

The publicity generated by the championship has led to one of the early toe-wrestlers visiting the Royal Oak and shedding light on the sport's origins. Toe-wrestling appears to have been started by Manchester University students in the late 1960s or early 1970s, when they were staying at the pub.

The rules of the sport have evolved, too. When George and I wrestled, we were sitting on stools; now, contestants sit on a mat on the floor, which is a lot safer – though the non-participating leg is still lifted. Also, contestants have to push their opponent's foot towards a side-wall several inches high, which means that 'toe-downs' happen much faster.

Contact: George Burgess, Ye Olde Royal Oak Inn, Wetton, Nr Ashbourne, Derbyshire, DE6 2AF, UK.
Tel: 013535 310287

The Tooth Fairy Tabloid

If man shed his skin, like a caterpillar or snake, then there would be a Slough Fairy to exchange the derma for a coin. As it is, our myths must centre on the relatively small area of the mouth; but there is still much to say about the tooth fairy – so much, that 1997 saw the launch of a specialist newsletter, *The Tooth Fairy Tabloid*.

The origins of the tooth fairy lie in the belief that the Devil or witches would use lost teeth to create spells to the detriment of the owner. To prevent this, teeth were burned, buried, or given to the fairies. But the myth of the tooth-fairy is not static. As the newsletter reports, there are many commercially-available tooth-fairy products, such as boxes to keep lost teeth in and tooth fairy dolls; numerous stories about the fairy, which describe what she does with the teeth (counts them, makes necklaces, etc); and many pictorial interpretations of the tooth fairy, whether by professional artists or by children. Enough material, indeed, to open a museum – which is exactly what the tabloids editor, Dr Rosemary Wells, has done. She describes herself as a Tooth Fairy Consultant.

'Santa Claus and the Easter Bunny are stereotyped,' she told me. 'That's not so with the tooth fairy.'

Contact: *The Tooth Fairy Tabloid*, PO Box 7196, Deerfield, IL 60015, USA. (An appointment to view the Tooth Fairy Museum can be made on 847 945 1129)

(The Institute of) Totally Useless Skills

Have you ever tried the invisible-ball-caught-in-a-paper-bag-trick? Throw up a non-existent ball, follow its trajectory with your eyes, and then flick the back of a paper bag to create the sound effect of the catch. Or perhaps, during your school years, you pretended that your pencil was made of rubber by moving it up and down in a wobbly way? Maybe, even, at some point in your life, you've pressed your arm hard against a door-frame, moved, and been amazed that the arm rises of its own accord? All these phenomena are of interest to the Institute of Totally Useless Skills.

The institute was established by an American, Rick Davis, who has a library of about 500 of these tricks, with new ones being added every week. From him I learned the technique of *arm shrinking*; stretch both arms out in front of you, scratch the back of your head with one hand, then stretch that arm out in front again. Sure enough, it's just that bit shorter! Or you might attempt the *two noses trick*: cross your fingers, place them at the tip of your nose, close your eyes and lightly rub . . . yep, your schnozzle has a *doppelgänger*.

Rick has formulated a definition of a useless skill: 'It must be fun, easy to do, rely on no special equipment, be safe and non-competitive and contribute nothing of practical value to society.' Totally useless skills, he believes, are the antidote to being totally responsible.

And his first totally useless skill? 'Taking a degree in philosophy,' he said.

Contact: Rick Davis, The Institute of Totally Useless Skills, PO Box 181, Temple, NH 03084, USA.
Website: www.jlc.net/~useless

The Toy Dish Collectors

I suppose one way of making *nouvelle cuisine* seem like a banquet is to display it on one of these collectables.

Actually, some toy dish enthusiasts are known to spend hours creating and painting clay replicas of turkeys, petit fours and other miniature food to give life and colour to their dishes.

Contact: Toy Dish Collectors, c/o F.J. Steffen, 9705 Mill Creek Drive, Eden Prairie, MN 55347-4307, USA.
Tel: 612 944 1041

Toy Sewing Machine Collectors

'As we were going to the locked case a man followed and said, "I want the toy sewing ma. . ." You can imagine, I bristled. I said, "Oh, me too." Good thing I had already asked for the case to be opened. Of course I got it – and ten per cent off. Another *minute* of hesitation and I would have lost out!'

The unfinished word in the above passage reminds me that the name for an incomplete line of literature is a *hemistich*: which suggests 'hem I stitch' or even 'hemi-stitch', or half-sized tacking. I can think of no better way of leading you into the world of Little Daisy Treadles and Seam Master Juniors: the subject-matter of *Toy Stitchers*, the world's only magazine for toy sewing machine collectors. (From which the passage is taken.)

Contact: Claire Toschi, *Toy Stitchers*, 623 Santa Florita Avenue, Millbrae, CA 94030-1203, USA.

Trainspotting

The 8.30am from London Victoria to Ashford in Kent does not appear on the railway timetable. One Saturday morning, a train with just such a route left the platform at just such a time – I suppose that made it a collector's item – for this was an excursion train, chartered by railway enthusiasts. I was a passenger, because I was spotting the trainspotters.

Of the 200 on board, all apart from a handful were men, but I managed to speak to one woman, who said that she had been obsessed by trains ever since she was carsick as a child. After she'd enthused about the power, the noise, the dirt, the excitement, I asked whether she ever became bored with trains. 'My problem is not getting enough of them,' she said.

The excursion, scheduled to last for eleven hours, appealed to different sorts of railway enthusiasts. For people into traction, we would be travelling on three trains: a 319 (a standard train), a 465 (state of the art), and an EPB (standing for electric-pneumatic brakes, which have been virtually phased out). Regardless of the train, whenever we stopped at a station, a hard core of spotters would dash outside to take photographs, front and rear, from every angle.

To many others on board, the route was the thrill. Track enthusiasts build up mileage travelled along certain lines; they can even be annoyed if the train stops more than two inches from the bumpers. Furthermore, the excursion was going along a few short sections of rare track, normally not seen by the public, like siding Number 28, near Grove Park Station.

So, we passed Clapham Junction, Brixton, Bromley South, Paddock Wood, Lewisham, Gravesend and much of the rest of the railway network of South-East England. There really wasn't much to do except talk about trains. I heard how spotters spend a fortune travelling the length of the United Kingdom, from Penzance to Aberdeen, collecting the full set of 4,000-odd locomotive numbers; some spotters will try to tick off the lot within a year and then start again.

But the more extreme of the spotters, I discovered, are known as 'bashers' – and in the extremest of extreme cases, there are bashers who are obsessed by *one individual locomotive*, which they follow all over the country. The train in question might be the last one in a particular class, loved especially because it is so difficult to find. Or maybe it has some minor modification which distinguishes it from the rest. Whatever the reason, I am told that in railway magazines there are articles like, 'My Favourite is Number 12'. Bashers become terribly upset if their favourite train is withdrawn or goes to the breaker's yard.

Yet even without going to such extremes, trainspotters probably have the worst image-problem of any hobby. In recent years, the word 'trainspotter' has even become a term of abuse, indicating someone who is obsessively attached to unimportant details. Perhaps as a reaction to this, trainspotting is changing. I have heard rumours that a new breed of 'cool' trainspotter has arrived on the scene. 'I think there *has* been some perceptible shift in the characteristics of your average trainspotter over the last few years,' I was told by Kit Wingate, the chairman of the group that organized the excursion. 'They have become upmarket, equipped with tape recorders and video cameras rather than tatty notepads and blunt pencils.'

To be honest, I feel a little guilty about calling this section 'Trainspotting'. It almost became 'Railway Enthusiasts'. But the ordering of the alphabet nicely links this section into the following one. . .

Note: There are many groups of rail enthusiasts throughout the English-speaking world. The following are two extremely useful initial contacts:

Contact: Southern Electric Group, c/o Kit Wingate, 12 Dorchester Gardens, Grand Avenue, Worthing, West Sussex, BN11 5AY, UK.
Website: http://www.carol.net/dolphin/southern/egrouphome.htm
Or: The Electric Railway Society, c/o Dr Iain Frew, 17 Catherine Drive, Sutton Coldfield, West Midlands, B73 6AX, UK.

The Transport Ticket Society

Michael Farr's fascination with railway tickets began fifty years ago. 'I used to go to school every day by train,' he told me, 'and most of my friends tended to stand at the end of the station platform taking train numbers. But I found that quite cold and draughty.' Instead, he managed to wheedle his way into the warmth of the ticket office – and this in turn led to an interest in collecting railway tickets as a hobby.

By various methods – rummaging in bins, asking friends to save all the tickets from their journeys, looking in library books for tickets used as bookmarks – Michael has accumulated *thousands* of tickets. When he opened a drawer in his lounge, I could see it was *stuffed* with tickets, packed tighter than . . . well, say, commuters on a Japanese train at rush-hour.

Michael is a leading member of the Transport Ticket Society. Some members like to collect an example of a ticket from every station; others collect tickets by type – not just 'singles' or 'returns' but special tickets for migrants, anglers, cyclists, or seamen on leave. 'And we've got one member who set out to collect tickets where the serial number was a prime number,' he said. 'And it's surprising how many prime numbers there are between 0 and 10,000.'

Contact: The Membership Secretary, The Transport Ticket Society, 4 Gladridge Close, Earley, Reading, RG6 7DL, UK.

Tree Climbers International

There is an old boast of Australian males, 'I'm climbing trees to get away from it.' The 'it' is sex, with the suggestion that the speaker is such a successful philanderer that he could almost do with a break. I recalled this saying when I saw a real tree climber go up a 70-foot beech. You see, the proper way of ascending a trunk requires proficiency in a certain body movement . . . now how can I put this delicately?

'The Americans call it tree humping,' said Mike Whyborn, as his pelvis gave a thrust. Mike, a British member of Tree Climbers International, was ten foot off the ground, standing at ninety degrees to the trunk, suspended by a rope attached to a waist-harness. During the thrust, a moveable knot on the rope is slid upwards, then a free end of the rope is released to lock the knot in place. If all this is done, the climber will be several inches higher than his original position. 'You could dangle here all day,' said Mike. 'It's perfectly safe.'

It is true that tree climbing, by this 'safe-sex' method, *does* have a perfect record: since 1983, when Tree Climbers International was founded, there have been no deaths and no injuries apart from the odd twisted ankle. The only problem is a psychological one – do you *believe* you are safe?

'Go as high as you want,' said Mike when it was my turn. 'If you only feel confident enough to go six inches off the ground, that's fine.' He had detected a degree of nervousness on my part – looking up at the towering beech, I was already wondering whether it was possible to start my training on something smaller: a bonsai, for example. I amazed myself by reaching a height of approximately fifteen feet and then just dangled. A foot or so above me was my objective, the first branch. Unfortunately, I started to swing around the trunk – and this induced a panic. I tried to ignore the feelings and progressed a little higher; but now the branch was level with my head – and fear overwhelmed me. What if I swung round and hit the branch? Objectively, it would not have been that painful ... but I wanted to be down, down on solid ground, anywhere but up a tree. It made it worse that the sliding knot was stuck and would not allow me to descend.

When I finally loosened it – this took the strength of both hands – and lowered myself, Mike told me that some climbers would not be bothered if they had to spend hours stranded in the branches. 'People like to sleep in trees,' he said. 'And some climbers, when they get to the top, just don't want to come down again. And when they *do* come down, the ground feels strange to them.'

The ground felt mighty safe to me. I was out of the woods, even if I was still in the forest.

Contact: Tree Climbers International, PO Box 5588, Atlanta, GA 30307, USA.
Tel: 404 377 3150 Website: http://www.treeclimbing.com/tci.htm

Trollaholics

Ellen Schmidt and Lisa Kerner are Trollaholics.

The addiction began for Ellen at the age of 22, when her mom gave her a surprise present: an old troll. 'I beamed with delight as she presented it to me,' she said. Once home, the troll received a thorough bath. The little hair that was left was washed and restyled. Finally, the troll was placed on a shelf in the guest room. Little did Ellen know that it would all become a ritual with each and every troll that would enter her home. She now has over 900 trolls.

The addiction began for Lisa at the age of 24, when her mom gave her a surprise present: an old troll. 'My troll needed a friend,' she said. 'He looked so homely and sad. So I said to myself, "I've got to start finding more".' Thus, she looked for trolls in flea markets, antique stores and basements. She now has over 6,000 trolls.

Ellen edits the newsletter *Troll'n*. Lisa edits the newsletter *Troll Monthly*.

Contact: Ellen Schmidt, *Troll'n*, 5714 Folsom Blvd. #199, Sacramento, CA 95819, USA.
Tel: 916 455 7678 E-mail: Trollaholic@worldnet.att.net
Or: Lisa Kerner, *Troll Monthly*, 3477 Howell Ct., Abingdon, MD 21009, USA.
Tel: 410 515 3233

The Tychonian Society

As wheel is to axle, so Earth is to sun. Thus did Copernicus put man in his place.

There were those at the time who disagreed, of course – like the Catholic Church. But for several hundred years, no-one has disputed what goes around what.

Well, almost no-one. Because there are still a few people who say, 'Stop the world – I want to get off.' These are the members of the Tychonian Society, subscribers to the geocentric view of the universe, the belief that the sun orbits the Earth. Taking its name from Tycho Brahe, the sixteenth-century scientist who opposed Copernicus, the Tychonian society is an international organization with its headquarters in the United States. And just before you shout that this is sheer lunacy – moon madness – I must tell you that the society was established by a man who has a doctorate in astronomy from a legitimate university.

I wrote to the Tychonian Society, in the hope that they had some contacts in Britain. I was eventually referred to a professional engineer whom (for reasons of confidentiality) I shall simply call Malcolm.

I must make it clear that Malcolm is not an out-and-out supporter of geocentrism. He was recommended to me because he is fully *au fait* with the reasons for believing that the sun goes around the Earth. His opinion is that geocentrism should not be ridiculed, or dismissed out of hand, and that it might possibly be correct. 'When I started to look at it,' he told me, 'I realized that there was more going for geocentrism than I had thought.' With that, he passed me a copy of the Tychonian Society's journal.

You can be blinded by the sun and you can be blinded by science. I am tempted to say that the two come together in the journal of the

Tychonian Society. I was immediately struck by the complexity of the articles and their erudition – or their apparent erudition. 'The mathematics of this model (of a particular geocentric universe),' I read, 'is arduous though straightforward to one acquainted with the conformal mappings of functions of complex variables.' There followed astronomical terms whose meanings I did not understand, lots of physics plus plenty of references to academic journals supposedly supporting the view that Copernicus got it wrong. I didn't have the technical knowledge to refute – or even comprehend – the arguments within the journal, but I was highly suspicious, as anyone born after the sixteenth century has a right to be. I turned to Malcolm and asked him why the Tychonians should be given any credence.

'Every attempt to detect the speed of the Earth going around the sun has failed,' he said. He reeled off a list of experiments. I heard about a scientist called Mascart, who tried to measure the twisting effect that the movement of the Earth through the ether should have upon polarized light. No effect was found. Another scientist called de Coudres tried to measure the effect that movement should have upon a pair of transformer coils in the inductance of current. No effect was found. Two more scientists, Troughton and Noble, tried to measure a similar effect upon a pair of capacitance plates. Again no effect was found.

The Earth, it seems, does not move. It does not even spin on its axis. We live on a planet that is absolutely fixed in space – while the rest of the universe turns around us. As I heard all this, I kept on thinking: this has to be wrong. What about space travel? Mission Control at NASA would have surely missed the moon if their underlying astronomical models were in error.

Malcolm had a reply. 'The Apollo moonshots actually assumed that the Earth was the centre of the universe,' he said, 'so as to simplify the mathematics.'

I wasn't beaten yet. Even I, with my limited knowledge of science, had heard of one test that *proves* the Earth rotates: the Foucault Pendulum. This is a pendulum whose angle of movement changes over time because the Earth is moving beneath it. But Malcolm told me that geocentrists remain unconvinced. They argue that the change in the angle could be explained by the forces of the rest of the universe (which to them is turning) acting upon the stationary Earth.

I doubt whether anything could persuade a geocentrist that he is wrong. For ultimately, geocentrists believe that there is biblical support for their science. As the Catholic churchmen who persecuted Galileo would have agreed, the Earth has a special place in the universe and so it *must* be at the centre. To emphasize this, the society recently changed its name to the Association for Biblical Astronomy. Yet even amongst fundamentalist Christians, who support the creation story of Genesis, geocentrism remains the extremest of extreme views. Malcolm, himself a fundamentalist, cannot quite go along with the Tychonians. 'Geocentrism is a hot potato amongst creationists,' he said. 'We have enough difficulty opposing evolution.'

Contact: The Association for Biblical Astronomy, 4527 Wetzel Ave, Cleveland, OH 44109, USA.

U

The Unicycling Society

So engrained is the idea of two wheels, that if asked to define a unicycle, I bet you'd call it a one-wheeled *bi*cycle.

Our lack of familiarity means that we're not aware of all the possibilities of unicycling, once the basics have been mastered. There are unicycle races not only of varying distance (100, 200, 400, 800, 1600 metres, and marathons) but also of varying types: backwards, pedalling with one foot, riding with the feet on the tyre rather than the pedals ('Walking the wheel'), and UMX (unicycle motocross).

As it says in the brochure of the Unicycle Society: 'Many are just showing off. All are having fun.'

Contact: Unicycling Society of America, PO Box 40534, Redford, MI 48240, USA.
Website: http://www.unicycling.org/usa

The Universal Perkehner Society

This is a borderline case for inclusion in the book – because the members of this society are all horses.

They're pretty borderline as horses, too. While there are many breed registries, those registered by their owners in the Universal Perkehner Society (UPS, pronounced oops) are equines with misfit traits. Members include Mr P, who derives no pleasure from grooming, patting or petting – but he does relish having just one spot under his tail scratched. He even condescends to requesting the pleasure by backing up to people and lifting his tail so they can scratch this secret spot of personal preference. If they ignore his requests, he gently bumps them with his butt and lifts his tail until he achieves his goal. Of course, strangers are bewildered and sometimes frightened by these actions but Mr P doesn't care. If they don't want to scratch him, what good are they anyhow?

While another member, Ole Blue, can clear a barn of any living thing with her Beaufort-scale blasts of gas. She also gets rid of visitors by aiming wet mushy sneezes at their clean clothes. It's a bull's eye every time.

Contact: Universal Perkehner Society, PO Box 1874, Cave Creek, Arizona 85327, USA.
Tel: 602 488 4131

The Unloved Soviet Socialist Register

They drive cars with window stickers saying 'My other car is a Zhaporozets.' They are the members of the Unloved Soviet Socialist Register (U.S.S.R.) – fans of Trabants and Eastern bloc cars in general. Don't such cars have a reputation for being, well, complete rubbish?

'Actually, Trabbies aren't as bad as people think they are,' says leading member Julian Nowill. 'They're reasonably put together. And when you drive one you feel you're doing something original. Nobody knows about them, they're unloved, and the maintenance is like a journey of discovery. Part of the charm of Eastern bloc cars is that they were developed on a completely different plane from western cars.'

I'll say. The Zhaporozets has a hatch in the floor for ice-fishing.

Contact: Julian Nowill, Earlsland House, Bradninch, Exeter, EX5 4QP, UK.
Tel: 01392 881748 Fax: 01392 410422

V

The Vampire Research Society

'I *did* get frightened many years ago,' I was told by Dr Sean Manchester, 'but I've lost all fear of fear for quite some time. I've reached the point where fear no longer exists.' Which is definitely an advantage when hunting vampires.

Some years ago, when I met the Dracula Society – fans of Gothic horror and the fictional portrayal of vampirism – I was shocked that some members contemplated the existence of vampires *for real*. Dr Manchester doesn't just acknowledge the possibility; he *knows* that vampires exist. In 1970, Dr Manchester, a Catholic priest, founded the Vampire Research Society – or, to give its full title, the International Society for the Advancement of Irrefutable Vampirological and Lycanthropic Research. He explained that many of the clichés from horror films are more-or-less true – for instance, garlic and stakes *can* be used as protection. As for the sign of the cross: 'Well, vampires do flee from holy things,' he said, but he added that the faith of the person is more important than the image, and the crucifix is the focus of faith.

'There are many recorded cases of vampirism, going back centuries,' he remarked. 'The ancients refer to demons and succubi – which are all part of the same phenomenon. There are references to these creatures being torpid and heavy from a banquet of blood. In the 1720s and 1730s there was a vampire plague which hit Europe – it was an epidemic. In modern times, you hear people describing alien abductions, and "Greys" – I suspect that, too, is a manifestation of vampirism.'

I wanted evidence. Dr Manchester referred to the outbreak of vampirism in the Highgate area of London from 1967 to 1982. 'There were hundreds of animals in the area drained of blood,' he said. The carcasses were completely desanguinated: animal welfare organizations couldn't even extract enough blood for a forensic examination. 'I found dozens of dead foxes myself,' he told me. And if that isn't enough evidence, he can simply hold up his left hand: it was lacerated by the Highgate vampire – and Dr Manchester still bears the scars.

Contact: The Vampire Research Society, PO Box 542, Highgate, London, N6 6BG, UK.

Variant Chess

You may have heard of the Möbius strip: a mathematical curio consisting of a long piece of paper, twisted once, and joined at the ends, to make a loop that starts at the beginning, derails itself, re-rails itself, and goes back to the beginning again. What I doubt is that you will ever have considered playing chess on such a surface. In the game known as Möbius chess, pieces move off one side of the board and reappear on the other, as if travelling upon the strip; and this is just one type of chess that interests the Chess Variants Society – whose members are dedicated to exploring unorthodox ways of playing the game. Let's consider some others:

There's kamikaze chess, where capturing a piece necessitates a sacrifice; zombie chess, where pieces rise from the dead, but in the colour of the captor; and pacifist chess, where all violence is rejected and you may neither take nor threaten your opponent's men. (The game ends when one player has no legal move. The winner is the one whose king is farthest from its initial position.) Then there are variants which introduce new pieces, like the zebra, a sort of lengthened knight, which does a (2,3) leap instead of the traditional (1,2). Indeed, there is a menagerie of new pieces: antelopes, spiders, octopuses, squirrels, even wildebeest – each species having its own distinctive move. Or perhaps progressive chess is more to your taste? It demands great imaginative powers, for in this variant, white has one move, then black two moves, then white three moves, and so on. Overall, there are *hundreds* of chess variants and new ones are being invented all the time: random chess, teleportation chess, losing chess, and not forgetting chess with reduced boards and chess with infinite boards . . .

What sort of person plays variant chess? A leading member of the society, George Jelliss, admitted to me that he finds normal chess boring. 'To get anywhere in the orthodox rankings,' he said, 'you really have to start at a very early age and absorb an awful lot of opening theory.' The joy of variant chess is that you start with a clean slate. Set against this, there is one minor problem: finding a partner to play against. George told me that he once arranged a meeting to bring variant players together, prior to the formation of the society. It was not a success – no games being played. 'Unfortunately,' he said, 'we couldn't agree on the rules.'

Contact: P.C. Wood, 39 Linton Road, Hastings, East Sussex, TN34 1TW, UK.

Varpa

In Valhalla, dead Vikings play at varpa; on the Isle of Gotland, live Swedes do so too.

Varpa is ancient – varpastones have been found in Viking graves. The object of the game is to toss one of these discus-sized flattened stones, attempting to get it as close as possible to an upright stick, situated 20 metres away.

There is a problem, though. Stones often break during the course of a game – so a varpa player has the heaviest sports holdall in the world: packed full of stones, all of which are likely to break during the course of a single competition. Because of this, modern Swedes often use aluminium-alloy 'stones', though these varpas must have exactly the same specific weight as the ancient ones: a rule, as it were, set in stone . . . about stone . . . set in metal.

Contact: Gotlands Turistförening, Box 1403, 621 25 Visby, Sweden.

Vertical Archery

Thank God that Cupid isn't Belgian: the only people to fall in love would be tightrope walkers, trapeze artists and tree surgeons. For Belgian archers specialize in shooting *skywards*.

The targets in the sport of *handboogschieten op de staande wip*, or shooting at the vertical pole, are 41 coloured 'jays' (plumes representing the bird), which are fixed to an iron frame, somewhat in a Christmas-tree arrangement, with the grandest jay at the top. The entire frame is then fixed to a 27-metre-high stake, and points are awarded to the archers for hitting the different jays, with the higher jays worth more.

So could a Belgian bow ever be the 'smoking gun' in a bizarre murder-mystery? *Death in the Penthouse*, perhaps? Probably not. For as the great Belgian detective Hercule Poirot would inform us, those fletchers in Flanders make special, *blunt* arrows for this sport.

Contact: De Koninklijke Nationale Bond der Belgische Wipschutters (K.N.B.B.W.), Willy Vander Heggen, Secretaris-Generaal, Steenweg 46, 9890 Gavere, Belgium.
Or: Volkessportconfederatie V.Z.W., Warandelaan 10B bus 2, 8340 Sijsele, Belgium.
Tel/Fax: 050 35 84 62 E-mail: VOSCO@snv.be

The Veteran-Cycle Club

So as to keep on the right side of the members, make certain that you refer to their bicycles by the correct name of *Ordinary* – *not* a Penny-Farthing.

Contact: The Veteran-Cycle Club, c/o Michael Morgan, 135a Radlett Road, Frogmore, St Albans, Hertfordshire, AL2 2LA, UK.
Tel: 01727 874137

Viking Longboat Racing

It is true that the boats are in the Viking style, complete with a figure-head; but you are as likely to see an oarsman with a baseball hat as a horned helmet. This is *not* a sport for re-enactors.

It did begin that way, though. The history of the Isle of Man Viking Longboat Race goes back to the early 1960s, when a mock invasion was held, and longboats stormed the beach. It became a matter of pride among the different crews to reach the beach first – and in 1963 the boats actually raced for the first time. Eventually, the re-enactment lost its popularity; but the racing went from strength to strength – and in due course, it became the Viking Longboat World Championship Race, with 60 teams taking turns to compete in timed trials.

In case you're wondering: Viking longboats *are* provided by the organizers.

Contact: Pat Sweeney, 13 Stanley Road, Peel, Isle of Man, IM5 1NY, UK.
Tel: 01624 843640

Vinegar Connoisseurs International

The British delicacy that is fish and chips is always sold to you with the accompanying question: 'Salt and vinegar?' When I went to the fish shop today, I had half a mind to respond: 'Yes – what sort of vinegars do you have?' and watch the bamboozlement on the faces.

The idea of being presented with a vinegar list, as one would a wine list, is by no means absurd. Just as there are people who attend wine tastings, so there are people who attend vinegar tastings – though the sampling procedures for vinegar are somewhat different. The acid makes the taste buds close, and thus to distinguish different vinegars in succession, you have to soak up the vinegar with a sugar cube, and then suck the vinegar out of the cube: this fools the taste buds so that they stay open, while allowing you to experience all the nuances and complexities of the vinegar. I learnt this technique from Vinegar Connoisseurs International.

The wonderful thing about these connoisseurs is that they glory in *all aspects* of vinegar. True, their *Vinegar Newsletter* does feature reviews of rare and exotic vinegars from around the world, but this is only part of their connoisseurship. Not only are there household hints on cleaning with vinegar – bathtub film can be removed by wiping with vinegar and then with soda – there are also snippets of exotic vinegar trivia. Did you know that vinegar could save your life if you're attacked by the box jellyfish? Seventy people in Australia have died from the sting, but if vinegar is put on the wound, it halts the spread of the venom. Did you know, too, that radio astronomers have located vinegar in a cloud of gas and dust 25,000 light years from earth?

I shall leave you with the words of a song written by the founder of Vinegar Connoisseurs International, L.J Diggs, aka the Vinegar Man:

> Here comes the Vinegar Man
> To help all his vinegar fans
> Here comes the Vinegar Man
> To make this a vinegar land
> It's the man of the hour
> With his great sour power
> In his vinegar dressings
> He brings us great blessings.

Contact: Vinegar Connoisseurs International, 30 Carlton St, PO Box 41, Roslyn, SD 57261, USA.
Tel/Fax: 605 486 4536
Website: http://itctel.com/~ldiggs/vinegar.html
E-mail: vinegar@itctel.com

The Volapük Centre

The saddest thing to say of an unusual leisure activity is that once, it was *not* unusual. The story of Volapük is an 100-year tale of decline.

Volapük, an artificial language, was launched in 1879 by the German priest and linguist Johann Martin Schleyer (1831–1912). It is said that Schleyer knew 85 languages – and his 86th, the one he created, achieved immediate success in science, culture and commerce. Soon clubs, courses and conferences were set up all over Europe, and the language then spread to Japan and America. So successful was Volapük that, in just ten years, there were more than a million speakers – plus 50 journals and 1,000 books for them to read. Steamboats, hats, pens, wines and other items took the now popular brand name Volapük. But . . .

From 1889, organizational and personal squabbles led to splinter groups, conflicting reshapings of the language and widespread disaffection. Esperanto, invented in 1887, picked up the pieces and continues today in its role as the sole international language in widespread use. Volapük is almost forgotten.

Though not entirely. For in Leigh-on-Sea, Essex, England, you will find the Volapük Centre, spiritual home of the remaining speakers of the language. (Estimated to number between a dozen and a score worldwide.) Even the man who runs the Centre, Brian Bishop, admits that he is far from fluent, as he has so little opportunity to use Volapük. 'I liken the Centre's work to steam locomotive preservation,' he said. The important thing is that Volapük should continue as a *living* language, should still be able to say of itself 'Binob!' (I am), rather than let others say of it 'It was' (äbinon, for those few who understand). Brian doesn't hold out any hopes for a grand revival – 'Volapük had its day,' he remarked.

Contact: Volapük Centre, Brian Bishop, 155 Leighton Avenue, Leigh-on-Sea, Essex, SS9 1PX, UK.

The Voluntary Human Extinction Movement

The Voluntary Human Extinction Movement (or VHEMT, pronounced Vehement), is the pressure group to end all pressure groups – literally. VHEMT is nothing less than an organization committed to the abolition of the human race.

Rallying around the slogan 'May we live long and die out', VHEMT was founded in 1991 by American schoolteacher and ecological campaigner Les Knight. 'I looked at all the problems of the world,' he told me, 'and I traced them back to a primary source: *homo sapiens.*' This simple realization led him to have a vasectomy, so as to avoid adding to the problem, and then to embark upon his life's work: to persuade mankind to phase itself out.

Now it does seem that there is an objection to this philosophy: is there not a fundamental need – a basic drive – to reproduce? Is not VHEMT's view about as incompatible with human nature as it is possible to be? Les thinks otherwise. Whilst he accepts the existence of sexual drives, he sees the need for *children* as 'cultural conditioning'. If pressed on the question of human instincts for mothering and fathering – desires to nurture – he believes that such desires could be channelled elsewhere: perhaps into gardening, or by adopting a stream, or by caring for old people, or simply by having a pet.

Even so, I put it to Les that VHEMT has not the slightest chance of achieving its aims. 'Success is achieved each time another person volunteers to make the moral choice to not reproduce and join the movement,' he told me. 'The odds may be against us, but the decision to live long and die out is still the morally correct one.'

Contact: Voluntary Human Extinction Movement, PO Box 86646, Portland, OR 97286-0646, USA.
Website: http://www.vhemt.org E-mail: les@vhemt.org

W

Wadlopen

This has been described as 'mountain climbing for a flat land'.

Every year, from May to September, about 25,000 people take part in the Dutch activity of *wadlopen*, or mudwalking. On Holland's north coast, they wait for the tide to go out, then set off across the shallow sea bottom towards a fringe of distant islands – a four-and-a-half-hour walk, on more than eleven miles of goop.

There are two pieces of advice if you want to try this pursuit. First, wear cheap, high-top shoes – cheap, because they are going to be ruined, and high enough to go over the ankles, because otherwise they'll be sucked right off your feet. Second, keep walking. If you stand still, the mud will ooze over your feet, and you'll lose the ability to compensate for weight shift. If that happens, you'll simply find yourself taking part in another Dutch sport: *wadzitten* . . . or mud*sitting*.

Contact: Stichting Wadloopcentrum, Postbus 1, 9968 ZG Pieterburen, Netherlands.
Tel: 0595 528300

The Wallpaper History Society

The paste is ready, you've got the scissors and the brushes, and the trestles are in place, it's just that . . . well, would it *matter* if you didn't bother stripping off that old wallpaper? It would save time. If there's the odd bump, well it's nothing, absolutely nothing.

Isn't that right?

Argue it out with yourself all you want, you'll have misgivings if you fail to peel the walls. I must tell you, though: relax, it's okay, you don't have to strip. There are people who will thank you for pasting ply upon ply, building up the layers over the years and making an artefact as significant as a rock stratification to a geologist. To quote from an article in this group's magazine: '[From old buildings] we often remove thick layers of paper, sometimes as many as twenty layers stuck one on top of the other. Once separated, they reveal important evidence of fashions in interior decoration.' I refer to the work of the Wallpaper History Society.

Contact: Lesley Hoskins, Executive Secretary, Wallpaper History Society, c/o Cole & Son (Wallpapers), 144 Offord Rd, London, N1 1NS, UK.
Tel: 0171 700 9122

The Waterless Regatta

What was that Nancy Sinatra song? 'These Boats are Made for Walking'?

All right, I know it's *boots* – but it's such a perfect description of the bottomless craft in the regatta at Alice Springs in Australia. Held on the dried-up bed of the Todd River, and dubbed Henley-on-Todd (after Britain's Henley-on-Thames regatta), the regatta features boats that are propelled by the legs of the crews, who struggle through the rough river sand to race against fierce competition. Different categories of craft enter, including 'rowing eights' (eight rowers – or runners – with little room to stretch their legs in a superstructure made of tubular steel and canvas), and 'yachts' (fore-and-aft sailed vessels, manned by ten dry river sailors, running in five rows of two, with cloth skirts trailing from the water line to cover up hairy legs).

About the only thing that can spoil the regatta is rain; and on rare occasions in the past, bulldozers have had to be brought to the riverbed to divert a small but unwanted flow of water that could have ruined the whole event.

Contact: Bill van Dijk, Executive Officer, Henley-on-Todd, PO Box 1385, Alice Springs, N.T. 0871, Australia.
Tel: 08 8955 0252 Fax: 08 8955 0544

Watermelon Seed-Spitting

I blame the melon.

The one I bought at my local store had small white seeds, rather than the large black ones recommended by the organizers of the Watermelon

Seed-Spitting Championship that takes place in Luling, Texas. I am sure this is why, when I opened my window and spat, the seed travelled all of six feet ... compared to the world record of 68ft 9¹/₈in set in 1989 by Luling local Lee Wheelis.

Contact: Luling Watermelon Thump Headquarters, PO Box 710, Luling, Texas 78648, USA.
Tel: 830 875 3214 Fax: (830) 875 2082
Website: http://www.bcsnet.net/lulingcc
E-mail: lulingcc@bcsnet.net

The Watsonians

Sympathy for the underdog is a common emotion; concern for the side-kick rather less so.

'I am sure that I am not alone in believing that the good doctor is as essential to the Holmes myth as is the Great Detective himself,' says Robert W. Hahn, the founder of the group known as the Watsonians, which holds an annual weekend to honour the doctor. 'The movies, especially, contributed to making Watson a kind of a boob. But he was a pretty reliable man, really. And apparently, fairly handsome. Holmes said many a time: "The women are your department, Watson." '

Contact: The Watsonians, c/o Robert W. Hahn, 2707 S. 7th Street, Sheboygan, WI 53081, USA.

The Wellies

The next time someone says, 'Fancy a drink at the local watering-hole?' be a little wary. Instead of a trip to the pub, you could find yourself walking into the countryside: past the last telephone kiosk, down a rough road, beyond the sewage works, until you reach a gate that leads to a large field. There you will be invited to bend down and sip from a muddy puddle of spring-water. This is the sort of activity pursued by well-enthusiasts, or 'wellies'.

'Some well-water is foul and some is wonderful – but all wells taste quite different,' I was informed by Tristan Gray Hulse, the editor of *Source*, the specialist journal for wellies. 'Of the hundreds of wells I've visited, there are only two where I haven't drunk. The first was completely silted up and the second contained a dead sheep.'

But *Source* does not aim to be the spring-water equivalent of a wine-taster's guide. Its focus is upon the traditions, legends, and spiritual practices which surround so-called holy-wells – wells which have a reputation for of granting wishes, or curing the sick.

Even today, there might still be such a thing as well-power – as I discovered, when exploring the reasons for Tristan's interest in wells. 'Some years ago, I was suffering from an arthritic condition which meant that I had to walk with a stick,' he said, 'and hearing about the curative traditions at St Winifred's Well in Clwyd, I decided to go there and bathe. My condition was so bad, I had to *hobble* to the well.' He recalled that the water was extraordinarily cold – it took his breath away. But a month later, he felt a distinct psychological improvement.

'And six weeks after that,' he said, 'I was able to throw away my stick.'

Contact: *Source* c/o Peter Read and Heather Hughes, Swn-y-Mor, 96 Terrace Rd, Mount Pleasant, Swansea, SA1 6HU, UK.
Tel: 01792 458665

The Westerners' Association

It was high noon in Bingley, West Yorkshire, northern England. I had strapped on the gunbelt and was practising my draw in the lounge of Allen Ambridge, one of the members of the Westerners' Association.

'I knew you'd want to try,' said Allen. In between spinning a gun on his trigger finger, he treated me to a display of the two methods of fast draw: thumb-busting, when only one hand is used, and fanning, when the other hand shifts across the body to cock the hammer. Allen is fast. He can pull his reproduction 1872 Colt out of the holster and fire in $33/100$ of a second. But there are faster. He has seen a man achieve $25/100$ – the quarter-second of a draw. To reach that standard would require hours of practice every day, in front of a mirror, in a showdown with your reflection. 'Fast draw is one of the legends of the West,' he said, 'and everyone in the Westerners' Association does it. Though it never actually happened. Face-to-face fast draw is pure Hollywood.'

Along with fellow Westerners, Allen goes to weekend camps, dressing up in full cowboy gear and eating beans and beef. Clothing is entirely authentic, so there are no modern contrivances like zippers. 'I even put on red long johns,' he said, 'though I do wear underpants for hygienic reasons.' Some members take authenticity a degree further: they don't bother to wash.

Contact: Allen Ambridge, British Westerners' Association, 6 Primrose Bank, Gilstead, Bingley, West Yorks, BD16 4RB, UK.
Tel: 01274 560286

Or: Westerners International, Cowboy Hall of Fame, 1700 N.E. 63rd Street, Oklahoma City, Oklahoma 73111, USA.
Tel: 405 478 2250

Whistling

You've got to be dedicated to fly to the other side of the world just to whistle. Reg Moores travelled all the way from Brighton in the UK to North Carolina in the USA to perform 'The Cuckoo Waltz' at a Whistlers' convention. 'I was given that special plaque,' he said, pointing to his mantelpiece, 'for the greatest distance travelled by anyone attending.' He proceeded to demonstrate his vibrato by rapidly shifting his tongue.

Contact: International Whistlers' Convention, PO Box 758, Louisburg, NC 27549, USA.
Tel: 919 496 1191/4771 Fax 919 496 1191 E-mail: adh4771@aol.com

The Wife Carrying World Championship

They say a man should carry his wife over the threshold. In Sonkajärvi in Finland a man carries his wife over a 253.5 metre track – a track which is partly sand, partly grass, and partly asphalt, with a hurdle and a water-filled pool as obstacles.

Indeed, in Sonkajärvi's World Wife Carrying Championship, the 'wife' doesn't have to be the man's spouse. As it says in the rules, 'The wife can be your own, a neighbour's, or you may have found her further afield. She must, however, be over 17 years of age.' The winner is the man who circles the track in the shortest possible time, carrying his wife either piggyback, or over the shoulder in a fireman's lift; though if he drops the wife, he'll be fined 15 secs. Contestants run the track two at a time, so each heat is a contest in itself.

The championship, which has been held every July since 1992, is based upon two aspects of local 19th-century history. Firstly, a brigand called

Ronkainen is said to have accepted in his troop only those men who had passed a test – they had to carry a live swine or heavy sack over an obstacle course. Secondly, in those days, it was common practice to steal women from the neighbouring villages.

One of the remarkable things about the modern event is that it started as a joke – with couples wearing fancy dress, and the wife flogging her man with birch twigs – but is now becoming serious. Lycra suits are the order of the day, and couples train specially for the event. Women, in particular, go on diets in preparation.

The training does have one drawback: the slimmer the wife, the smaller the prize. The winner receives his wife's weight in beer.

Contact: Eero Pitkänen, Kulttuuritoimisto, PL 20, 74301 Sonkajärvi, Finland.

The Wild Turkey Calling Contest

So what sound does a wild turkey make?

Trick question. If you gave an answer then you obviously haven't listened to wild turkeys, and you're unlikely to win the Wild Turkey Calling Contest – because wild turkeys make sounds, in the plural. In the contest you will be expected to imitate five in all: the Mating Call, the so-called Lost Call (of the old hen in spring), the Cluck of an assembly of turkeys, the Kee-Kee of a young bird in the fall, and finally the Early Morning Fly-Down Cackle.

Contact: Yellville Chamber of Commerce, National Wild Turkey Calling Contest, PO Box 369, Yellville, AR 72687, USA.
Tel: 501 449 4676 or 449 4066

The Wood Collectors' Society

If bookworms are people who like books, are woodworms people who like wood? By liking wood, I do not mean a preference for mahogany over plastic. I mean a devotion to *pieces* of wood – collecting timber as a hobby. The trouble is, there is no generally accepted name for such a collector; and 'woodworm' might jar . . .

'I have had the odd nightmare about woodworm getting into my collection,' said Ken Southall. 'And I don't even like to think about the possibility of fire.'

The room was dominated by a cabinet. Ken had made it himself, and he told me the dimensions: 11ft long, 4ft high, 21in deep, with 36 drawers. This cabinet was home to 4,000 different types of wood: every piece was cut to the same size – he quoted dimensions again (6in long, 3in wide, ½in thick) – and each bore a label showing the wood's name. These samples were then kept in strict alphabetical order, so that altogether the cabinet represented a *dictionary* of timber.

'Have you got a wood for *every* letter of the alphabet?' I asked. He nodded. 'What's "X" then?'

He opened a drawer and let me see the row of labels that read xylia, xylocarpus, xylomelims . . .

'I just love wood,' he said. 'I love the feel and the colours and the *smell* of wood.' He opened a drawer and offered me a piece to sniff: it brought back memories of sharpening pencils at school – for this was *juniperus virginiana*, otherwise known as pencil cedar.

Even today, Ken is always on the look-out for specimens to add to his collection. He will search for wood at rubbish dumps and among park-keepers' refuse; he will attempt to scrounge a log if he sees someone pruning an unusual tree; and he will purchase objects made of wood, if they are going to yield samples. (Recently, he bought a chopping-board, and chopped it up, simply because he wanted a piece of the board's rubberwood.) Many exotic types of wood, though, are obtained by swapping timbers with wood-enthusiasts who live overseas – which is one of the advantages of being a member of the 1600-strong International Wood Collectors' Society.

'I heard about the society in 1979,' said Ken, 'and I was delighted to discover that there were other people devoted to collecting wood. I had always thought it was just a funny little whim I had.'

Contact: Myrtle & Bill Cockrell, International Wood Collectors' Society, 2300 West Range Line Road, Greencastle, IN 46135-9574, USA.
Tel: 317 653 6483
Or: Ken Southall, Aspen Cottage, Nettlestead, Ipswich, Suffolk, IP8 4QT, UK.
Tel: 01473 831174

Worm Charming

I toyed with renaming this pursuit 'annelid alluring', on the grounds that puzzlement is preferable to disgust.

On the grounds ... that's also where the World Worm Charming Championship takes place, on the grounds of a school in Cheshire, England. Competitors charm worms to the surface of the soil, pick them up and put them in a jar – and the person charming the greatest number in a 30-minute period is the winner. The world record stands at 511, set in 1980.

The traditional method of charming is to stick a garden fork into the ground and twang it back and forth. The vibrations are thought to resemble rainfall – the worms think their burrows are going to be flooded, so they come to the surface. Other methods have been tried over the years, including bringing along a horse, to stamp its hooves on the soil; but competitors are not allowed to dig, nor pour on water.

The worms are released at midnight, after the birds have gone to roost.

Contact: Mike Forster, 83 Wistaston Road, Willaston, Nr Nantwich, Cheshire, CW5 6QP, UK.
Tel: 01270 663957

X

The Xtal Set Society

No letter of the alphabet has a greater mystique than 'X'. Its presence in the title undoubtedly attracts some viewers to the TV programme, *The X-Files*; and an 'X' in the spelling gives a fresh image to the word 'crystal' – and may attract new listeners to old radios. That is the hope of the Xtal Set Society, a group of 500 enthusiasts, spread across the globe, who are dedicated to building crystal sets, a type of radio that was invented in 1902 and had its heyday in the 1920s, in the pre-valve era. Perhaps because I, too, have succumbed to the power of 'X', I went to visit a British member of the society, Ron Pearce, a clock and watch repairer from Bungay, Suffolk.

'You really need a background that's dead quiet to hear a crystal set,' commented Ron. 'I turn the central heating off because it bubbles a bit.' He remarked, too, that years of listening to crystal sets had improved the sensitivity of his ears. When he passed me the earpiece, I could barely hear anything but he said: 'For me, that's blasting.'

'Couldn't you put an amplifier on it?' I asked.

'Yes, I could,' he said. 'But that would offend purists like myself. It wouldn't be a crystal set any longer.'

'You mean you actually *like* listening to weak signals?'

'Well, you have to understand that it's the difficulty with crystal sets that's part of their appeal.'

Ron explained that, on a crystal set, it is extremely difficult to pick up *anything* beyond local stations; thus, crystal sets pose an immediate *challenge*. You have to make minute adjustments to the tuning dial, to separate one station from another – and Ron has developed extremely dextrous fingers. 'It's probably helped that I'm a watch repairer,' he said. 'I like to see how many stations I can receive. I get a buzz from picking up a very distant station on something I've made myself – last night I picked up Radio Israel, and you can bet your life that I was the only person listening to that programme on a crystal set. It gives me a real sense of achievement.'

Contact: The Xtal Set Society, PO Box 3026, St Louis, MO 63130, USA.
Tel: 314 725 1172 E-mail: xtalset@midnightscience.com

Y

(Advanced) Yo-Yo

You walk the dog and rock the baby, via a windmill, then spaghetti, a loop-the-loop, a flying saucer, and finish by catching the yo-yo in your pocket. That's the meaning of *advanced* yo-yo.

The essential newsletter for yo-yo enthusiasts is *Yo-Yo Times*. Here, you will find many new tricks. My favourite is sled dog, which is walking the dog when there's snow on the ground. The yo-yo digs a neat hole, but if you give a tug, it comes flying out.

Contact: *Yo-Yo Times*, PO Box 1519-UGU, Herndon, VA 20172-1519, USA.
Tel: 703 715 6187
Website: http://members.aol.com/YoYoTime/index.html
E-mail: YoYoTime@aol.com
Or: American Yo-Yo Association, 627-163rd Street South, Spanaway, Washington 98387, USA
Website: http://AYYA.pd.net

Z

Zen Archery

Once, a master of the Japanese art of Zen archery travelled west, and further west, until he came to England. Upon studying the native language and history, he learnt that the English longbow of Agincourt fame owed its power to the wood of the yew-tree. 'How right and truly appropriate,' he thought, 'that this English word "yew" sounds exactly like their word of identity, "you". It is as if to confirm that whenever an arrow is released its path depends entirely upon one person – you, yourself and no-one else.' A small bow-shaped smile came to his lips as he realized how easily the English might have discovered the essence of his Japanese art . . .

I wrote that mock-parable after travelling to Dartford in Kent, to the headquarters of the Association for Japanese Archery. There, wearing his kimono, was Don Slade-Southam, the association's president. He bade me take off my shoes and we stepped onto the *dojo*, the archery-court – in fact, the only permanent archery-court in England which is equipped to traditional Japanese standards. But what exactly is Japanese archery?

In *Kyudo*, 'The Way of the Bow' – or Zen archery, as it is often called – hitting the target is of secondary importance; what counts is the archer's state of mind. Ideally, the archer should be empty of intention and filled with the pure awareness of the present moment. There should be no desire to succeed. It is the paradox of releasing an arrow without being interested in hitting the target that captures the Zen-essence of this sport-cum-philosophy-cum-art.

'Kyudo begins where other martial arts end,' I was told by John Carder-Bush, one of the association's leading members. 'After you've done karate or judo for ten or fifteen years, you come to realize that your only opponent is yourself. In Kyudo, you are up against yourself from the word go. You cannot run away.' Other members agreed that Kyudo is about you versus you. If you miss the target, you look inwards and ask 'Why?' – always to be reminded that internal attitude is the key to success or failure.

Like the Japanese tea ceremony, Zen archery is entirely ritualized. There are no random movements – if, in the course of conducting a ritual, you drop an arrow, there is yet another ritual for picking it up. I watched as the members demonstrated *Yawatashi*, a ceremonial shoot involving a master and two assistants. First the master moves, then the assistant, then the second assistant, like a wave. It is all very slow, a confrontation with your own impatience; but eventually an assistant draws down the master's kimono to bear a shoulder and a breast; only then is an arrow released . . .

It is said that a master of Zen archery can tell if a shot has been successful simply by listening to the sound of the string.

Don beckoned to me and handed me a bow. In no sense can this Zen weapon be called user-friendly. Unlike the English longbow, the Japanese bow is asymmetrical, with the lower limb being much shorter than the upper; this perversion of shape means that the arrow will veer off-target, to the right – unless, that is, the archer has mastered the Japanese technique of simultaneously spinning the bow-shaft in the hand to the left. 'Well,' I thought, 'I'll leave that for a later lesson.' The important thing was to get an arrow in the air.

I found that I couldn't even draw back the string. The archers smiled. 'There's a secret to it,' they said. Muscle-power alone will never draw back the string of a Zen bow.

I think I am too impatient by nature to learn Zen archery. Don admitted that there was one female member who trained for *eight months* before she released her first arrow. Part of her problem was fear – for the bowstring is drawn back a long way indeed, way behind the head . . . and as that string comes twanging forward, there is always the possibility that it will strike the archer and maybe *slice* the archer, re-enacting that scene from *Reservoir Dogs* involving an ear.

I am reminded of the old Zen *koan*, or riddle, which asks: 'What is the sound of one hand clapping?' Perhaps the answer is: 'Well, there were really two hands, but the master was a bit hard of hearing following his archery session.'

Contact: Don Slade-Southam, 7 Barn End Drive, Wilmington, Kent DA2 7BX, UK.
Tel: 01322 222145